THE BENJAMIN FRANKLIN PAPERS

THE PAPERS OF THE FOUNDING FATHERS

❦

THE

BENJAMIN FRANKLIN

PAPERS

BY

FRANK DONOVAN

DODD, MEAD & COMPANY

NEW YORK

To
Bob and Lee,
Brian and Mara

AN EXPLANATION

Among scholars, the papers of the Founding Fathers are sacred documents. Tampering with them in any way is a form of heresy. This poses a problem for one who would present them in a manner most understandable to twentieth-century readers. In the eighteenth century, customs relating to punctuation, capitalization, italics, contractions and spelling differed from those of today. And there was the annoying long *s*.

Franklin, particularly, used capitals, italics, punctuation and contractions in a way that made his documents hard to read by one accustomed to modern practices. Consider the following paragraph:

Courteous and kind Reader,

THIS is the fifth Time I have appear'd in Publick, chalking out the future Year for my honeft Countrymen, and foretelling what fhall, and what may, and what may not come to pafs; in which I have the Pleafure to find that I have given general Satisfaction. Indeed, among the Multitude of our aftrological Predictions, 'tis no wonder if fome few fail; for, without any Defect in the Art itfelf, 'tis well known that a fmall Error, a fingle wrong Figure overfeen in a Calculation, may occafion great Miftakes: But however we Almanack-makers may *mifs it* in other Things, I believe it will be generally allow'd *That we always hit the Day of the Month*, and that I fuppofe is efteem'd one of the moft ufeful Things in an Almanack.

Franklin had what he considered a reason for doing this. In a letter to his son he said that when his "Edict of the King of

Prussia" was reprinted in the *London Chronicle,* it was ". . . stripped of all the capitalling and italicking that intimate the allusions and mark the emphasis of written discourses, to bring them as near as possible to those spoken. Printing such a piece all in one even small character, seems to me like repeating one of Whitfield's sermons in the monotony of a school boy." The savant was annoyed when any change was made in his copy. He told a printer to see that the compositor observed "strictly the Italicking, Capitalling and Pointing."

At the risk of offending the shade of the worthy Doctor, spelling and the use of capitals, italics and contractions have been changed in this book to conform with modern practice to make it easier to read. However, not one word that Franklin wrote has been changed—that would really be heresy.

Franklin also opposed the abridgment of anything that he wrote. Of an editor who had freely curtailed one of his contributions he said, "He has drawn the teeth and pared the nails of my paper, so that it can neither scratch nor bite. It seems only to paw or mumble." Every writer sympathizes with the good Doctor, but an unabridged edition of the Franklin papers requires months, if not years, to read and digest. Yale University is currently publishing such an edition which will comprise at least forty large volumes.

In this single volume only a few of Franklin's papers can be presented. An attempt has been made to select those that are of particular significance or that are typical of a point of view or an idea or a discovery that has lasting meaning. And even some of these must be abridged. Franklin frequently wrote about many diverse things in a single document or letter. He said that "ideas will string themselves like ropes of onions." In 1751 he wrote a letter advocating a union of the colonies—the earliest record of such a proposal. In the same letter he discussed the location of a fort to guard against Indian attack and the desirability of limiting German emigration to Pennsylvania. Surely the great man would permit us to leave out the part about the fort and the Germans when the former is no longer necessary and the latter have become the ancestors of some of our First Families.

Nothing in this volume has been abridged to change the meaning in any way.

CONTENTS

༄

CHAPTER I

THE REBELLIOUS TEEN-AGER

ॐ

LET US THEREFORE beware of being lulled into a dangerous security; of being weakened by internal contentions and divisions; of being shamefully extravagant in contracting private debts, while we are backward in discharging those of the public; of neglect in military exercises and discipline, and in providing arms and munitions of war, to be ready on occasion; for all these are circumstances that give confidence to enemies, and diffidence to friends, and the expenses required to prevent a war are much lighter than those that will, if not prevented, be absolutely necessary to maintain it.

These words suggest a mental image of a current Chief Executive standing at a lectern facing a bank of television cameras as he addresses the nation; or of a recent President sitting by his fireside as he chatted with the people on the radio.

When they were written there was no television or radio. There was no President of the United States. The year was 1784. Benjamin Franklin was offering some advice to the new nation in America.

The principal merit of the papers of the Founding Fathers lies, not in their historical significance, but in the ageless truths which these men discerned and presented. Their ideas on politics, economics, philosophy; on the rights, duties and responsibilities of the individual and the state, and—in Franklin's case —science, were radical and earth shaking at the time. But they were as basically true as the Ten Commandments. Today, in America, we take these ideas for granted: "We hold these truths to be self-evident." This is not a safe thing to do. They are being challenged. We must defend them. It is well to know what we are defending and how it all came about.

Benjamin Franklin differed from the other Founding Fathers in several respects. Born on January 17, 1706, he was a generation older. The year Washington was born Franklin published the first issue of *Poor Richard's Almanac*. Franklin was cosmopolitan. His interests and knowledge were so diverse as to embrace almost every aspect of human affairs. Washington was a soldier and a statesman, a farmer and a surveyor; Jefferson was a statesman, an architect and a planter with an inquiring mind. Franklin did so many things that it is easier to list what he did not do than what he did. And after trying to think of something which his nimble genius did not touch, one might come up with the statement, "Well, he couldn't fly a plane."

The first half of Franklin's life was devoted to making a living as a printer. During the second half his business was politics and diplomacy. When he stopped working for a living he devoted himself to science—which was then called philosophy, an inquiry into the nature of things. For the forty-odd years of his career as a public servant, this was his relaxation. And, throughout the eighty-four years of his life, a concern for human welfare was an avocation.

Franklin's wide acquaintance included men of three centuries. In his boyhood he heard Increase Mather preach. Shortly before he died, he gave Abiel Holmes, father of Oliver Wendell Holmes, a library of books. Between the birth of Increase

Mather and the death of the elder Holmes, both of whom came within the orbit of Franklin's life, lies a stretch of two hundred years.

His greatest single contribution to the founding of the United States was negotiating the treaty under which France lent the rebelling colonies an army, a navy and $5,000,000. But his participation in all phases of the birth of the new nation is evidenced by the fact that he is the only man who signed all four of the great documents marking that birth: the Declaration of Independence, the treaty with France, the peace treaty with England and the Constitution. He was young America's master diplomat, but his best-known piece of writing is philosophical rather than political—the verses and proverbs of *Poor Richard's Almanac*. And at the time that he was writing these, he was also reporting on experiments that made him the acknowledged world leader on the theory of electricity. During this period, in his spare time, he promoted the organization of the Philadelphia militia, founded a school that became the University of Pennsylvania, established America's first fire insurance company, started the American Philosophical Society, organized the first free hospital, reorganized the Philadelphia police department and the Post Office, led in establishing the first public library— and he had something to say about street cleaning, too.

The school-taught image of Benjamin Franklin is a dignified man, and perhaps a dull one, a paragon of virtue whose life would serve as a model for all small boys. This is not quite correct. He was dignified when the occasion demanded dignity, but humor and charm were more characteristic of Franklin than dignity. He was virtuous, but he was also a lusty man, and an earthy one, some of whose humorous writings are not quite suitable for mixed company. By certain standards of polite discourse he was sometimes vulgar. The creed that he preached was "industry and frugality." The former he practiced all his life—his brain could not be idle. The latter he conformed to until it had gained him financial independence. After that he preached it for others who were not so well off, and made a show of observing it in his dress—but for the last half of his life Franklin did not live frugally.

When Franklin started to write, in his native Boston, he was a rebellious teen-ager, defying the ordered existence and channeled thinking of an adult concept. His early boyhood had been checkered. First, a year in grammar school, starting at the age of eight with the idea that he would be a minister. Then, when it was obvious that money would not be available for a college education, a year in another school for writing and arithmetic. This ended, as did Franklin's formal education, when he failed the latter subject. Next, there were two years working for his father, a candle maker, followed by a brief period working for his uncle, a cutler. At the age of twelve Franklin had two interests—books and the sea. His father used the first to curb the second. Franklin says, in his autobiography:

THIS BOOKISH INCLINATION at length determined my father to make me a printer, though he already had one son of that profession. In 1717 my brother James returned from England with a press and letters to set up in business in Boston. I liked it much better than that of my father, but still had a hankering for the sea. To prevent the apprehended effect of such an inclination, my father was impatient to have me bound to my brother. I stood out some time, but at last was persuaded, and signed the indentures when I was but twelve years old. I was to serve as an apprentice till I was twenty-one years of age.

Franklin's first writing was published when he was thirteen. It consisted of two news stories in the form of poems. One was entitled "The Lighthouse Tragedy" and dealt with the drowning of a lighthouse keeper in Boston harbor. The other was an

account of the death of Blackbeard the pirate. He wrote them,
set them in type, printed them and sold them, at his brother's
orders, on the streets of Boston. "They were wretched stuff,"
says Franklin, "in the Grub-street ballad style."

There are no copies of these poems that are surely authentic.
In 1941 the *Boston Post* reported that some verses, printed in
Old English characters on a tattered and yellow sheet, were
found in "a tumbledown closet in the ruins of an old house" on
an island in Boston harbor. They were titled "The Lighthouse
Tragedy." This may be a copy of the first published work of
Benjamin Franklin. The poem began:

> Oh, George, this wild November
> We must not pass with you
> For Ruth, our fragile daughter,
> Its chilly gales will rue.

In 1765 the *Worcestershire Garland* printed a poem about
the downfall of Blackbeard—whose real name was Teach—
which many scholars think was a reprint of Franklin's second
poem. There is no proof, but it seems unlikely that anyone would
compose a new poem on this subject more than forty-five years
after the event, and the second line of the first stanza indicates
that it was written at the time of Blackbeard's demise. Franklin
is the only one who is known to have written such a poem when
the incident happened. These verses started:

> Will you hear of a bloody battle,
> Lately fought upon the seas,
> It will make your ears to rattle,
> And your admiration cease
>
> Have you heard of Teach the Rover,
> And his knavery on the main;
> How of gold he was a lover
> How he loved ill got gain?

If this is Franklin's doggerel it does not show the promise of
the great writer that was latent in the thirteen-year-old. Young
Franklin realized that he had a lot to learn. He describes how
he went about learning it.

AT ABOUT THIS TIME I met with an odd volume of the
Spectator. . . . I thought the writing excellent, and wished,
if possible, to imitate it. With this view I took some of the
papers, and, making short hints of the sentiment in each
sentence, laid them by a few days, and then, without looking at the book, tried to complete the papers again, by expressing each hinted sentiment at length, and as fully as it
had been expressed before, in any suitable words that
should come to hand. Then I compared my *Spectator* with
the original, discovered some of my faults, and corrected
them. But I found I wanted a stock of words, or a readiness
in recollecting and using them, which I thought I should
have acquired before that time if I had gone on making
verses; since the continual occasion for words of the same
import, but of different length, to suit the measure, or of
different sound for the rhyme, would have laid me under a
constant necessity of searching for variety. . . . Therefore I
took some of the tales and turned them into verse; and,
after a time, when I had pretty well forgotten the prose,
turned them back again. . . . By comparing my work
afterward with the original, I discovered many faults and
amended them; but I sometimes had the pleasure of fancying that, in certain particulars of small import, I had been
lucky enough to improve the method or the language, and
this encouraged me to think I might possibly in time come
to be a tolerable English writer, of which I was extremely
ambitious. . . .

I met with an English grammar, at the end of which there
were two little sketches of the arts of rhetoric and logic, the
latter finishing with a specimen of a dispute in the Socratic

method; and soon after I procured Xenophon's *Memorable Things of Socrates,* wherein there are many instances of the same method. I was charmed with it, adopted it, dropped my abrupt contradiction and positive argumentation, and put on the humble inquirer and doubter. . . . I found this method safest for myself and very embarrassing to those against whom I used it; therefore I took a delight in it, practiced it continually, and grew very artful and expert in drawing people, even of superior knowledge, into concessions, the consequences of which they did not foresee, entangling them in difficulties out of which they could not extricate themselves, and so obtaining victories that neither myself nor my cause always deserved. I continued this method for some years, but gradually left it, retaining only the habit of expressing myself in terms of modest diffidence; never using, when I advanced anything that may possibly be disputed, the words *certainly, undoubtedly,* or any others that give the air of positiveness to an opinion. . . . This habit, I believe, has been of great advantage to me when I have had occasion to inculcate my opinions, and persuade men into measures that I have been from time to time engaged in promoting; and, as the chief ends of conversation are to inform or to be informed, to please or to persuade, I wish well-meaning, sensible men would not lessen their power of doing good by a positive, assuming manner, that seldom fails to disgust, tends to create opposition, and to defeat every one of those purposes for which speech was given to us, to wit, giving or receiving information or pleasure.

The Socratic method of dispute which sixteen-year-old Franklin studied and practiced so deliberately led to his great powers of persuasion as a diplomat which, sixty years later, enabled him to convince Vergennes, minister to Louis XVI, to the alliance with the colonies that was the decisive factor in the American Revolution.

Franklin shortly put his newfound writing skill to practice. His brother published a newspaper, the *New England Courant.* Much of the "news" consisted of letters from contributors expressing opinions on varied subjects, signed with fictitious names. Young Benjamin had ideas. He wanted to express them. He describes the subterfuge that he used to get his writing into print:

. . . BEING STILL A BOY, and suspecting that my brother would object to printing anything of mine in his paper if he knew it to be mine, I contrived to disguise my hand, and, writing an anonymous paper, I put it in at night under the door of the printing-house. It was found in the morning, and communicated to his writing friends when they called as usual. They read it, commented on it in my hearing, and I had the exquisite pleasure of finding it met with their approbation, and that, in their different guesses at the author, none were named but men of some character among us for learning and ingenuity. I suppose now that I was rather lucky in my judges, and that perhaps they were not really so very good ones as I then esteemed them.

The pen name that Franklin selected was Silence Dogood, a fictitious widow whose early life Franklin described in his first letter. This is the earliest known authentic paper of this Founding Father, and is an indication of the "pixy" sense of humor that he carried through his life.

TO THE AUTHOR of the *New England Courant.*

Sir: It may not be improper in the first place to inform your readers that I intend once a fortnight to present them, by the help of this paper, with a short epistle, which I presume will add somewhat to their entertainment.

And since it is observed, that the generality of people, nowadays, are unwilling either to commend or dispraise what they read, until they are in some measure informed who or what the author of it is, whether he be poor or rich, old or young, a scholar or a leather apron man, etc., and give their opinion of the performance, according to the knowledge which they have of the author's circumstances, it may not be amiss to begin with a short account of my past life and present condition, that the reader may not be at a loss to judge whether or no my lucubrations are worth his reading.

At the time of my birth, my parents were on ship-board on their way from London to New England. My entrance into this troublesome world was attended with the death of my father, a misfortune, which though I was not then capable of knowing, I shall never be able to forget; for as he, poor man, stood upon the deck rejoicing at my birth, a merciless wave entered the ship, and in one moment carried him beyond reprieve. . . .

When we arrived in Boston (which was not long after) I was put to nurse in a country place, at a small distance from the town, where I went to school, and passed my infancy and childhood in vanity and idleness, until I was bound out apprentice, that I might no longer be a charge to my indigent mother. . . .

My master was a country minister, a pious good-natured young man, and a bachelor: he labored with all his might to instill virtuous and godly principles into my tender soul. . . . He endeavored that I might be instructed in all that knowledge and learning which is necessary for our sex, and denied me no accomplishment that could possibly be attained in a country place, such as all sorts of needle-work, writing, arithmetic, etc., and observing that I took a more than ordinary delight in reading ingenious books, he gave me the free use of his library. . . .

I will not abuse your patience with a tedious recital of all the frivolous accidents of my life, that happened from this time until I arrived to years of discretion, only inform you that I lived a cheerful country life, spending my leisure time either in some innocent diversion with the neighboring females, or in some shady retirement, with the best of company, books. Thus I passed away the time with a mixture of profit and pleasure, having no affliction but what was imaginary, and created in my own fancy; as nothing is more common with us women, than to be grieving for nothing, when we have nothing else to grieve for.

As I would not engross too much of your paper at once, I will defer the remainder of my story until my next letter; in the mean time desiring your readers to exercise their patience, and bear with my humors now and then, because I shall trouble them but seldom. I am not insensible of the impossibility of pleasing all, but I would not willingly displease any; and for those who will take offense where none is intended, they are beneath the notice of

Your humble servant,
SILENCE DOGOOD

There were fourteen Dogood papers in all. In the second, Franklin continued to delineate his fictitious widow. In describing her character, he set down his teen-age views and opinions on some important principles—attitudes which did not change throughout his life.

. . . I SHALL CONCLUDE this with my own character, which (one would think) I should be best able to give. Know then, that I am an enemy to vice, and a friend to virtue. I am one of an extensive charity, and a great forgiver of private injuries: a hearty lover of the clergy and all good men, and a mortal enemy to arbitrary government and unlimited power. I am naturally very jealous for the rights and liberties of my country; and the least appearance of an encroachment on those valuable privileges is apt to make my blood boil exceedingly. I have likewise a natural inclination to observe and reprove the faults of others, at which I have an excellent faculty. I speak this by way of warning to all such whose offenses shall come under my cognizance, for I never intend to wrap my talent in a napkin. To be brief; I am courteous and affable, good-humored (unless I am first provoked), and handsome, and sometimes witty, but always, Sir,

Your friend, and
humble servant,
SILENCE DOGOOD

Successive Dogood papers dealt with women, widows, old maids, drunkenness, religion, freedom of speech, the dangers of fashionable dress, the poor quality of poetry in New England and the night life of Boston. An early one was a rather vicious satire on a college education, written perhaps in a mood of sour grapes. Young Franklin was of an age to enter college when he wrote it. Had he been able to, his attitude toward the advantages of a higher education might have been different. He starts this letter by describing a conversation between Silence Dogood and her "Reverend Boarder" whom he calls Clericus. The minister advises Silence to send her son to college. Silence falls asleep and Franklin describes her dream:

I FANCIED I was traveling over pleasant and delightful fields and meadows, and through many small country towns and villages; and as I passed along, all places resounded with the fame of the Temple of Learning: every peasant, who had wherewithal, was preparing to send one of his children at least to this famous place; and in this case most of them consulted their own purses instead of their children's capacities: So that I observed a great many, yea, the most part of those who were traveling thither, were little better than dunces and blockheads. Alas! Alas!

At length I entered upon a spacious plain, in the midst of which was erected a large and stately edifice. . . . In the middle of the great hall stood a stately and magnificent throne which was ascended to by two high and difficult steps. On the top of it sat Learning in awful state; she was appareled wholly in black, and surrounded almost on every side with innumerable volumes in all languages. . . . On her right hand sat English with a pleasant smiling countenance, and handsomely attired; and on her left were seated several antique figures with their faces veiled. I was considerably puzzled to guess who they were, until one informed me (who stood beside me) that those figures on her left hand were Latin, Greek, Hebrew, etc., and that they were very much reserved, and seldom or never unveiled their faces here, and then to few or none, though most of those who have in this place acquired so much learning as to distinguish them from English, pretended to an intimate acquaintance with them. I then inquired of him what could be the reason why they continued veiled, in this place especially. He pointed to the foot of the throne, where I saw Idleness, attended with Ignorance, and these (he informed me) were they who first veiled them, and still kept them so.

Now I observed that the whole tribe who entered into the Temple with me began to climb the throne; but the work proving troublesome and difficult to most of them, they withdrew their hands from the plow and contented themselves to sit at the foot, with Madame Idleness and her maid Ignorance, until those who were assisted by diligence and a docible [docile] temper, had well nigh got up to the first step. But the time drawing nigh in which they could no way avoid ascending, they were fain to crave the assistance of those who had got up before them, and who, for the reward perhaps of a pint of milk, or a piece of plumcake, lent the lubbers a helping hand, and sat them in the eye of the world upon a level with themselves.

The other step being in the same manner ascended, and the usual ceremonies at an end, every beetle-skull seemed well satisfied with his own portion of learning, though perhaps he was even just as ignorant as ever. And now the time of their departure being come, they marched out of doors to make room for another company, who waited for entrance. And I, having seen all that was to be seen, quitted the hall likewise, and went to make my observations on those who were just gone out before me.

Some I perceived took to merchandising, others to traveling, some to one thing, some to another, and some to nothing; and many of them henceforth, for want of patrimony, lived as poor as church mice, being unable to dig, and ashamed to beg, and to live by their wits it was impossible. . . .

Now I bethought myself in my sleep, that it was time to be at home, and as I fancied I was traveling back thither, I reflected in my mind on the extreme folly of those parents who, blind to their children's dullness, and insensible of the solidity of their skulls, because they think their purses can afford it, will needs send them to the Temple of Learning . . . from whence they return, after abundance of trouble and charge, as great blockheads as ever, only more proud and self-conceited.

While I was in the midst of these unpleasant reflections, Clericus (who with a book in his hand was walking under the trees) accidentally awakened me; to him I related my dream with all its particulars, and he, without much study, presently interpreted it, assuring me, that it was a lively representation of Harvard College.

Most of the contributors to James Franklin's paper were young men, some of them medical students. When Cotton

Mather endorsed inoculation for smallpox, the paper published pieces ridiculing him. Wrathfully, the younger Mather compared the *Courant* contributors to the infamous Hell-fire Club of London and said ". . . we find a notorious, scandalous paper, called the *Courant,* full freighted with nonsense, unmanliness, profaneness, immorality, arrogance, calumnies, lies, contradictions and what not, all tending to quarrels and divisions, and to debauch and corrupt the minds and manner of New England." Increase Mather added that if the civil authorities did not take action ". . . some awful judgment will come upon the land and the wrath of God will arise and there will be no remedy." The Mathers did not like to be crossed—although the clergymen had some cause for complaint. The *Courant* was a sensationalized sheet, most of its contributors young radicals.

When James topped his disrespect for the intolerent clergymen by criticizing the local government, he went to jail for thirty days, during which sixteen-year-old Benjamin managed the paper. When he was released, James was forbidden to publish the *Courant*. To get around this, Franklin's indentures as an apprentice were canceled and he became the publisher of record of the paper. A new set of secret indentures was drawn up between the brothers.

About this time the brothers started to quarrel. Benjamin claims that his older brother was harsh and intolerant, although he admits that the praise which he received on the Dogood papers, when their authorship became known, may have gone to his head. In any event, he says:

AT LENGTH, a fresh difference arising between my brother and me, I took upon me to assert my freedom, presuming that he would not venture to produce the new indentures. It was not fair of me to take this advantage, and this I therefore reckon one of the first errata of my life; but the unfairness of it weighed little with me, when under the impressions of resentment for the blows his passion too often urged him to bestow upon me, though he was not otherwise an ill-natured man; perhaps I was too saucy and provoking.

When James blackballed his rebellious brother with every other printer in Boston, seventeen-year-old Benjamin left home, going first to New York and then to Philadelphia, arriving on that memorable Sunday morning described in every "Boy's Life of Benjamin Franklin" for the past century which tells of him walking along the street munching on one roll and carrying two others under his arm while his future wife, Deborah Read, laughs at him from her doorway.

Another aspect of his teen-age rebellion was his attitude toward religion. At the age of fifteen he came across some books attacking deism—a school of thought which advocated a natural rather than an inspired religion—a religion in which reason tempered faith. Franklin said, "It happened that they wrought an effect on me quite contrary to what was intended of them; for the arguments of the deists, which were quoted to be refuted, appeared to me much stronger than the refutations; in short, I soon became a thorough deist."

During his late teens he thought seriously on all questions relating to a personal religion and the nature of the universe. When he was nineteen he wrote a little metaphysical piece entitled *A Dissertation on Liberty and Necessity, Pleasure and Pain,* which was, he later said, "to prove the doctrine of fate, from the supposed attributes of God, in some manner as this: that in erecting and governing the world, as he was infinitely wise, he knew what would be best; infinitely good, he must be disposed, and infinitely powerful, he must be able to execute it: consequently all is right." Later, he said that "this pamphlet was another erratum."

Franklin has been accused of being an atheist. He was not. Although he was a member of the Presbyterian and, later, the Episcopal church, he was never a staunch churchman or sectarian. He believed that there was good in even the "worst" religion and that good works were far more important, in the sight of the Lord, than orthodoxy. Only three years after his deist period, he wrote a set of *Articles of Belief and Acts of Religion*—a sort of personal prayer book in which he said, in part:

BEING MINDFUL that I address the Deity, my soul ought to be calm and serene, free from passion and perturbation, or otherwise elevated with rational joy and pleasure, I ought to use a countenance that expresses a filial respect, mixed with a kind of smiling, that signifies inward joy, and satisfaction, and admiration.

O wise God, my good Father!

Thou beholdest the sincerity of my heart and of my devotion; grant me a continuance of thy favor!

1. O Creator, O Father! I believe that thou art good, and that thou art pleased with the pleasure of thy children. —Praised be thy name forever!

2. By thy power hast thou made the glorious sun, with his attending worlds; from the energy of thy mighty will, they first received their prodigious motion, and by thy wisdom hast thou prescribed the wondrous laws by which they move. —Praised be thy name forever!

3. By thy wisdom thou formed all things. Thou hast created man, bestowing life and reason, and placed him in dignity superior to thy other earthly creatures. —Praised be thy name forever!

4. Thy wisdom, thy power, and thy goodness are everywhere clearly seen; in the air and in the water, in the heaven and on the earth; thou providest for the various winged fowl, and the innumerable inhabitants of the water; thou givest cold and heat, rain and sunshine, in their season, and to the fruits of the earth increase. —Praised be thy name forever!

5. Thou abhorrest in thy creatures treachery and deceit, malice, revenge, intemperance, and every other hurtful vice;

but thou art a lover of justice and sincerity, of friendship and benevolence, and every virtue. Thou art my friend, my Father, and my benefactor. —Praised be thy name forever, O God, forever! Amen! . . .

Inasmuch as by reason of our ignorance we cannot be certain that many things, which we often hear mentioned in the petitions of men to the Deity, would prove real goods, if they were in our possession, and as I have reason to hope and believe that the goodness of my Heavenly Father will not withhold from me a suitable share of temporal blessings, if by a virtuous and holy life I conciliate his favor and kindness, therefore I presume not to ask such things, but rather, humbly and with a sincere heart, express my earnest desires that he would graciously assist my continual endeavors and resolutions of eschewing vice and embracing virtue; which kind of supplications will at least be thus far beneficial, as they remind me in a solemn manner of my extensive duty.

This does not sound like atheism, but at a time when the religious leaders of the colonies considered all faiths other than Protestantism as evil, any departure from orthodox thought might be branded as atheistic. Certainly Franklin's religious views and practices distressed his parents. Years later, in reply to a letter from his father, he wrote:

HONORED FATHER, I have your favors of the twenty-first of March, in which you both seem concerned lest I have imbibed some erroneous opinions. Doubtless I have my share; and when the natural weakness and imperfection of human understanding is considered, the unavoidable influence of education, custom, books, and company upon our ways of thinking, I imagine a man must have a good deal of vanity who believes, and a good deal of boldness who affirms, that all the doctrines he holds are true, and all he rejects are false. And perhaps the same may be justly said of every sect, church and society of men, when they assume to themselves that infallibility which they deny to the Pope and councils.

I think opinions should be judged of by their influences and effects; and, if a man holds none that tend to make his less virtuous or more vicious, it may be concluded he holds none that are dangerous; which I hope is the case with me.

I am sorry you should have any uneasiness on my account; and if it were a thing possible for one to alter his opinions in order to please another, I know none whom I ought more willingly to oblige in that respect than yourselves. But, since it is no more in a man's power to think than to look like another, methinks all that should be expected from me is to keep my mind open to conviction, to hear patiently and examine attentively, whatever is offered me for that end; and, if after all I continue in the same errors, I believe your usual charity will induce you to rather pity and excuse than blame me. In the meantime, your care and concern for me is what I am very thankful for. . . .

I think vital religion has always suffered when orthodoxy is more regarded than virtue; and the scriptures assure me that at the last day we shall not be examined what we thought, but what we did; and our recommendation will not be that we said, "Lord! Lord!" but that we did good to our fellow creatures. See Matt. xxv.

Although Franklin did not consider churchgoing as a positive sign of virtue for himself, he saw merit in it for others, particularly his daughter Sarah, to whom he wrote:

GO CONSTANTLY TO CHURCH, whoever preaches. The act of devotion in the *Common Prayer Book* is your principal business there, and if properly attended to, will do more toward amending the heart than sermons generally can do. For they were composed by men of much greater piety and wisdom than our common composers of sermons can pretend to be; and therefore I wish you would never miss the prayer days; yet I do not mean you should despise sermons, even of the preachers you dislike, for the discourse is often much better than the man, as sweet and clear waters come through very dirty earth. I am the more particular on this head, as you seemed to express a little before I came away some inclination to leave our church, which I would not have you do.

For the rest, I would only recommend to you in my absence to acquire those useful accomplishments, arithmetic and bookkeeping. This you might do with ease, if you would resolve not to see company on the hours you set apart for those studies. . . .

To his daughter Sarah, papa Franklin says, in effect, "Go to church regularly, even though I do not, and do your home work instead of having so many dates." Parents were ever thus.

CHAPTER II

SUCCESS STORY

ॐ

When Benjamin Franklin walked into Philadelphia in 1723 he was alone, friendless in the Quaker city, and his capital was one Dutch dollar. When he retired from business twenty-five years later he was the most famous man in Philadelphia and had enough money so that he need never work again. He did it by applying to his trade as a printer his creed of industry and frugality—and a certain amount of genius.

While working as a journeyman for a printer named Keimer, he attracted the attention of the Governor of the colony, William Keith, who proposed to set him up in business for himself and sent young Franklin to London to buy the necessary equipment, telling him that letters of introduction and credit were in the mail pouch on the ship. When Franklin arrived in London there were no letters—Keith was a dreamer. Again, at the age of eighteen, he was in an unfamiliar city, a stranger and broke. He worked as a printer in London for two years. Then a Quaker named Denham, whom he had met on the ship coming over, offered him a post as a clerk in a store that he was opening in Philadelphia and advanced passage money home.

Within a year Denham died and Benjamin went back to work

for Keimer until the father of a fellow worker financed a print shop for his son and Franklin. At the age of twenty-two he was in business for himself with a partner. The next year he started his first newspaper, the *Pennsylvania Gazette*. The following year he became the official printer for Pennsylvania, the sole owner of the print shop and newspaper, and married Deborah Read—the girl who supposedly laughed at him on his first day in town.

In the same year in which he started his print shop he organized the Junto, a discussion group, debating and wine-drinking society of a dozen young men who met every Friday evening. The club was a combination social group, forum, self-improvement society and Junior Chamber of Commerce—with emphasis on self-improvement. Franklin wrote the rules.

RULES FOR A CLUB ESTABLISHED

FOR MUTUAL IMPROVEMENT

Previous Question, to be answered at every meeting

Have you read over these queries this morning in order to consider what you might have to offer the Junto touching on one of them? viz.,

1. Have you met with anything, in the author you last read, remarkable or suitable to be communicated to the Junto, particularly in history, morality, poetry, physic, travels, mechanic arts, or other parts of knowledge?

2. What new story have you lately heard agreeable for telling in conversation?

3. Has any citizen in your knowledge failed in his business lately, and what have you heard of the cause?

4. Have you lately heard of any citizen's thriving well, and by what means?

5. Have you lately heard how any present rich man, here or elsewhere, got his estate?

6. Do you know of a fellow citizen who has lately done a worthy action, deserving praise and imitation; or who has lately committed an error, proper for us to be warned against and avoid?

7. What unhappy effects of intemperance have you lately observed or heard; of imprudence, of passion, or of any other vice or folly?

8. What happy effects of temperance, of prudence, of moderation, or of any other virtue?

9. Have you or any of your acquaintance been lately sick or wounded? If so, what remedies were used, and what were their effects?

10. Whom do you know that are shortly going on voyages or journeys, if one should have occasion to send by them?

11. Do you think of anything at present in which the Junto may be serviceable to mankind, to their country, to their friends, or to themselves?

12. Hath any deserving stranger arrived in town since last meeting that you have heard of? And what have you heard or observed of his character or merits? And whether, think you, it lies in the power of the Junto to oblige him, or encourage him as he deserves?

13. Do you know of any deserving young beginner lately set up, whom it lies in the power of the Junto any way to encourage?

14. Have you lately observed any defect in the laws of your country of which it would be proper to move the legislature for an amendment? Or do you know of any beneficial law that is wanting?

15. Have you lately observed any encroachment on the just liberties of the people?

16. Hath anybody attacked your reputation lately. And what can the Junto do toward securing it?

17. Is there any man whose friendship you want, and which the Junto, or any of them, can procure for you?

18. Have you lately heard any member's character attacked, and how have you defended it?

19. Hath any man injured you, from whom it is in the power of the Junto to procure redress?

20. In what manner can the Junto, or any of them, assist you in any of your honorable designs?

21. Have you any weighty affair on hand in which you think the advice of the Junto may be of service?

22. What benefits have you lately received from any man not present?

23. Is there any difficulty in matters of opinion, of justice and injustice, which you would gladly have discussed at this time?

24. Do you see anything amiss in the present customs or proceedings of the Junto which might be amended?

Any person, to be qualified, [is] to stand up and lay his hand upon his breast and be asked these questions, viz.:

1. Have you any particular disrespect to any present members? *Answer.* I have not.

2. Do you sincerely declare that you love mankind in general, of what profession or religion soever? *Answer.* I do.

3. Do you think any person ought to be harmed in his body, name, or goods, for mere speculative opinions, or his external way of worship? *Answer.* No.

4. Do you love truth for truth's sake, and will you endeavor impartially to find and receive it yourself, and communicate it to others? *Answer.* Yes.

Franklin left some notes on queries that he asked the Junto to discuss—together with some of his own answers. These are things that he was thinking about in his early twenties.

"How shall we judge the goodness of writing? Or what qualities should a writing have to be good and perfect of its kind?" Franklin answered, "It should be smooth, clear and short."

"What is wisdom?" Franklin thought: "The knowledge of what is best for us on all occasions, and the best way of obtaining it."

"Is any man wise at all times and in all things?" Answer, according to Franklin: "No, but some are more frequently wise than others."

Some questions he did not answer. "Can a man arrive at perfection in this life, as some believe; or is it impossible, as others believe?"

"Wherein consists the happiness of a rational creature?"

"If the sovereign power attempts to deprive a subject of his right (or, which is the same thing, what he thinks is his right), is it justifiable for him to resist, if he is able?"

"Which is best: to make a friend of a wise and good man that is poor or of a rich man that is neither wise nor good?"

"Whence comes the dew that stands on the outside of a tankard that has cold water in it in the summertime?"

Through the years the Junto became a force in the community. Among other things it started the first circulating library in the colonies, formed the nucleus of the American Philosophical Society, carried some weight politically and swung some printing and publishing business to its founder.

Possibly stimulated by discussions in the Junto, Franklin at about this time conceived of what he describes as "a great and extensive project" and made some notes on it. In the last years of his life he expressed his great disappointment that he had never found the leisure to carry out this project—which he had tentatively named "The Society of the Free and Easy." It is unfortunate that he did not for, in a sense, his notes suggest the earliest groping for some kind of a United Nations.

OBSERVATIONS on my reading history, in Library, May 19, 1731.

That the great affairs of the world, the wars, revolutions, etc., are carried on and affected by parties.

That the view of these parties is their present general interest, or what they take to be such.

That the different views of these different parties occasion all confusion.

That while a party is carrying on a general design, each man has his particular private interest in view.

That as soon as a party has gained its general point, each member becomes intent upon his particular interest; which, thwarting others, breaks that party into divisions, and occasions more confusion.

That few in public affairs act from a mere view of the good of their country, whatever they may pretend; and though their actions bring real good to their country, yet men primarily considered that their own and their country's interest was united, and did not act from a principle of benevolence.

That fewer still, in public affairs, act with a view to the good of mankind.

There seems to me at present to be great occasion for raising a United Party for Virtue, by forming the virtuous and good men of all nations into a regular body, to be governed by suitable good and wise rules, which good and wise men may probably be more unanimous in their obedience to, than common people are to common laws.

I at present think that whoever attempts this aright, and is well qualified, can not fail of pleasing God, and of meeting with success.

On his way to the top financially, Franklin used his wits as well as industry and skill. When he decided to publish his newspaper he explained his plans to a man he proposed to hire. This individual promptly disclosed the project to Keimer, who rushed into print with a newspaper of his own. There was already one paper in Philadelphia, the *American Weekly Mercury,* published by a third printer, William Bradford. To wreck Keimer's enterprise, Franklin contributed a series of clever and entertaining essays to the *Mercury.* They were so successful in diverting readers from Keimer's dull paper that it failed and Franklin bought it for a song a few months later. In these contributions to the *Mercury,* Franklin used something of the same technique as in the Dogood papers, signing them "Busy-Body." The first of them explains what he proposed to do in the series.

I DESIGN THIS to acquaint you, that I, who have long been one of your courteous readers, have lately entertained some thoughts of setting up for an author myself; not out of the least vanity, I assure you, or desire for showing my parts, but purely for the good of my country.

I have often observed with concern that your *Mercury* is not always equally entertaining. The delay of ships expected in, and want of fresh advices from Europe, make it frequently very dull; and I find the freezing of our river has the same effect on news as on trade. With more concern have I continually observed the growing vices and follies of my country-folk; and, though reformation is properly the concern of every man; that is, everyone ought to mend one; yet 'tis too true in this case, that what is everybody's business is nobody's business; and the business is done accordingly. I therefore, upon mature deliberation, think fit to take nobody's business wholly into my own hands; and out of zeal for the public good, design to erect myself into a kind of *Censor Morum;* proposing, with your allowance, to make use of the *Weekly Mercury* as a vehicle in which my remonstrances shall be conveyed to the world.

I am sensible I have in this particular undertaken a very unthankful office, and expect little besides my labor for my pains. Nay, 'tis probable I may displease a great number of your readers, who will not very well like to pay ten shillings a year for being told of their faults. But, as most people delight in censure when they themselves are not the object of it, if any are offended at my publicly exposing their private vices, I promise they shall have the satisfaction, in a very little time, of seeing their good friends and neighbors in the same circumstances.

However, let the fair sex be assured that I shall always treat them and their affairs with the utmost decency and respect. I intend now and then to dedicate a chapter wholly to their service; and if my lectures any way contribute to the embellishment of their minds and brightening of their understandings, without offending their modesty, I doubt not of having their favor and encouragement.

Sometimes I propose to deliver lectures of morality or philosophy, and (because I am naturally inclined to be meddling with things that don't concern me) perhaps I may sometimes talk politics. And if I can by any means furnish out a weekly entertainment for the public that will give a rational diversion, and at the same time be instructive to the readers. I shall think my leisure hours well employed. . . .

While he was writing the Busy-Body essays to confound a competitor, Franklin's fertile mind turned to a chronic problem in America, then as now—money. There was not enough of it. Franklin saw a way to correct this situation and, at the same time, pick up some printing business. He tells about it in his autobiography:

ABOUT THIS TIME there was a cry among the people for more paper money, only fifteen thousand pounds being extant in the province, and that soon to be sunk. The wealthy inhabitants opposed any addition, being against all paper currency, from an apprehension that it would depreciate, as it had done in New England, to the prejudice of all creditors. We had discussed this point in our Junto, where I was on the side of an addition, being persuaded that the first small sum struck in 1723 had done much good by increasing the trade, employment, and number of inhabitants in the province. . . .

Our debates possessed me so fully of the subject that I wrote and printed an anonymous pamphlet on it, entitled *The Nature and Necessity of a Paper Currency*. It was well received by the common people in general; but the rich men disliked it, for it increased and strengthened the clamor for more money, and they happening to have no writers among them that were able to answer it, their opposition slackened, and the point was carried by a majority in the House. My friends there, who conceived I had been of some service, thought fit to reward me by employing me in printing the money; a very profitable job and a great help to me. This was another advantage gained by my being able to write.

The pamphlet on paper currency was a long, logical exposition of all of the potential benefits of a greater quantity of legal tender. One part of it is of particular interest in connection with Franklin the economist because it states exactly the same doctrine—the theory of labor as a standard of value—that the famous economist Adam Smith propounded forty-six years later in *The Wealth of Nations*. At the time he wrote it, Franklin was only twenty-three years old.

IT REMAINS NOW that we inquire whether a large addition to our paper currency will not make it sink in value very much. And here it will be requisite that we first form just notions of the nature and value of money in general.

As Providence has so ordered it that not only different countries, but even different parts of the same country, have

their peculiar most suitable productions; and likewise that
different men have geniuses adapted to variety of different
arts and manufactures, therefore, commerce, or the exchange
of one commodity or manufacture for another, is highly
convenient and beneficial to mankind. As for instance, A
may be skillful in the art of making cloth, and B understand
the raising of corn; A wants corn, and B cloth; upon which
they make an exchange with each other for as much as each
has occasion, to the mutual advantage and satisfaction of
both.

But as it would be very tedious, if there were no other
way of general dealing, but by an immediate exchange of
commodities; because a man that had corn to dispose of
and wanted cloth for it, might perhaps, in his search for a
chapman to deal with, meet with twenty people that had
cloth to dispose of, but wanted no corn; and twenty others
that wanted his corn, but had no cloth to suit him with. To
remedy such inconveniences, and facilitate exchange, men
have invented *money,* properly called a medium of exchange, because through or by its means labor is exchanged
for labor, or one commodity for another. And whatever particular thing men have agreed to make this medium of,
whether gold, silver, copper or tobacco, it is, to those who
possess it (if they want anything), that very thing which they
want, because it will immediately procure it for them. It is
cloth to him that wants cloth, and corn to those that want
corn; and so of all other necessaries, it *is* whatever it will
procure. . . .

For many ages, those parts of the world which are engaged in commerce have fixed upon gold and silver as the
chief and most proper materials for this medium; they being
in themselves valuable metals for their fineness, beauty and
scarcity. By these, particularly by silver, it has been usual
to value all things else. But as silver itself is of no certain
permanent value, being worth more or less according to its

scarcity or plenty, therefore it seems requisite to fix upon something else, more proper to be made a measure of values, and this I take to be labor.

It has been said that Franklin was the first American economist. Through the years he wrote numerous papers on money, national wealth, credit, wages, the movements of population and other economic subjects. Also, much of the material in the prefaces to *Poor Richard's Almanac* was in this area, as were many of his contributions to the European press. In some ways his views on economics were similar to those of many mid-twentieth-century economists, in that he often considered economics the handmaiden of political expediency.

While pursuing the almighty dollar, editing a newspaper and spreading his comments on morals, religion, economics and other aspects of human affairs, Franklin had time for continual soul searching in connection with his own code of virtue and conduct. In his autobiography he describes how he undertook to improve himself morally and ethically.

IT WAS ABOUT THIS TIME I conceived the bold and arduous project of arriving at moral perfection. I wished to live without committing any fault at any time; I would conquer all that either natural inclination, custom, or company might lead me into. As I knew, or thought I knew, what was right and wrong, I did not see why I might not always do the one and avoid the other. But I soon found I had undertaken a task of more difficulty than I had imagined. While my care was employed in guarding against one fault, I was often surprised by another; habit took the advantage of inattention; inclination was sometimes too strong for reason. I concluded, at length, that the mere speculative conviction that it was our interest to be completely virtuous was not sufficient to prevent our slipping; and that the contrary habits must be broken, and good ones acquired and established, before we can have any dependence upon a steady, uniform rectitude of conduct. For this purpose I therefore contrived the following method.

In the various enumerations of the moral virtues I had met with in my reading, I found the catalogue more or less numerous, as different writers included more or fewer ideas under the same name. Temperance, for example, was by some confined to eating and drinking, while by others it was extended to mean the moderating every other pleasure, appetite, inclination, or passion, bodily or mental, even to our avarice and ambition. I proposed to myself, for the sake of clearness, to use rather more names, with fewer ideas annexed to each, than a few names with more ideas; and I included, under thirteen names of virtues, all that at that time occurred to me as necessary or desirable, and annexed to each a short precept, which fully expressed the extent I gave to its meaning.

These names of virtues, with their precepts, were:

1. TEMPERANCE
Eat not to dullness; drink not to elevation.

2. SILENCE
Speak not but what may benefit others or yourself; avoid trifling conversation.

3. ORDER
Let all your things have their places; let each part of your business have its time.

4. RESOLUTION
Resolve to perform what you ought; perform without fail what you resolve.

5. FRUGALITY
Make no expense but to do good to others or yourself; i.e., waste nothing.

6. INDUSTRY

Lose no time; be always employed in something useful; cut off all unnecessary actions.

7. SINCERITY

Use no hurtful deceit; think innocently and justly, and, if you speak, speak accordingly.

8. JUSTICE

Wrong none by doing injuries, or omitting the benefits that are your duty.

9. MODERATION

Avoid extremes; forbear resenting injuries so much as you think they deserve.

10. CLEANLINESS

Tolerate no uncleanliness in body, clothes, or habitation.

11. TRANQUILLITY

Be not disturbed at trifles, or at accidents common or unavoidable.

12. CHASTITY

Rarely use venery but for health or offspring, never to dullness, weakness, or the injury of your own or another's peace or reputation.

13. HUMILITY

Imitate Jesus and Socrates.

My intention being to acquire the habitude of all these virtues, I judged it would be well not to distract my attention by attempting the whole at once, but to fix it on one of them at a time; and, when I should be master of that, then to proceed to another, and so on, till I should have gone through the thirteen; and, as the previous acquisition of some might facilitate the acquisition of certain others, I arranged them with that view, as they stand above. Temperance first, as it tends to procure that coolness and clearness of head, which is so necessary where constant vigilance was to be kept up, and guard maintained against the unremitting attraction of ancient habits, and the force of perpetual temptations. This being acquired and established, Silence would be more easy; and my desire being to gain knowledge at the same time that I improved in virtue, and in considering that in conversation it was obtained rather by the use of the ears than of the tongue, and therefore wishing to break a habit I was getting into of prattling, punning and joking, which only made me acceptable to trifling company, I gave Silence the second place. This and the next, Order, I expected would allow me more time for attending to my project and my studies. Resolution, once become habitual, would keep me firm in my endeavors to obtain all the subsequent virtues; Frugality and Industry freeing me from my remaining debt, and producing affluence and independence, would make more easy the practice of Sincerity and Justice, etc., etc. Conceiving then that . . . daily examination would be necessary, I contrived the following method for conducting that examination.

I made a little book, in which I allotted a page for each of the virtues. I ruled each page with red ink, so as to have seven columns, one for each day of the week, marking each column with a letter for the day. I crossed these columns with thirteen red lines, marking the beginning of each line with the first letter of one of the virtues, on which line, and in its proper column, I might mark by a little black spot every fault I found upon examination to have been committed respecting that virtue upon that day.

I determined to give a week's strict attention to each of the virtues successively. Thus, in the first week, my great guard was to avoid every the least offense against Temperance, leaving the other virtues in their ordinary chance, only marking every evening the faults of the day. Thus, if in the first week I could keep my first line, marked T, clear of spots, I supposed the habit of that virtue so much strengthened, and its opposite weakened, that I might venture extending my attention to include the next, and for the following week keep both lines clear of spots. . . .

In truth, I found myself incorrigible with respect to Order; and now I am grown old, and my memory bad, I feel very sensibly the want of it. But, on the whole, though I never arrived at the perfection I had been so ambitious of obtaining, but fell far short of it, yet I was, by the endeavor, a better and a happier man than I otherwise should have been if I had not attempted it; as those who aim at perfect writing by imitating the engraved copies, though they never reach the wished-for excellence of those copies, their hand is mended by the endeavor, and it is tolerable while it continues fair and legible.

Through the 1730's and the early forties Franklin's fortunes rose. He added a stationery shop to his newspaper and press as a money-making enterprise. He described his success as follows:

I BEGAN NOW gradually to pay off the debt I was under for the printing-house. In order to secure my credit and character as a tradesman, I took care not only to be in reality industrious and frugal, but to avoid all appearances to the contrary. I dressed plainly; I was seen at no places of idle diversion. I never went out a fishing or shooting; a book, indeed, sometimes debauched me from my work, but that was seldom, snug, and gave no scandal; and, to show that I was not above my business, I sometimes brought home the paper I purchased at the stores through the streets on a wheelbarrow. Thus being esteemed an industrious, thriving young man, and paying duly for what I bought, the merchants who imported stationery solicited my custom;

FORM OF THE PAGES

TEMPERANCE							
Eat not to Dulness. *Drink not to Elevation.*							
	SUN.	MON.	TUES.	WED.	THURS.	FRI.	SAT.
T [Temperance]							
S [Silence]	● ●	●		●		●	
O [Order]	●	●	●		●	●	●
R [Resolution]			●			●	
F [Frugality]		●			●		
I [Industry]			●				
S [Sincerity]							
J [Justice]							
M [Moderation]							
Cl. [Cleanliness]							
T [Tranquility]							
Ch. [Chastity]							
H [Humility]							

Benjamin Franklin's Notebook of Virtues

others proposed supplying me with books, and I went on swimmingly. . . .

Reading was the only amusement I allowed myself. I spent no time in taverns, games, or frolics of any kind; and my industry in my business continued as indefatigable as it was necessary. I was indebted for my printing-house; I had a young family coming on to be educated, and I had to contend with for business two printers, who were established in the place before me. My circumstances, however, grew daily easier. My original habits of frugality continuing, and my father having, among his instructions to me when a boy, frequently repeated a proverb of Solomon, "Seest thou a man diligent in his calling, he shall stand before kings, he shall not stand before mean men," I from thence considered industry as a means of obtaining wealth and distinction, which encouraged me, though I did not think that I should ever literally "stand before kings," which, however, has since happened; for I have stood before five, and even had the honor of sitting down with one, the King of Denmark, to dinner.

As his business progressed he turned some of the work over to journeymen and apprentices and undertook more outside activities. In 1736 he became clerk of the General Assembly— a job that did not pay much but that gave him access to an original news source and from which he secured contracts to print votes, laws and paper money. In 1737 he became a justice of the peace and the deputy-postmaster of Philadelphia. His competitor, Bradford, had held this job and, while he had it, Franklin had to bribe the post-riders to carry the *Gazette*— Bradford permitted them to carry only his own *Mercury*. Now Franklin controlled out-of-town distribution and had first access to incoming news. He says that he did not retaliate on Bradford, but the latter was soon out of business, leaving a monopoly of the printing and publishing business to Franklin except for a couple of small German-language printers.

As clerk of the Assembly, Franklin was required to attend all the sessions—some of which were long and dull. Franklin's mind could not be idle. Like a small boy hiding a comic book inside a text book, he made "magic squares" among his clerkly papers while the legislators droned on. He had come a long way in handling numbers since he failed in arithmetic at the age of nine. In a letter, written many years later, he described, and belittled, this mathematical exercise. ". . . I then confessed to him, that in my younger days, having once some leisure, (which I still think I might have employed more usefully) I had amused myself in making these kind of magic squares, and, at length, had acquired such a knack at it, that I could fill the cells of any magic square, of reasonable size, with a series of numbers as fast as I could write them, disposed in such a manner, as that the sums of every row, horizontal, perpendicular, or diagonal, should be equal. . . ."

52	61	4	13	20	29	36	45
14	3	62	51	46	35	30	19
53	60	5	12	21	28	37	44
11	6	59	54	43	38	27	22
55	58	7	10	23	26	39	42
9	8	57	56	41	40	25	24
50	63	2	15	18	31	34	47
16	1	64	49	48	33	32	17

Franklin's "Magic Squares"

During this time Franklin made the first of his inventions—
the famed Franklin stove. He mentions it in his autobiography
and, at the same time, expresses his attitude on patents and
explains why he never sought to make money from his many
inventions.

HAVING, IN 1742, invented an open stove for the better
warming of rooms, and at the same time saving fuel, as the
fresh air admitted was warmed in entering, I made a present
of the model to Mr. Robert Grace, one of my early friends,
who, having an iron-furnace, found the casting of the plates
for these stoves a profitable thing, as they were growing in
demand. To promote that demand, I wrote and published
a pamphlet entitled "An account of the new-invented Pennsylvania fireplaces; wherein their construction and manner
of operation is particularly explained; their advantages
above every other method of warming rooms demonstrated;
and all objections that have been raised against the use of
them answered and obviated," etc. This pamphlet had a
good effect. Governor Thomas was so pleased with the construction of this stove, as described in it, that he offered to
give me a patent for the sole vending of them for a term of
years; but I declined it from a principle which has ever
weighed with me on such occasions, viz., that as we enjoy
great advantages from the inventions of others, we should
be glad of an opportunity to serve others by any invention
of ours; and this we should do freely and generously.

In connection with the stove pamphlet, one early biographer
wrote, "The test of literary genius is the ability to be fascinating
about stoves."

From stoves Franklin's nimble brain jumped to the need for
an organization for the exchange of views and information on
scientific progress, and the American Philosophical Society was
born. Although the nucleus of this was a half dozen associates in

the Junto, it had members throughout the other colonies and correspondents in England. Franklin started it with:

A PROPOSAL FOR PROMOTING USEFUL KNOWLEDGE AMONG THE BRITISH PLANTATIONS IN AMERICA
(Philadelphia, May 14, 1743)

The English are possessed of a long tract of continent, from Nova Scotia to Georgia, extending north and south through different climates, having different soils, producing different plants, mines and minerals, and capable of different improvements, manufactures, etc.

The first drudgery of settling new colonies, which confines the attention of the people to mere necessaries, is now pretty well over; and there are many in every province in circumstances that set them at ease, and afford leisure to cultivate the finer arts and improve the common stock of knowledge. To such of these who are men of speculation, many hints must from time to time arise, many observations occur, which, if well examined, pursued, and improved, might produce discoveries to the advantage of some or all of the British plantations, or to the benefit of mankind in general.

But as from the extent of the country such persons are widely separated, and seldom can see and converse or be acquainted with each other, so that many useful particulars remain uncommunicated, die with the discoverers, and are lost to mankind; it is, to remedy this inconvenience for the future, proposed,

That one society be formed of *virtuosi* or ingenious men, residing in the several colonies, to be called The American Philosophical Society, who are to maintain a constant correspondence.

As in all of Franklin's grand plans, this document started by proposing a new idea, and continued with a practical, detailed proposal for making the idea effective. Philadelphia, "being the city nearest the center" of the colonies, should be the headquarters. There should always be seven members in Philadelphia: "a physician, a botanist, a mathematician, a chemist, a mechanician, a geographer, and a general natural philosopher." Philadelphia members should meet once a month and correspond with distant members about "all new-discovered plants, herbs, trees, roots . . . new methods of curing or preventing diseases; all new-discovered . . . mines, minerals and quarries . . . new mechanical inventions for saving labor . . . all new arts, trades and manufactures that may be proposed or thought of . . . surveys, maps and charts . . . nature of soil and productions; new methods of improving the breed of useful animals . . . and all philosophical experiments that let light into the nature of things, tend to increase the power of man over matter, and multiply the conveniences and pleasures of life."

The balance of the proposal was a detailed plan for organization, meetings, dues, etc. This society, which Franklin organized almost 220 years ago, is still going strong.

Franklin's interest in community affairs was growing during this period. He had spark-plugged the building of a large, nonsectarian meeting house; had written a plan for reorganizing the city watch—the police department; had promoted the first volunteer fire department. Then, in 1747, he sprang into civic prominence by organizing a militia.

Philadelphia was not concerned about the war of France and Spain against England until some French and Spanish privateers sailed up the Delaware and sacked two plantations and captured a ship a few miles below the city. Even then, nothing was done. The Quakers dominated the assembly and their religion opposed even defensive violence. The wealthy merchants would not spend money for the defense of Quaker property as well as their own. Franklin said it reminded him of the story of "him who refused to pump in a sinking ship because one on board

whom he hated would be saved by it as well as himself." The
Germans and Scotch-Irish on interior farms would not contribute to the defense of the city folk—and the urbanites would
not support a force to ward off Indian attacks on outlying farms.
In the emergency, Franklin sprang into the breach. He says:

I DETERMINED TO TRY what might be done by a voluntary
association of the people. To promote this, I first wrote and
published a pamphlet entitled *Plain Talk,* in which I stated
our defenseless situation in strong lights, with the necessity
of union and discipline for our defense, and promised to
propose in a few days an association to be generally signed
for that purpose. The pamphlet had a sudden and surprising
effect. I was called upon for the instrument of association,
and having settled the draft of it with a few friends, I appointed a meeting of the citizens in the large building before
mentioned. The house was pretty full; I had prepared a
number of printed copies, and provided pens and ink dispersed all over the room. I harangued them a little on the
subject, read the paper, and explained it, and then distributed the copies, which were eagerly signed, not the least
objection being made.

When the company separated and the papers were collected, we found above twelve hundred hands; and other
copies being dispersed in the country, the subscribers
amounted at length to upward of ten thousand. These all
furnished themselves as soon as they could with arms,
formed themselves into companies and regiments, chose
their own officers, and met every week to be instructed in
the manual exercise and other parts of military discipline.
The women, by subscriptions among themselves, provided
silk colors which they presented to the companies, painted
with different devices and mottoes which I supplied.

The officers of the companies composing the Philadelphia

regiment, being met, chose me for their colonel; but conceiving myself unfit, I declined that station.

In *Plain Talk* Franklin went over the head of the Quaker-dominated Assembly and the rich upper class with a ringing appeal to the people. Though most of his writing is noted for its clarity, simplicity and logic, he could be a dramatic rabble rouser when the need arose.

YOU HAVE, my dear countrymen and fellow citizens, riches to tempt a considerable force to unite and attack you, but are under no ties or engagements to unite for your defense. Hence, on the first alarm terror will spread over all; and as no man can with certainty depend that another will stand by him, beyond doubt very many will seek safety by a speedy flight. Those that are reputed rich will flee through fear of torture to make them produce more than they are able. The man that has a wife and children will find them hanging on his neck, beseeching him with tears to quit the city and save his life, to guide and protect them in that time of general desolation and ruin. All will run into confusion, amidst cries and lamentations and the hurry and disorder of departers, carrying away their effects. The few that remain will be unable to resist. Sacking the city will be the first, and burning it, in all probability, the last act of the enemy. This, I believe, will be the case if you have timely notice. But what must be your condition if suddenly surprised, without previous alarm, perhaps in the night! Confined to your houses, you will have nothing to trust to but the enemy's mercy. Your best fortune will be to fall under the power of commanders of king's ships, able to control the mariners; and not into the hands of licentious privateers. Who can, without the utmost horror, conceive the miseries of the latter, when your persons, fortunes, wives and daughters shall be subject to the wanton and unbridled rage,

rapine and lust of Negroes, mulattos and others, the vilest
and most abandoned of mankind. A dreadful scene, which
some may represent as exaggerated. I think it my duty to
warn you: Judge for yourselves.

'Tis true, with very little notice the rich may shift for
themselves. . . . But most unhappily circumstanced indeed
are we, the middling people, the tradesmen, shopkeepers
and farmers of this province and city! . . . We . . . and
what little we have gained by hard labor and industry, must
bear the brunt: the weight of contributions extorted by the
enemy (as it is of taxes among ourselves) must be surely
borne by us. Nor can it be avoided as we stand at present;
for though we are numerous we are quite defenseless, having neither forts, arms, union nor discipline. And though
it were true that our trade might be protected at no great
expense, and our country and our city easily defended if
proper measures were but taken, yet who shall take these
measures? Who shall pay that expense? On whom may we
fix our eyes with the least expectation that they will do any
one thing for our security? Should we address that wealthy
and powerful body of people, who have ever since the war
governed our elections and filled almost every seat in our
Assembly; should we entreat them to consider, if not as
Friends, at least as legislators, that *protection* is as truly due
from the government to the people, as *obedience* from the
people to the government? . . . Should we remind them that
the public money, raised from all, belongs to all? . . . That
though they themselves may be resigned and easy under this
naked, defenseless state of the country, it is far otherwise
with a very great part of the people—with us, who can have
no confidence that God will protect those that neglect the
use of rational means for their security? . . . Should we con-
jure them by all the ties of neighborhood, friendship, justice
and humanity to consider these things? . . . All would be in
vain, for they have already been by great numbers of peo-

ple petitioned in vain. . . . Their religious prepossessions are unchangeable, their obstinancy invincible. Is there then the least hope remaining that from that quarter any thing should arise for our security?

And is our prospect better if we turn our eyes to the strength of the opposite party, those great and rich men, merchants and others, who are ever railing at Quakers for doing what their principles seem to require, and what in charity we ought to believe they think their duty, but take no one step themselves for the public safety? They have so much wealth and influence, if they would use it. . . . But envy seems to have taken possession of their hearts, and to have eaten out and destroyed every generous, noble, public-spirited sentiment. Rage at the disappointment of their little schemes for power gnaws their souls, and fills them with such cordial hatred to their opponents, that every proposal . . . is rejected with indignation. "What," say they, "shall we lay out our money to protect the trade of Quakers? Shall we fight to defend Quakers? No, let the trade perish and the city burn; let what will happen, we shall never lift a finger to prevent it." Yet the Quakers have conscience to plead for their resolution not to fight, which these gentlemen have not. . . .

Thus unfortunately we are circumstanced at this time, my dear countrymen and fellow citizens; we, I mean the middling people, the farmers, shopkeepers and tradesmen of this city and country. Through the dissensions of our leaders, through mistaken principles of religion, joined with a love of worldly power on the one hand, through pride, envy and implacable resentment on the other, our lives, our families and little fortunes, dear to us as any great man's can be to him, are to remain continually exposed to destruction from an enterprising, cruel, now well-informed and, by success, encouraged enemy. . . . It seems as if our greatest men, our *cives nobilissimi* of both parties, had sworn the ruin of the country, and invited the French, our most inveterate enemy, to destroy it. . . . Our case indeed is dangerously bad, but perhaps there is yet a remedy if we have but the prudence and the spirit to apply it.

If this now flourishing city and greatly improving colony is destroyed and ruined, it will not be for want of numbers of inhabitants able to bear arms in its defense. 'Tis computed that we have at least (exclusive of the Quakers) 60,-000 fighting men, acquainted with firearms, many of them hunters and marksmen, hardy and bold. All we want is order, discipline and a few cannon. At present we are like the separate filaments of flax before the thread is formed, without strength, because without connection; but *Union* would make us strong and even formidable. Though the great should neither help nor join us; though they should even oppose our uniting, from some mean views of their own, yet if we resolve upon it, and it please God to inspire us with the necessary prudence and vigor, it *may* be effected. Great numbers of our people are of British race, and though the fierce fighting animals of those happy islands are said to abate their native fire and intrepidity when removed to a foreign clime, yet with the people 'tis not so. . . .

Nor are there wanting amongst us thousands of that warlike nation whose sons have, ever since the time of Caesar, maintained the character he gave their fathers of joining the most obstinate courage to all other military virtues; I mean the brave and steady Germans, numbers of whom have actually borne arms in the service of their respective princes; and if they fought well for their tyrants and oppressors, would they refuse to unite with us in defense of their newly acquired and most precious liberty and property? Were this union formed, were we once united, thoroughly armed and disciplined, was everything in our power done for our security, as far as human means and foresight could provide, we might then, with more propriety, humbly ask the assistance of Heaven and a blessing on our lawful endeavors. The very fame of our strength and readiness would be a means of discouraging our enemies; for 'tis a wise and true saying that "one sword often keeps another in the scabbard." The way to secure peace is to be prepared for war. . . . We have yet a winter before us, which may afford a good and almost sufficient opportunity for this, if we seize and improve it with a becoming vigor. . . .

May the God of Wisdom, Strength and Power, the Lord of the armies of Israel, inspire us with prudence in this time of danger; take away from us all the seeds of contention and division, and unite the hearts and counsels of all of us, of whatever sect or nation, in one bond of peace, brotherly love and generous public spirit; may He give us strength and resolution to amend our lives, and remove from us everything that is displeasing to Him; afford us His most gracious protection, confound the designs of our enemies, and give peace in all our borders, is the sincere prayer of

A Tradesman of Philadelphia.

Although he turned down the rank of colonel in the militia, Franklin accepted a commission to go to New York to try to get some cannon. Here the shrewd businessman showed that he was not above taking advantage of the governor in his cups to get what he wanted. He says:

Meanwhile, Colonel Lawrence, William Allen, Abram Taylor, Esq., and myself were sent to New York by the associators, commissioned to borrow some cannon of Governor George Clinton. He at first refused us peremptorily; but at dinner with his council, where there was great drinking of Madeira wine, as the custom of that place then was, he softened by degrees, and said he would lend us six. After a few more bumpers he advanced to ten, and at length he very good-naturedly conceded eighteen. They were fine cannon, eighteen-pounders, with their carriages, which we soon transported and mounted on our battery, where the associators kept a nightly guard while the war lasted, and amongst the rest I regularly took my turn of duty there as a common soldier.

Franklin's influence was spreading. He had financed print shops in South Carolina, Rhode Island, Connecticut, Jamaica and New York, taking one-third of the profits. Then, in 1748, he took in a partner in Philadelphia, David Hall. He left Hall to run the business and retired, with an income from his partnerships and real estate of about £1,000 a year—equal to that of the governor of the colony.

He said, "My business was now continually augmenting and my circumstances growing daily easier, my newspaper having become very profitable, as being for a time almost the only one in this and the neighboring provinces. I experienced, too, the truth of the observation that 'after getting the first hundred pounds, it is more easy to get the second,' money itself being of a prolific nature."

CHAPTER III

THE POOR MAN'S CONFUCIUS

ॐ

If a popular poll were held to determine the best-known thing that Benjamin Franklin ever wrote, the winner would probably be:

> Early to bed, and early to rise,
> Makes a man healthy, wealthy, and wise.

It was one of the maxims in *Poor Richard's Almanac* for the year 1735. And Benjamin Franklin probably did not write it.

In colonial days there were but two pieces of printed matter in most homes—a Bible and an almanac. The latter was a paper-bound, pocket-size booklet which both city and country folk considered indispensable. It was a combination calendar, miniature encyclopedia, moral counselor and source of all kinds of tidbits of miscellaneous information. It noted the holidays, the tides, the quarters of the moon, the dates of the fairs and of the court sessions. It contained jokes, poems, maxims and sometimes recipes.

The almanac had a mysterious, magical quality for those who believed in astrology—which was then in great vogue. It forecast the weather and foretold the future. Farmers selected their days for planting from it; mariners their days for sailing. For businessmen it determined the best day to close a deal. Women used it to forecast the future of a newborn child, and children to learn to read.

A printer might not make money from books or a newspaper, but he was sure of a profit from an almanac. In 1732 Bradford was printing four, Franklin two. When Franklin lost his almanac customers that year, he decided to bring out his own annual book. He described its beginning in his autobiography:

IN 1732 I first published my *Almanac,* under the name of Richard Saunders; it was continued by me about twenty-five years, commonly called *Poor Richard's Almanac.* I endeavored to make it both entertaining and useful, and it accordingly came to be in such demand that I reaped considerable profit from it, vending annually near ten thousand. And observing that it was generally read, scarce any neighborhood in the province being without it, I considered it as a proper vehicle for conveying instructions among the common people, who bought scarcely any other books; I therefore filled all the little spaces that occurred between the remarkable days in the calendar with proverbial sentences, chiefly such as inculcated industry and frugality, as the means of procuring wealth, and thereby securing virtue; it being more difficult for a man in want to act always honestly, as, to use here one of those proverbs: "It is hard for an empty sack to stand upright."

Ironically, there was little that was original with Franklin in his best-known literary legacy. He took the name from *Poor Robin's Almanac,* which was published by his brother. The *Richard* came from the name of an actual English astrologer, Richard Saunders. Few of the famous proverbs in *Poor Richard* originated with Franklin—over two-thirds of them have been traced to their original sources. But Franklin did not copy them.

He changed them to conform to his smooth, clear, concise and vigorous style. In their original form they would have been long forgotten. In Franklin's form they became part of the language.

The original Scotch proverb "A listening damsel and a speaking castle shall never end with honor" became, in Franklin's version, "Neither a fortress nor a maid will hold out long after they begin to parley." The English proverb "God restoreth health and the physician hath the thanks" was changed to "God heals and the doctor takes the fee." "Fresh fish and new-come guests smell, but that they are three days old"—"Fish and visitors smell in three days." "The maintaining of one vice costeth more than ten virtues"—"What maintains one vice would bring up two children." "A muffled cat is no good mouser"—"The cat in gloves catches no mice."

In making changes to sharpen the proverbs, Franklin sought balance and brevity. He changed "The greatest talkers are the least doers" to "Great talkers, little doers." Frequently he introduced alliteration—for instance, "Men and melons are hard to know," or "Sloth and silence are fool's virtues." Sometimes the change of a single word would point up a sentence to make it more meaningful. "Many strokes fell great oaks" became "Little strokes fell great oaks"—a much more graphic concept of the idea. In other cases Franklin added a thought to give the original a whole new meaning, as in the proverb "The king's cheese goes half away in parings," which he changed to "The king's cheese is half wasted in parings; but no matter, 'tis made of the people's milk."

Franklin said that he found his proverbs in "the wisdom of many ages and many nations." Since age-old wisdom spoke with many tongues, Franklin, during the early years of *Poor Richard,* taught himself to read French, Spanish, Italian, German and Latin.

Each almanac started with a preface. The first one described Richard Saunders and contained a publicity stunt to launch his new venture.

COURTEOUS READER:

I might in this place attempt to gain thy favor by declaring that I write almanacs with no other view than that of the public good; but in this I would not be sincere, and men are nowadays too wise to be deceived by pretenses how specious soever. The plain truth of the matter is, I am excessive poor, and my wife, good woman, is, I tell her, excessive proud. She cannot bear, she says, to sit spinning in her shift of tow, while I do nothing but gaze at the stars, and has threatened more than once to burn all my books and rattling-traps (as she calls my instruments) if I do not make some profitable use of them for the good of my family. The printer has offered me some considerable share of the profits, and I have thus begun to comply with my dame's desire.

Indeed this motive would have had force enough to have made me publish an almanac many years since, had it not been overpowered by my regard for my good friend and fellow student Mr. Titan Leeds, whose interest I was extremely unwilling to hurt. But this obstacle (I am far from speaking it with pleasure) is soon to be removed, since inexorable death, who has never known to respect merit, has already prepared the mortal dart, the fatal sister has already extended her destroying shears, and that ingenious man must soon be taken from us. He dies, by my calculation made at his request, on October 17, 1733. By his own calculation he will survive till the 26th of the same month. . . . Which of us is most exact, a little time will now determine. As therefore these provinces may not longer expect to see any of his performances after this year, I think myself free to take up the task, and request a share of the public encouragement, which I am the more apt to hope for on this account, that the buyer of my almanac may consider himself not only purchasing an useful utensil, but as performing an act of charity to his poor friend and servant.

R. SAUNDERS

Titan Leeds was a rival writer of an almanac published by Bradford—no "good friend and fellow student" of Franklin's. As the wily publicist anticipated, Leeds rushed into print to assure people that he was not dead and waxed indignant at Franklin for this base deceit. The feud attracted attention and sold books. Franklin kept it going for another year. In the preface to the 1737 *Almanac* he said:

THERE IS HOWEVER (and I cannot speak it without sorrow), there is the strongest probability that my dear friend is no more; for there appears in his name, as I am assured, an almanac for the year 1734, in which I am treated in a very gross and unhandsome manner; in which I am called "a false predicter, an ignorant, a conceited scribbler, a fool, and a liar." Mr. Leeds was too well bred to use any man so indecently and so scurrilously, and moreover his esteem and affection for me was extraordinary; so that it is to be feared that pamphlet may be only a contrivance of somebody or other who hopes perhaps to sell two or three years' almanacs still, by the sole force and virtue of Mr. Leeds' name; but certainly, to put words into the mouth of a gentleman and a man of letters, against his friend, which the meanest and most scandalous of people might be ashamed to utter even in a drunken quarrel, is an unpardonable injury to his memory and an imposition upon the public.

Even this Leeds hoax was not an original idea of Franklin's. He picked it up from a trick that Dean Jonathan Swift had maliciously played in 1707 when he predicted the death of one John Partridge, an almanac publisher, on March 29 of the following year. On March 30, Swift wrote and published "An Elegy on Mr. Partridge, the almanac maker, who died on the twenty-ninth of this instance." Since Swift's writings were far more widely read than Partridge's, the poor publisher spent the rest of his days denying that he was dead.

In twenty-five years of *Poor Richard* there were enough maxims to fill a good-sized book. Here are some samples under each of five headings:

MAXIMS ON VIRTUE AND THE GOOD LIFE

The noblest question in the world is, "What good may I do in it?"

There is no man so bad but he secretly respects the good.

Wish not so much to live long as to live well.

A good example is the best sermon.

He that cannot obey cannot command.

'Tis easier to suppress the first desire than to satisfy all that follow it.

Death takes no bribes.

Content makes poor men rich; discontent makes rich men poor.

Nothing brings more pain than too much pleasure; nothing more bondage than too much liberty.

Would you live with ease, do what you ought, and not what you please.

MAXIMS ON FOLLIES AND FAULTS

Sin is not hurtful because it is forbidden, but it is forbidden because it is hurtful.

The proud hate pride—in others.

Tim was so learned that he could name a horse in nine languages. So ignorant, that he bought a cow to ride on.

All blood is alike ancient.

Glass, china and reputation are easily cracked, and never well mended.

Anger is never without a reason, but seldom with a good one.

Who has deceived thee so oft as thyself?

A learned blockhead is a greater blockhead than an ignorant one.

When the wine enters, out goes the truth.

He that lieth down with dogs shall rise up with fleas.

MAXIMS ON WOMEN AND MARRIAGE

There are no ugly loves, nor handsome prisons.

Why does a blind man's wife paint herself?

If you would be loved, love and be lovable.

Keep your eyes wide open before marriage, half shut afterwards.

A ship under sail and a big-bellied woman are the handsomest two things that can be seen common.

Let thy maidservant be faithful, strong, and homely.

He that takes a wife takes care.

Where there's marriage without love, there will be love without marriage.

When a man and woman die, as poets sung,

His heart's the last part moves—her last, the tongue.

MAXIMS ON PEOPLE

Mankind are very odd creatures. One half censure what they practice, the other half practice what they censure; the rest always say and do as they ought.

To err is human, to repent divine; to persist devilish.

Love your neighbor; yet don't pull down your hedge.

The same man cannot be both friend and flatterer.

When you're good to others, you are best to yourself.

He is not well bred that cannot bear ill-breeding in others.

A mob's a monster; heads enough but no brains.

To serve the public faithfully, and at the same time please it entirely, is impracticable.

Write with the learned, pronounce with the vulgar.

MAXIMS ON WISDOM

The doors of wisdom are never shut.

Three may keep a secret, if two of them are dead.

All would live long, but none would be old.

He that would catch fish must venture his bait.

Write injuries in dust, benefits in marble.

He who pursues two hares at once does not catch the one and lets the other go.

There's a time to wink as well as to see.

The wise and brave dares own that he was wrong.

Lost time is never found again.

Franklin's interest in health and medicine—which later made him a member of both the English and French medical societies—was first evidenced in the *Almanac*. The same advice on dieting which he published in 1742 is being handed out by doctors today in modern words. At a time when metabolism was unknown, Franklin realized that a "phlegmatic" person required less food than a "choleric" one. Franklin had never heard of calories, but somehow he knew that greater quantities of some foods could be eaten—"they being of lighter digestion."

EAT AND DRINK such an exact quantity as the constitution of thy body allows of, in reference to the services of the mind.

They that study much, ought not to eat so much as those that work hard, their digestion being not so good.

Excess in all other things whatever, as well as in meat and drink, is also to be avoided.

Youth, age, and sick require a different quantity.

And so do those of contrary complexions; for that which is too much for a phlegmatic man is not sufficient for a choleric.

That quantity that is sufficient, the stomach can perfectly concoct and digest, and it sufficeth the due nourishment of the body.

A greater quantity of some things may be eaten than of others, some being of lighter digestion than other.

The difficulty lies in finding out an exact measure; but eat for necessity, not pleasure, for lust knows not where necessity ends.

Wouldst thou enjoy a long life, a healthy body, and a vigorous mind, and be acquainted also with the wonderful works of God, labor in the first place to bring thy appetite into subjection to reason.

Much has been written about the influence of *Poor Richard* in

Europe—particularly in France. Actually, few copies of the almanac went overseas. The fame of *Poor Richard* spread to the other side of the ocean through the broadcast of the preface of the 1757 *Almanac* in which Franklin collected all of the proverbs on industry and frugality that had been published in the previous almanacs for twenty-five years. He describes it as follows:

THESE PROVERBS, which contained the wisdom of many ages and nations, I assembled and formed into a connected discourse prefixed to the *Almanac* of 1757, as the harangue of a wise old man to the people attending an auction. The bringing all these scattered counsels thus into a focus enabled them to make greater impression. The piece, being universally approved, was copied in all the newspapers of the Continent; reprinted in Britain on a broadside to be stuck up in houses; two translations were made of it in French, and great numbers bought by the clergy and gentry to distribute gratis among their poor parishioners and tenants. In Pennsylvania, as it discouraged useless expense in foreign superfluities, some thought it had its share of influence in producing that growing plenty of money which was observable for several years after its publication.

The thrifty French took this sermon—entitled *The Way to Wealth*—very much to heart. As a result, the creator of "Bonhomme Richard" became a hero to the French middle class, a role which strengthened his position immeasurably when, twenty years later, he sought the support of their government for the struggling colonies. *The Way to Wealth* may seem somewhat out of date in this era of credit cards and "buy-now-pay-later," but one sage remarked that "for the past two centuries, Franklin's homely aphorisms and observations have influenced more Americans than the learned wisdom of all the formal philosophers put together."

COURTEOUS READER,

I have heard that nothing gives an author so great pleasure as to find his words respectfully quoted by other learned authors. This pleasure I have seldom enjoyed; for though I have been, if I may say it without vanity, an eminent author of almanacs annually now a full quarter of a century, my brother authors in the same way, for what reason I know not, have ever been very sparing in their applauses, and no other author has taken the least notice of me, so that did not my writings produce me some solid pudding, the great deficiency of praise would have quite discouraged me.

I concluded at length that the people were the best judges of my merit, for they buy my works; and besides, in my rambles, where I am not personally known, I have frequently heard one or other of my adages repeated with "as Poor Richard says" at the end on it. This gave me some satisfaction, as it showed that not only my instructions were regarded, but discovered likewise some respect for my authority; and I own that to encourage the practice of remembering and repeating those wise sentences, I have sometimes quoted myself with great gravity.

Judge, then, how much I must have been gratified by an incident I am going to relate to you. I stopped my horse lately where a great number of people were collected at a vendue of merchant goods. The hour of sale not being come, they were conversing on the badness of the times, and one of the company called to a plain clean old man, with white locks, "Pray, Father Abraham, what think you of the times? Won't these heavy taxes quite ruin the country? How shall we be ever able to pay them? What would you advise us to?" Father Abraham stood up, and replied, "If you'd have my advice, I'll give it to you in short, for *A word to the wise is enough,* and *Many words won't fill a bushel,* as Poor Richard says." They joined in desiring him to speak his mind, and gathering round him, he proceeded as follows:

"Friends," says he, "and neighbors, the taxes are indeed very heavy, and if those laid on by the government were the only ones we had to pay, we might more easily discharge them; but we have many others, and much more grievous to some of us. We are taxed twice as much by our idleness, three times as much by our pride, and four times as much by our folly; and from these taxes the commissioners cannot ease or deliver us by allowing an abatement. However, let us hearken to good advice, and something may be done for us. *God helps them that help themselves,* as Poor Richard says in his *Almanac* of 1733.

"It would be thought a hard government that should tax its people one-tenth part of their time, to be employed in its service. But idleness taxes many of us much more, if we reckon all that is spent in absolute sloth, or doing of nothing, with that which is spent in idle employments or amusements that amount to nothing. Sloth, by bringing on diseases, absolutely shortens life. *Sloth, like rust, consumes faster than labor wears; while the used key is always bright,* as Poor Richard says. *But dost thou love life, then do not squander time, for that's the stuff life is made of,* as Poor Richard says. How much more than is necessary do we spend in sleep, forgetting that *The sleeping fox catches no poultry,* and that *There will be sleeping enough in the grave,* as Poor Richard says.

"*If Time be of all things the most precious, wasting time must be,* as Poor Richard says, *the greatest prodigality;* since, as he elsewhere tells us, *Lost time is never found again; and what we call time enough always proves little enough.* Let us then up and be doing, and doing to the purpose; so by diligence shall we do more with less perplexity. *Sloth makes all things difficult, but industry all easy,* as Poor Richard says; and *He that riseth late must trot all day, and shall scarce overtake his business at night,* while *Laziness travels so slowly that poverty soon overtakes him,* as we read in

Poor Richard, who adds, *Drive thy business, let not that drive thee;* and *Early to bed, and early to rise, makes a man healthy, wealthy, and wise.*

"So what signifies wishing and hoping for better times? We may make these times better, if we bestir ourselves. *Industry need not wish,* as Poor Richard says, *and he that lives upon hope will die fasting. There are no gains without pains; then help hands, for I have no lands,* or if I have they are smartly taxed. And, as Poor Richard likewise observes, *He that hath a trade, hath an estate; and he that hath a calling, hath an office of profit and honor;* but then the trade must be worked at and the calling well followed, or neither the estate nor the office will enable us to pay our taxes. If we are industrious, we shall never starve, for, as Poor Richard says, *At the workingman's house hunger looks in, but dares not enter.* Nor will the bailiff or the constable enter, for *Industry pays debts, while despair increaseth them,* says Poor Richard. What though you have found no treasure, nor has any rich relation left you a legacy, *Diligence is the mother of good luck,* as Poor Richard says, *and God gives all things to industry. Then plow deep while sluggards sleep, and you shall have corn to sell and to keep,* says Poor Dick. Work while it is called today, for you know not how much you may be hindered tomorrow, which makes Poor Richard say, *One today is worth two tomorrows,* and farther, *Have you somewhat to do tomorrow, do it today.* If you were a servant, would you not be ashamed that a good master should catch you idle? Are you then your own master, *Be ashamed to catch yourself idle,* as Poor Dick says. When there is so much to be done for yourself, your family, your country, and your gracious king, be up by peep of day; *Let not the sun look down and say, Inglorious here he lies.* Handle your tools without mittens; remember that *The Cat in gloves catches no mice,* as Poor Richard says. 'Tis true there is much to be done, and perhaps you are weak-handed;

but stick to it steadily and you will see great effects, for *Constant dropping wears away stones,* and *By diligence and patience the mouse ate in two the cable;* and *Little strokes fell great oaks,* as Poor Richard says in his *Almanac,* the year I cannot just now remember.

"Methinks I hear some of you say, 'Must a man afford himself no leisure?' I will tell thee, my friends, what Poor Richard says, *Employ thy time well, if thou meanest to gain leisure; and, since thou art not sure of a minute, throw not away an hour.* Leisure is time for doing something useful; this leisure the diligent man will obtain, but the lazy man never; so that, as Poor Richard says, *A life of leisure and a life of laziness are two things.* Do you imagine that sloth will afford you more comfort than labor? No, for as Poor Richard says, *Trouble springs from idleness, and grievous toil from needless ease. Many without labor would live by their wits only, but they break for want of stock.* Whereas industry gives comfort, and plenty, and respect: *Fly pleasures, and they'll follow you. The diligent spinner has a large shift; and now I have a sheep and a cow, everybody bids me good morrow;* all which is well said by Poor Richard.

"But with our industry, we must likewise be steady, settled and careful, and oversee our own affairs with our own eyes, and not trust too much to others; for, as Poor Richard says:

> *I never saw an oft-removed tree,*
> *Nor yet an oft-removed family,*
> *That throve so well as those that settled be.*

"And again, *Three removes is as bad as a fire;* and again, *Keep thy shop, and thy shop will keep thee;* and again, *If you would have your business done, go; if not, send.* And again,

> *He that by the plow would thrive,*
> *Himself must either hold or drive.*

"And again, *The eye of a master will do more work than both his hands;* and again, *Want of care does us more damage than want of knowledge;* and again, *Not to oversee workmen, is to leave them your purse open.* Trusting too much to other's care is the ruin of many; for, as the *Almanac* says, *In the affairs of this world, men are saved, not by faith, but by the want of it;* but a man's own care is profitable; for, saith Poor Dick, *Learning is to the studious, and riches to the careful, as well as power to the bold, and heaven to the virtuous,* and farther, *If you would have a faithful servant, and one that you like, serve yourself.* And again, he adviseth to circumspection and care, even in the smallest matters, because sometimes *A little neglect may breed great mischief;* adding, *For want of a nail the shoe was lost; for want of a shoe the horse was lost; and for want of a horse the rider was lost, being overtaken and slain by the enemy; all for want of care about a horse-shoe nail.*

"So much for industry, my friends, and attention to one's own business; but to these we must add frugality, if we would make our industry more certainly successful. A man may, if he does not know how to save as he gets, keep his nose all his life to the grindstone, and die not worth a groat at last. *A fat kitchen makes a lean will,* as Poor Richard says; and

> *Many estates are spent in the getting,*
> *Since women for tea forsook spinning and knitting,*
> *And men for punch forsook hewing and splitting.*

"*If you would be wealthy,* says he, in another *Almanac, Think of saving as well as of getting: The Indies have not made Spain rich, because her outgoes are greater than her incomes.*

"Away then with your expensive follies, and you will not then have so much cause to complain of hard times, heavy taxes, and chargeable families; for, as Poor Dick says,

> *Women and wine, game and deceit,*
> *Make the wealth small and the wants great.*

"And farther, *What maintains one vice, would bring up two children.* You may think, perhaps, that a little tea, or a little punch now and then, diet a little more costly, clothes a little finer, and a little entertainment now and then, can be no great matter; but remember what Poor Richard says, *Many a little makes a mickle;* and farther, *Beware of little expense; a small leak will sink a great ship;* and again, *Who dainties love, shall beggars prove;* and moreover, *Fools make feasts, and wise men eat them.*

"Here you are all got together at this vendue of fineries and knicknacks. You call them *goods;* but if you do not take care, they will prove evils to some of you. You expect they will be sold cheap, and perhaps they may for less than they cost; but if you have no occasion for them, they must be dear to you. Remember what Poor Richard says: *Buy what thou hast no need of, and ere long thou shalt sell thy necessaries.* And again, *At a great pennyworth pause a while.* He means that perhaps the cheapness is apparent only, and not real; or the bargain, by straitening thee in thy business, may do thee more harm than good. For in another place, he says, *Many have been ruined by buying good pennyworths.* Again, Poor Richard says, *'Tis foolish to lay out money in a purchase of repentance;* and yet this folly is practiced every day at vendues, for want of minding the *Almanac. Wise men,* as Poor Dick says, *learn by others' harms, fools scarcely by their own.* Many a one, for the sake of finery on the back, have gone with a hungry belly, and half-starved their families. *Silks and satins, scarlet and velvets,* as Poor Richard says, *put out the kitchen fire.*

"These are not the necessaries of life; they can scarcely be called the conveniences; and yet only because they look pretty, how many want to have them! The artificial wants of mankind thus become more numerous than the natural; and, as Poor Richard says, *For one poor person, there are a hundred indigent.* By these, and other extravagancies, the genteel are reduced to poverty and forced to borrow of those whom they formerly despised, but who through industry and frugality have maintained their standing; in which case it appears plainly that *A plowman on his legs is higher than a gentleman on his knees,* as Poor Richard says. Perhaps they have had a small estate left them, which they knew not the getting of; they think, *'tis day, and will never be night;* that a little to be spent out of so much, is not worth the minding; *A child and a fool,* as Poor Richard says, *imagine twenty shillings and twenty years can never be spent* but, *always taking out of the meal tub, and never putting in, soon comes to the bottom;* as Poor Dick says, *When the well's dry, they know the worth of water.* But this they might have known before, if they had taken his advice; *If you would know the value of money, go and try to borrow some, for he that goes a borrowing, goes a sorrowing;* and indeed so does he that lends to such people, when he goes to get it again. Poor Dick farther advises, and says,

> *Fond pride of dress is sure a very curse;*
> *E'er fancy you consult, consult your purse.*

"And again, *Pride is as loud a beggar as Want, and a great deal more saucy.* When you have bought one fine thing, you must buy ten more, that your appearance may be all of a piece; but Poor Dick says, *'Tis easier to suppress the first desire than to satisfy all that follow it.* And 'tis as truly folly for the poor to ape the rich, as for the frog to swell, in order to equal the ox.

> *Great estates may venture more,*
> *But little boats should keep near shore.*

" 'Tis, however, a folly soon punished; for *Pride that dines on vanity, sups on contempt,* as Poor Richard says. And in another place, *Pride breakfasted with plenty, dined with poverty, and supped with infamy.* And, after all, of what use is this pride of appearance, for which so much is risked, so much suffered? It cannot promote health or ease pain; it makes no increase of merit in the person; it creates envy, it hastens misfortune.

> *What is a butterfly? At best*
> *He's but a caterpillar drest*
> *The gaudy fop's his picture just,*

as Poor Richard says.

"But what madness must it be to run in debt for these superfluities! We are offered, by the terms of this vendue, six months' credit; and that perhaps has induced some of us to attend it, because we cannot spare the ready money, and hope now to be fine without it. But, ah, think what you do when you run in debt; you give to another power over your liberty. If you cannot pay at the time, you will be ashamed to see your creditor; you will be in fear when you speak to him; you will make poor pitiful sneaking excuses, and by degrees come to lose your veracity, and sink into base downright lying; for, as Poor Richard says, *The second vice is lying, the first is running in debt.* And again, to the same purpose, *Lying rides upon debt's back.* Whereas a free-born Englishman ought not to be ashamed or afraid to see or speak to any man living. But poverty often deprives a man of all spirit and virtue: *'Tis hard for an empty bag to stand upright,* as Poor Richard truly says.

"What would you think of that prince, or that government, who should issue an edict forbidding you to dress like a gentleman or a gentlewoman, on pain of imprisonment or servitude? Would you not say that you were free, have a right to dress as you please, and that such an edict would be a breach of your privileges, and such a government tyrannical? And yet you are about to put yourself under that tyranny when you run in debt for such dress! Your creditor has authority at his pleasure to deprive you of your liberty by confining you in a gaol for life, or to sell you for a servant, if you should not be able to pay him! When you have got your bargain, you may, perhaps, think little of payment; but *Creditors,* Poor Richard tells us, *have better memories than debtors;* and in another place, says, *Creditors are a superstitious sect, great observers of set days and times.* The day comes round before you are aware, and the demand is made before you are prepared to satisfy it. Or if you bear your debt in mind, the term which at first seemed so long will, as it lessens, appear extremely short. Time will seem to have added wings to his heels as well as shoulders. *Those have a short Lent,* saith Poor Richard, *who owe money to be paid at Easter.* Then since, as he says, *The borrower is a slave to the lender, and the debtor to the creditor,* disdain the chain, preserve your freedom, and maintain your independency. Be industrious and free; be frugal and free. At present, perhaps, you may think yourself in thriving circumstances, and that you can bear a little extravagance without injury; but

> *For age and want, save while you may;*
> *No morning sun lasts a whole day,*

as Poor Richard says. Gain may be temporary and uncertain, but ever, while you live, expense is constant and certain; and *'Tis easier to build two chimneys than to keep one in fuel,* as Poor Richard says. So, *Rather go to bed supperless than rise in debt.*

> *Get what you can, and what you get hold;*
> *'Tis the stone that will turn all your lead into gold,*

as Poor Richard says. And when you have got the philosopher's stone, sure you will no longer complain of bad times or the difficulty of paying taxes.

"This doctrine, my friends, is reason and wisdom; but after all, do not depend too much upon your own industry and frugality and prudence, though excellent things, for they may all be blasted without the blessing of heaven; and therefore, ask that blessing humbly, and be not uncharitable to those that at present seem to want it, but comfort and help them. Remember, Job suffered, and was afterward prosperous.

"And now to conclude, *Experience keeps a dear school, but fools will learn in no other, and scarce in that;* for it is true, *We may give advice, but we cannot give conduct,* as Poor Richard says. However, remember this, *They that won't be counseled, can't be helped,* as Poor Richard says; and farther, that *If you will not hear Reason, she'll surely rap your knuckles.*"

Thus the old gentleman ended his harangue. The people heard it and approved the doctrine, and immediately practiced the contrary, just as if it had been a common sermon; for the vendue opened, and they began to buy extravagantly, notwithstanding his cautions and their own fear of taxes. I found the good man had thoroughly studied my *Almanacs,* and digested all I had dropped on these topics during the course of five and twenty years. The frequent mention he made of me must have tired anyone else, but my vanity was wonderfully delighted with it, though I was conscious that not a tenth part of the wisdom was my own, which he ascribed to me, but rather the gleanings I had made of the sense of all ages and nations. However, I resolved to be the better for the echo of it; and though I had at first determined to buy stuff for a new coat, I went away resolved to wear my old one a little longer. Reader, if thou wilt do the same, thy profit will be as great as mine. I am, as ever, thine to serve thee,

RICHARD SAUNDERS

In a way it is unfortunate that Benjamin Franklin ever compiled *The Way to Wealth*. The 1,300 editions of it that have been issued since his day—1,000 in English and about 300 in other languages—are responsible for an image of him that has been handed to posterity: a priggish, parsimonious, commercial moneygrubber; the patron saint of savings banks and forerunner of Horatio Alger and Dale Carnegie. Most early historians failed to grasp the purpose of the document. It was addressed mainly to young people, most of them as poor as he had been, at a time when there was no middle class and in an era of scarcity when only production through incressant labor and thrift could create a middle class with its attendant relative leisure and independence. Franklin advised *how* this could be done. He was saying to young men, "If you want to be free from the dictates of a boss, you must discipline yourself to work."

He cared nothing for wealth as such. He could have been as rich as Rockefeller merely by patenting his inventions. True, he despised needless luxuries such as jewelry or fashionable, expensive clothes. To his sister he once wrote, "I have been thinking what would be a suitable present for me to make, and you to receive, as I hear you have grown a celebrated beauty. I had almost determined on a tea-table; but when I considered that the character of a good housewife was far preferable to that of being only a pretty gentlewoman, I concluded to send you a spinning-wheel."

To accept the acquisition of money for money's sake as Franklin's purpose, one must ignore many of the other maxims of Poor Richard such as "Avarice and happiness never saw each other. How then could they become aquainted?" "Wealth is not his that has it, but his that enjoys it." "He does not possess wealth, it possesses him." "Poverty wants some things, luxury many things, avarice all things."

Franklin wanted wealth for only one purpose—leisure to do as he pleased. He worked six or, sometimes, seven days a week until he reached that goal. But, prorated over his lifetime, Franklin worked an average three-day week at making money. His leisure was devoted to science, because that was what he wanted to do, and to public service because he considered it his duty to serve when called upon. He summarized this well in a letter to his mother when he said, "So the years roll by and the last will come, when I would rather have it said 'He lived usefully' than 'He died rich'!"

CHAPTER IV

THE WIZARD OF RACE STREET

ૐ

Had there been no American Revolution, no historic documents for Benjamin Franklin to sign, his name would still be world renowned. Instead of being linked with Washington, Jefferson and Adams, he would be grouped with Newton, Cavendish and Lavoisier. Although he devoted most of his time to scientific research for only seven years—thereafter it was an occasional sideline to his duties as a public figure—he stood in the front rank of eighteenth-century "philosophers." When he became interested in electricity it was little more than a curiosity. Franklin's theories and experiments laid the foundation for modern electrical science.

It is possible that Franklin retired from business when he did because of his preoccupation with electricity. He said that he first became interested in the subject when he heard a Dr. Spence lecture in Boston in 1746. History knows no Dr. Spence—there was a Dr. Spencer who had an electrical "act" at that time, at the climax of which he hung a boy in the air by silk cords and pulled sparks from his nose and ears. This is undoubtedly the man to whom Franklin refers.

Franklin bought Spencer's electrical equipment and started to

experiment. He was interrupted by the emergency which led to
his writing *Plain Talk* and taking leadership in organizing the
militia. When this was over he moved from the building that
housed his shop and store on busy Market Street to a house on
quiet, outlying Race Street. He intended to devote the remainder
of his life to inquiring into the nature of things—physical, moral
and spiritual. He said, "I am in a fair way to having no other
tasks than such as I shall like to give myself and of enjoying
what I look upon as a great happiness: leisure to read, study,
make experiments, and converse at large with such ingenious
and worthy men who are pleased to honor me with their friendship or acquaintance, on such points as may produce something
for the common benefit of mankind, uninterrupted by the little
cares and fatigues of business."

In the sixth century B.C. Thales mentioned that rubbed amber
attracted light substances. Three hundred years later Theo-
phrastus more fully described the phenomenon and extended it
to many gems. Almost two thousand years later William Gilbert,
physician to Queen Elizabeth, wrote a book on magnetism in
which he discussed the attractive power of amber, gems, crystal
and sulphur when rubbed. He called these things "electrums"—
from the Latin word for amber—and so named electricity.

By Franklin's time it was known that electricity was not a
form of magnetism. Sulphur or glass globes had been created to
produce electricity when rubbed. It had been learned that it
could be transmitted by some substances and not by others and
gathered in an insulated conductor—usually a musket barrel
hung by silk threads. It was known that some charged substances
attracted and others repelled. European scientists believed that
this was based on the nature of the material that was rubbed—
that there were two kinds of electrical fluid, vitreous and resinous. The condenser had just been invented—the Leyden jar—
a foil-wrapped glass bottle, filled with water or metal shot, with
a wire running down through the cork. The principal use
to which electricity had been put was to startle, amaze and

amuse. Abbé Nollet, electrician of the French court, lined up seven hundred monks, each joined to his neighbor by a bit of wire which he held. The monk at one end was connected to a prime conductor, at the other end to a condenser. Louis XV was delighted as all the monks jumped into the air in unison when the circuit was completed.

This was electricity when Franklin took over. Peter Collinson, the London agent of the Philadelphia Library, had sent over an electrical tube about three feet long and as thick as your wrist— a substitute for the glass sphere as a generator. Franklin started to experiment with this, building laboratory equipment around it from such common materials as a salt cellar, a vinegar cruet, a pump handle and gold in the binding of a book. One early writer said, "He could make an experiment with less apparatus and conduct his experimental inquiry to a discovery with more ordinary materials than any other philosopher we ever saw."

Franklin applied his clear, concise writing style to his scientific work. Of one theory he said, "If my hypothesis is not the truth itself, it is at least as naked for I have not, with some of our learned moderns, disguised my nonsense in Greek, clothed it in algebra or adorned it with fluxions. You have it in *puris naturalibus.*"

Virtually all records of Franklin's contribution to electrical science are contained in a series of private letters which he wrote to Peter Collinson in London. He wrote no scientific papers, as such. Of these letters he said, in his autobiography:

OBLIGED AS WE WERE to Mr. Collinson for his present of the tube, etc., I thought it right he should be informed of our success in using it, and wrote him several letters containing accounts of our experiments. He got them read in the Royal Society, where they were not at first thought worth so much notice as to be printed in their Transactions. One paper, which I wrote for Mr. Kinnersley, on the sameness of lightning with electricity, I sent to Dr. Mitchel, an acquaintance of mine, and one of the members also of that society, who wrote me word that it had been read, but was laughed at by the connoisseurs. The papers, however, being shown to Dr. Fothergill, he thought them of too much value to be stifled, and advised the printing of them. Mr. Collinson then gave them to Edward Cave for publication in his *Gentleman's Magazine;* but he chose to print them separately in a pamphlet, and Dr. Fothergill wrote the preface.

This book, published in 1751, was the first of many editions of Franklin's "collected papers."

Franklin's first letter to Collinson was a short thank-you note for the tube that the latter had sent, saying that Franklin and other members of the Library Company were experimenting with it and had "observed some particular phenomena that we look upon as new. I shall therefore communicate them to you in my next." Franklin's "next" contained several observations that were news to the old world—the conception of electricity as a single fluid, the substitution of "positive and negative" for vitreous and resinous, and the discovery of the effectiveness of pointed bodies in drawing or throwing a charge. Franklin described the experiments on which his conclusions were based:

PLACE AN IRON SHOT of three or four inches in diameter on the mouth of a clean dry glass bottle. By a fine silken thread from the ceiling, right over the mouth of the bottle, suspend a small cork ball about the bigness of a marble; the thread of such a length as that the cork ball may rest against the side of the shot. Electrify the shot, and the ball will be repelled to the distance of four or five inches, more or less, according to the quantity of electricity. When in this state, if you present to the shot the point of a long slender sharp bodkin, at six or eight inches distance, the repellancy is instantly destroyed, and the cork flies to the shot. A blunt body must be brought within an inch, and draw a spark, to produce the same effect. . . .

To show that points will *throw off* as well as *draw off* the electrical fire; lay a long sharp needle upon the shot, and you cannot electrize the shot so as to make it repel the cork ball. Or fix a needle to the end of a suspended gun-barrel, or iron rod, so as to point beyond it like a little bayonet; and while it remains there, the gun-barrel or rod, cannot by applying the tube to the other end be electrized so as to give a spark, the fire continually running out silently at the point. In the dark you may see it make the same appearance as it does in the case before mentioned.

Later in the same letter, Franklin described the experiment from which he developed the conception of positive and negative electricity—probably the most fundamental thing ever done in the field of electricity:

1. A person standing on wax, and rubbing the tube, and another person on wax drawing the fire, they will both of them (provided they do not stand so as to touch one another), appear to be electrized, to a person standing on the floor; that is, he will perceive a spark on approaching each of them with his knuckle.

2. But, if the persons on wax touch one another during the exciting of the tube, neither of them will appear to be electrized.

3. If they touch one another after exciting the tube, and drawing the fire as aforesaid, there will be a stronger spark between them than was between either of them and the person on the floor.

4. After such strong spark, neither of them discover any electricity.

These appearances we attempt to account for thus: We suppose, as aforesaid, that electrical fire is a common element, of which every one of the three persons above mentioned has his equal share, before any operation is begun with the tube. *A*, who stands on wax and rubs the tube, collects the electrical fire from himself into the glass; and his communication with the common stock being cut off by the wax, his body is not again immediately supplied. *B* (who stands on wax likewise) passing his knuckles along near the tube, received the fire which was collected by the glass from *A;* and his communication with the common stock being likewise cut off, he retains the additional quantity received. To *C* standing on the floor, both appear to be electricized; for he having only the middle quantity of electrical fire, receives a spark on approaching *B*, who has an over quantity; but gives one to *A* who has an under quantity. If *A* and *B* approach to touch each other, the spark is stronger, because the difference between them is greater. After such touch there is no spark between either of them and *C*, because the electrical fire in all is reduced to the original equality. If they touch while electrizing, the equality is never destroyed, the fire only circulating. Hence have arisen some new terms among us: we say *B* (and bodies like circumstanced) is electrized *positively; A, negatively*. Or rather, *B* is electrized *plus; A, minus*. And we daily in our experiments electrize bodies *plus* or *minus*, as we think proper. . . .

Franklin next made a thorough analysis of the Leyden jar and came to the conclusion that the glass in which the electricity resided need not be in the shape of a jar. So he invented, and named, the battery.

UPON THIS we made what we called an electrical battery, consisting of eleven panes of large sash-glass, armed with thin leaden plates, pasted on each side, placed vertically, and supported at two inches distance on silk cords, with thick hooks of leaden wire, one from each side, standing upright, distant from each other, and convenient communications of wire and chain from the giving side of one pane to the receiving side of the other; that so the whole might be charged together, and with the same labor as one single pane; and another contrivance to bring the giving sides, after charging, in contact with one long wire, and the receivers with another, which two long wires would give the force of all the plates of glass at once through the body of any animal forming the circle with them.

Franklin's theory of electricity, developed in this first experimental period, explained all known electrical phenomena. It completely defined the condenser; proved that there was one kind of electrical "fire," not two; presented the merits of pointed conductors; and accounted for the phenomenon of attraction and repulsion. Now, he and his fellow experimenters from the Library Company relaxed with electricity.

CHAGRINED A LITTLE that we have hitherto been able to produce nothing in this way of use to mankind, and the hot weather coming on, when electrical experiments are not so agreeable, it is proposed to put an end to them for this season, somewhat humorously, in a party of pleasure on the banks of the Schuylkill. Spirits, at the same time, are to be fired by a spark sent from side to side through the river, without any other conductor than the water; an experiment which we some time since performed, to the amazement of many. A turkey is to be killed for our dinner by the electrical shock, and roasted by the electrical jack, before a fire kindled by the electrified bottle; when the healths of all the famous electricians in England, Holland, France and Germany are to be drunk in electrified bumpers, under the discharge of guns from the electrical battery.

In a footnote to the above letter, Franklin described an

"electrical bumper" as "a small thin glass tumbler nearly filled with wine, and electrified as the bottle. This, when brought to the lips, gives a shock if the party be close shaved and does not breathe on the liquor."

To the layman, Franklin's greatest contribution to electricity is the famous kite experiment which supposedly proved the identity of lightning and electricity. Actually, the identity of lightning and electricity was not first proven with a kite experiment, and Franklin was not the first to prove it.

This important discovery started on November 7, 1749, with a notation that Franklin made in "the minutes I used to keep on the experiments I made, with memorandums of such as I proposed to make," which read:

ELECTRICAL FLUID agrees with lightning in these particulars: 1. Giving light. 2. Color of the light. 3. Crooked direction. 4. Swift motion. 5. Being conducted by metals. 6. Crack or noise on exploding. 7. Subsiding in water or ice. 8. Rending bodies it passes through. 9. Destroying animals. 10. Melting metals. 11. Firing inflammable substances. 12. Sulphurous smell.

The electrical fluid is attracted by points. We do not know whether this is a property of lightning. But since they agree in all particulars wherein we can already compare them, is it not probable that they agree likewise in this? Let the experiment be made.

In May, 1750, Franklin wrote to Collinson:

THERE IS SOMETHING, however, in the experiments of points, sending off or drawing on the electrical fire, which is not fully explained, and which I intend to supply in my next. For the doctrine of points is very curious, and the effects of them truly wonderful; and, from what I have observed on experiments, I am of the opinion that houses, ships, and even towers and churches may be effectually secured from the strokes of lightning by their means; for if, instead of the round balls of wood or metal which are commonly placed on the tops of weathercocks, vanes or spindles of churches, spires and masts, there should be a rod of iron eight or ten feet in length, sharpened gradually to a dull point like a needle, and gilt to prevent rusting, or divided into a number of points, which would be better, the electrical fire would, I think, be drawn out of a cloud silently, before it could come near enough to strike; and a light would be seen at the point, like the sailor's corposant [St. Elmo's fire]. This may seem whimsical, but let it pass for the moment until I send the experiments at large.

Luckily nobody acted on Franklin's first suggestion for a lightning rod. He had neglected to ground it.

In his next letter to Collinson, on July 29, 1750, Franklin corrected his error and added "a wire down the outside of a building into the ground, or down round one of the shrouds of a ship till it reached the water." This letter continued to describe an experiment that would prove the lightning-electricity theory.

TO DETERMINE THE QUESTION whether the clouds that contain lightning are electrified or not, I would propose an experiment to be tried where it may be done conveniently. On the top of some high tower or steeple, place a kind of sentry-box, big enough to contain a man and an electrical stand. From the middle of the stand let an iron rod rise and pass bending out of the door, and then upright twenty or thirty feet, pointed very sharp at the end. If the electrical stand be kept clean and dry, a man standing on it when such clouds are passing low might be electrified and afford sparks, the rod drawing fire to him from a cloud.

Franklin did not make this experiment. Also, he obviously

did not know how dangerous it was. His description of it was published in the first collection of his electrical papers in 1751 and translated into French. In a suburb of Paris a scientist named D'Alibard set up an iron rod forty feet high on a wooden plank mounted on three wine bottles. On May 10, 1752, there was a single flash of lightning. D'Alibard was absent, but a dragoon who was guarding the experiment ran to the rod with an electric phial and charged it amidst crackling sparks. The identity of lightning and electricity was proved.

Louis XV was so impressed by the lightning experiment that he ordered a letter written to express his thanks and appreciation to "Mr. Franklin in Philadelphia." When Collinson conveyed this flattering news to Franklin, the modest genius replied: "The *Tatler* tells us of a girl who was observed to grow suddenly proud, and none could guess the reason till it came to be known that she had got on a pair of new silk garters. . . . I fear I have not so much reason to be proud as the girl had; for a feather in the cap is not so useful a thing, or so serviceable to the wearer, as a pair of good silk garters."

But what of the kite? When was this experiment made? Franklin never said. In October, six months after the French experiment had been made, Franklin described the kite experiment, telling, impersonally, how it could be done.

MAKE A SMALL CROSS of two light strips of cedar, the arms so long as to reach to the four corners of a large thin silk handkerchief when extended. Tie the corners of the handkerchief to the extremities of the cross, so you have the body of a kite, which, being properly accommodated with a tail, loop and string, will rise in the air like those made of paper; but this being of silk, is fitter to bear the wet and wind of a thunder-gust without tearing. To the top of the upright stick of the cross is to be fixed a very sharp-pointed wire, rising a foot or more above the wood. To the end of the twine, next the hand, is to be tied a silk ribbon,

and where the silk and twine join, a key may be fastened.
This kite is to be raised when a thunder-gust appears to be
coming on, and the person who holds the string must stand
within a door or window or under some cover, so that the
silk ribbon may not be wet; and care must be taken that
the twine does not touch the frame of the door or window.
As soon as any of the thunderclouds come over the kite,
the pointed wire will draw the electric fire from them, and
the kite, with all the twine, will be electrified, and the loose
filaments of the twine will stand out every way, and be
attracted by an approaching finger. And when the rain has
wet the kite and twine, so that it can conduct the electric
fire freely, you will find it stream out plentifully from the
key on the approach of your knuckle.

The only account of the actual kite experiment as Franklin
made it was published fifteen years after the event by Joseph
Priestley. It is known that Franklin saw Priestley's manuscript
before it was published, so it is probably accurate.

THE DOCTOR, having published his method of verifying his
hypothesis concerning the sameness of electricity with the
matter of lightning, was waiting for the erection of a spire
[on Christ Church] in Philadelphia to carry his views into
execution; not imagining that a pointed rod of a moderate
height could answer the purpose; when it occurred to him
that by means of a common kite he could have better access
to the regions of thunder than by any spire whatsoever.
Preparing, therefore, a large silk handkerchief and two
cross-sticks of a proper length on which to extend it, he
took the opportunity of the first approaching thunderstorm
to take a walk in the fields, in which there was a shed convenient for his purpose. But, dreading the ridicule which
too commonly attends unsuccessful attempts in science, he

communicated his intended experiment to nobody but his son . . . who assisted him in raising the kite.

The kite being raised, a considerable time elapsed before there was any appearance of its being electrified. One very promising cloud had passed over it without any effect; when, at length, just as he was beginning to despair of his contrivance, he observed some loose threads of the hempen string to stand erect, and to avoid one another, just as if they had been suspended on a common conductor. Struck with this promising appearance, he immediately presented his knuckle to the key, and (let the reader judge of the exquisite pleasure he must have felt at that moment) the discovery was complete. He perceived a very evident electric spark. Others succeeded, even before the string was wet, so as to put the matter past all dispute, and when the rain had wet the string he collected electric fire very copiously. This happened in June, 1752, a month after the electricians in France had verified the same theory, but before he had heard of anything they had done.

The conflict of dates between Priestley's June, and October, when Franklin announced the experiment, is a minor mystery, but there is no doubt that the French experiment that proved Franklin's theory was the first to be made.

The lightning rod caught on in America, but in the old world there was much superstitious aversion to it. In provincial France, thirty years after its invention, it was still illegal. In England one scientist, Benjamin Wilson, disagreed with Franklin and claimed that blunt lightning rods were safer than pointed ones. When the American Revolution started, George III ordered that Wilson's blunt rods were to be substituted for Franklin's pointed ones on Kew Palace—the American type rods were not patriotic. Franklin's comment on this was: "The King's changing his pointed conductors for blunt is a matter of small importance to me. If I had a wish about it, it would be that he rejected them altogether as ineffectual. For it is only since he thought himself and family safe from the thunder of Heaven, that he dared to use his own thunder in destroying his innocent subjects."

Most of Franklin's original inquiries in all fields of science were what is now called "pure research"—the search for the "why" in the laws of nature without having any particular application in mind. The comment he made when he saw the first balloon is a classic defense of pure research. When a bystander queried, "What good is it?" Franklin replied, "What good is a newborn baby?" But he usually sought for a means of applying his newly gained knowledge for the benefit of mankind, as in the case of the lightning rod. His pragmatism is suggested by a sentence from a letter to his wife, describing an occasion when he was almost shipwrecked. He said, "Were I a Roman Catholic perhaps I would build a chapel to some saint, but as I am not, if I were to vow at all it would be to build a lighthouse." Of the practical importance of knowing the basic laws of science without applying them, he said, "It is of real use to know that china left in the air unsupported will fall and break; but *how* it comes to fall and *why* it breaks are matters of speculation. It is a pleasure indeed to know them, but we can preserve our china without it."

In his search to find practical uses for electricity, Franklin experimented with electrocution to determine whether the flesh of animals killed in this way would be more tender.

IT HAS BEEN OBSERVED that lightning, by rarefying and reducing into vapor the moisture contained in solid wood, in an oak, for instance, has forcibly separated its fibers, and broken it into small pieces; that by penetrating intimately the hardest metals, as iron, it has separated the parts in an instant, so as to convert a perfect solid into a state of fluidity. It is not then improbable that the same subtile matter, passing through the bodies of animals with rapidity, should possess sufficient force to produce an effect nearly similar. The flesh of animals, freshly killed in the usual manner, is firm, hard and not in a very eatable state, because the particles adhere too forcibly to each other. At a certain period, the cohesion is weakened, and in its progress toward putrefaction, which tends to produce a total separation, the flesh becomes what we call tender, or is in that state most proper to be used as our food. It has frequently been remarked that animals killed by lightning putrefy immediately. This cannot be invariably the case, since a quantity of lightning, sufficient to kill, may not be sufficient to tear and divide the fibers and particles of flesh, and reduce them to that tender state which is the prelude to putrefaction.

If his theory can be applied, the meat-packing industry has not yet caught up to Franklin. In the experiment which he made to prove it he was well on the way to inventing the electric chair.

HAVING PREPARED A BATTERY of six large glass jars (each from twenty to twenty-four pints) as for the Leyden experiment, and having established a communication as usual, from the interior surface of each with the prime conductor, and having given them a full charge, a chain which communicates with the exterior of the jars must be wrapped round the thighs of the fowl; after which the operator, holding it by the wings, turned back and made to touch behind, must raise it so high that the head may receive the first shock from the prime conductor. The animal dies instantly. Let the head be immediately cut off to make it bleed, when it may be plucked and dressed immediately. This quantity of electricity is supposed sufficient for a turkey of ten pounds weight, and perhaps for a lamb. Experience alone will inform us of the requisite proportions for animals of different forms and ages. . . . As six jars, however, discharged at once, are capable of giving a very violent shock, the operator must be very circumspect lest he should happen to make the experiment on his own flesh, instead of that of the fowl.

All of Franklin's fundamental contributions to electricity were made between 1746 and 1752; they created something of a sensation in scientific circles at the time. Harvard, Yale and William and Mary gave him honorary degrees. The Royal Academy in London made him a member and awarded him a gold medal. But Franklin the scientist was not concerned only with electricity. At one time or another his writings contributed to knowledge in the fields of geology, meteorology, seismology, physics, chemistry, astronomy, mathematics, hydrography, aeronautics, navigation, ethnology, agriculture, botany, paleontology, medicine and hygiene.

In 1748, amidst his electrical experiments, he told a Swedish botanist about an experiment he had made to determine whether ants had something like speech. Ants had got into a little pot of molasses. Franklin shook all of them out but one ant. Then he hung the pot by a string from a nail in the ceiling. When the single ant had eaten its fill, it crawled up the string. Within half an hour a swarm of ants arrived—obviously the first ant had directed them to the molasses.

During the same year, Franklin bought a farm in New Jersey. He was soon writing letters describing his experiments in scientific farming and bemoaning the fact that farmers were reluctant to apply modern methods. He said: "But if the farmers in your neighborhood are as unwilling to leave the beaten road of their ancestors as they are near me, it will be difficult to persuade them to attempt any improvement. Where the cash is to be laid out on a probability of a return, they are very averse to the running any risk at all, or even expending freely, where a gentleman of a more public spirit has given them ocular demonstration of the success."

Franklin's "ocular demonstration" had to do with his urging the adoption of plaster of Paris as a fertilizer. As an object lesson to other farmers, he wrote with plaster in a field along the highway, "THIS FIELD HAS BEEN PLASTERED." The white letters soon disappeared, but when the crop came up, the message reappeared in the greener, more lush growth of the fertilized letters.

While he was inventing the lightning rod in 1752, he took time off to invent the first flexible catheter in America—a medical instrument—for the use of his brother John, to whom he wrote: "Reflecting yesterday on your desire to have a flexible catheter, a thought struck into my mind how one might probably be made; and lest you should not speedily conceive it by any description of mine, I went immediately to the silversmith's and gave directions for making one (sitting by till it was finished) that it might be ready for this post."

In 1753, when Franklin was appointed Postmaster General of the colonies, it was obvious to him that he was not going to be allowed to devote the remainder of his life to reading, study, experimenting and conversation with "ingenious and worthy men." Rather sadly, he sent to Collinson "a small philosophical packet" of letters which he had recently written to fellow scientists in America. They dealt mainly with conjectures, observations and suppositions in physics and meteorology—mostly simple, everyday thoughts prompted by the things around him, like this one on thermal conduction.

MY DESK AND ITS LOCK ARE, I suppose, of the same temperament [temperature] when they have long been exposed to the same air; but now, if I lay my hand on the wood, it does not seem so cold to me as the lock; because (as I imagine) wood is not so good a conductor, to receive and convey away the heat from my skin and the adjacent flesh, as metal is. Take a piece of wood of the size and shape of a dollar between the thumb and fingers of one hand, and a dollar in like manner with the other hand; place the edges of both, at the same time, in the flame of a candle; and though the edge of the

wooden piece takes flame and the metal piece does not, yet
you will be obliged to drop the latter before the former, it
conducting the heat more suddenly to your fingers. . . .
Perhaps it is for the same reason that woolen garments keep
the body warmer than linen ones equally thick; woolen
keeping the natural heat in, or in other words, not conducting it out to the air.

One of these letters—a short one—indicates the diversity of
Franklin's interests. In it he speaks of linseed oil, hemp land,
swamp draining, variations in climate, northeast storms, the
cause of springs on mountains, sea shells in rocks, taxation and
smuggling.

Franklin sought neither wealth nor worldly acclaim from his
scientific discoveries. As with the stove, he refused to patent the
lightning rod, although the rods were called "Franklin rods." It
was enough for him if his ideas and theories stimulated discoveries that would help mankind. He cared not who got the
credit. He explained his feelings in a letter to Collinson:

THESE THOUGHTS, my dear friend, are many of them crude
and hasty; and if I were merely ambitious of acquiring some
reputation in philosophy I ought to keep them by me till
corrected and improved by time and further experience. But
since even short hints and imperfect experiments in any new
branch of science, being communicated, have oftimes a good
effect in exciting the attention of the ingenious to the
subject, and so become the occasion of more exact disquisi-
tion and more complete discoveries, you are at liberty to
communicate this paper to whom you please; it being of
more importance that knowledge should increase than that
your friend should be thought an accurate philosopher.

Franklin the philosopher—the searcher for the hidden truths

of nature's laws—was perhaps best summarized by a fellow scientist, Sir Humphry Davy, who said:

THE EXPERIMENTS adduced by Dr. Franklin . . . were most ingeniously contrived and happily executed. A singular facility of induction guided all his researches, and by very small means he established very grand truths. The style and manner of his publication [on electricity] are almost as worthy of admiration as the doctrines it contains. He has endeavored to remove all mystery and obscurity from the subject; he has written equally for the uninitiated and for the philosopher; and he has rendered his details amusing as well as perspicuous—elegant as well as simple. Science appears in his language in a dress wonderfully decorous, the best adapted to display her native loveliness. He has in no case exhibited that false dignity by which philosophy is kept aloof from common applications; and he has sought rather to make her a useful inmate and servant in the common habitations of man than to preserve her merely as an object of admiration in temples and palaces.

CHAPTER V

THE GERMAN'S GENERAL

❧

"When I disengaged myself . . . from private business, I flattered myself that, by the sufficient though moderate fortune I had acquired, I had secured leisure during the rest of my life for philosophical studies and amusements . . . but the public, now considering me a man of leisure, laid hold of me for their purposes, every part of our civil government, and almost at the same time, imposing some duty on me."

Colonial America did not consider scientific research productive employment. Franklin's ability should be put to more useful purpose—he was too much of a public figure to remain a philosopher. The governor appointed him to a peace commission. He was made an alderman of Philadelphia and elected to the Assembly of the province. The Masons made him Grand Master of the Pennsylvania Lodge.

Although these positions were thrust upon him without his solicitation, he accepted them gracefully, particularly the Assembly appointment, of which he "conceived by becoming a member would enlarge my power of doing good. I would not, however, insinuate that my ambition was not flattered by all these promotions. It certainly was; for, considering my low beginning, they were great things to me."

Certainly it was by choice that he let his electric tubes gather dust while he founded the academy that would become the University of Pennsylvania, and a mere request for an endorsement of the project led him to take the leadership in promoting the first free hospital in the colonies.

As early as 1743 Franklin had recognized the need for a college in Pennsylvania. Massachusetts had Harvard; Connecticut, Yale; Virginia, William and Mary; and New Jersey was organizing an institution that would become Princeton. He had not pushed his early proposal, but in 1749 he said, "I turned my thoughts again to the affair of establishing an academy. The first step I took was to associate in the design a number of active friends, of whom the Junto furnished a good part; the next was to write and publish a pamphlet entitled *Proposals Relating to the Education of Youth in Pennsylvania.*" *Plain Talk* had been exciting and dramatic to arouse the emotions of all the people. *Proposals* was a serious, logical document designed to coax money from the pockets of those who could best afford to endow a school. It started by pointing out the need.

IT HAS LONG BEEN regretted as a misfortune to the youth of this province that we have no academy, in which they might receive the accomplishments of a regular education.

. . . The good education of youth has been esteemed by wise men in all ages as the surest foundation of the happiness both of private families and of commonwealths. Almost all governments have therefore made it a principal object of their attention to establish and endow with proper revenues such seminaries of learning as might supply the succeeding age with men qualified to serve the public with honor to themselves and to their country.

Many of the first settlers of these provinces were men who had received a good education in Europe, and to their wisdom and good management we owe much of our present prosperity. But their hands were full and they could not do all things. The present race are not thought to be generally of equal ability; for though the American youth are allowed not to want capacity, yet the best capacities require cultivation, it being truly with them, as with the best ground which, unless well tilled and sowed with profitable seed, produces only ranker weeds.

That we may obtain the advantages arising from an increase of knowledge, and prevent as much as may be the mischievous consequences that would attend a general ignorance among us, the following hints are offered toward forming a plan for the education of the youth of Pennsylvania, viz.: . . .

The "viz." was a complete and detailed plan for organization, physical plant, curriculum and faculty. It proposed that the Academy should be, if possible, "not far from a river, having a garden, orchard, meadow, and a field or two"—a far cry from University of Pennsylvania's present downtown campus. It should have a library "with maps of all countries, globes, some mathematical instruments, an apparatus for experiments in natural philosophy and for mechanics; prints of all kinds, prospects, buildings, machines, etc." There should be a sports program under which the students "be frequently exercised in leaping, wrestling and swimming." The boys should "diet together plainly, temperately, and frugally.

"As to their studies, it would be well if they could be taught everything that is useful, and everything that is ornamental. But art is long, and their time is short. It is therefore proposed that they learn those things that are likely to be most useful and more ornamental, regard being had to the several professions for which they are intended."

Franklin then laid out a curriculum which included writing "a fair hand, and swift," drawing, arithmetic, grammar, reading,

English composition, and oratory—"Not with an even tone which underdoes, nor a theatrical which overdoes, nature." History and geography were to be taught, as well as morality and the Christian religion.

The free hospital was not Franklin's idea, but his writing and political cunning made it possible. He described how it was done.

IN 1751, Dr. Thomas Bond, a particular friend of mine, conceived the idea of establishing a hospital in Philadelphia (a very beneficent design, which has been ascribed to me, but was originally his) for the reception and cure of poor sick persons, whether inhabitants of the province or strangers. He was zealous and active in endeavoring to procure subscriptions for it, but the proposal being a novelty in America, and at first not well understood, he met with but small success.

At length he came to me with the compliment that he found there was no such thing as carrying a public-spirited project through without my being concerned in it. "For," says he, "I am often asked by those to whom I propose subscribing, Have you consulted Franklin upon this business? And what does he think of it? And when I tell them that I have not (supposing it rather out of your line), they do not subscribe, but say they will consider of it." I inquired into the nature and probable utility of his scheme, and receiving from him a very satisfactory explanation, I not only subscribed to it myself, but engaged heartily in the design of procuring subscriptions from others.

Franklin introduced a bill in the Assembly to provide two thousand pounds in addition to the subscriptions from the public. When the country members opposed it on the grounds that the hospital would benefit only Philadelphians, Franklin amended it to provide that the money from the government would be paid only if private subscribers first raised an equal amount.

THIS CONDITION carried the bill through; for the members who had opposed the grant, and now conceived they might have the credit of being charitable without the expense, agreed to its passage; and then, in soliciting subscriptions among the people, we urged the conditional promise of the law as an additional motive to give, since every man's donation would be doubled: thus the clause worked both ways. The subscriptions accordingly soon exceeded the requisite sum, and we claimed and received the public gift, which enabled us to carry the design into execution. . . . I do not remember any of my political maneuvers, the success of which gave me at the time more pleasure, or wherein, after thinking of it, I more easily excused myself for having made some use of cunning.

As a newspaper publisher Franklin could enlist public support for measures that he introduced into the legislative body. One of his first bills was a protest against Britain sending over convicts for the "improvement and well peopling of America." To attract attention to the bill he published in the *Gazette* a humorous proposal for repayment to the mother country, signing it "Americanus."

IN SOME OF THE uninhabited parts of these provinces there are numbers of venomous reptiles we call rattlesnakes; felons-convict from the beginning of this world. These, whenever we meet with them, we put to death, by virtue of an old law: Thou shalt bruise his head. But as this is a sanguinary law, and may seem too cruel; and as, however mischievous those creatures are with us, they may possibly change their natures if they were to change the climate; I would humbly propose that this general sentence of death be changed to transportation. In the spring of the year, when they first creep out of their holes, they are feeble, heavy, slow, and easily taken; and if a small bounty were allowed per head, some thousands might be collected annually and transported to Britain. . . .

Rattlesnakes seem the most suitable returns for the human serpents sent to us by our mother country.

This item in the *Gazette* was Franklin's first warning that England would have to change her ways in dealing with her colonies.

Before his retirement from business, Franklin had become a prominent Philadelphian. Shortly, in the assembly, he became a leading Pennsylvanian. Then he started on the long road to becoming the first American as his influence spread to the other colonies. The initial step was his appointment as Deputy Post-master-General for the colonies, the one public office which he sought through a letter in which he asked Collinson to use his influence.

The main value of this appointment in Franklin's development was the contacts that he made and the recognition that he gained in other colonies through his trips to reorganize their post offices, establish new routes, and introduce a uniform system of accounting. His intercolonial influence was strengthened by membership, in 1754, on a congress of commissioners of all the northern colonies to meet with the chiefs of the Six Nations at Albany on the eve of the French and Indian War. It was here that he proposed a plan for a defensive union of the colonies, saying:

THE UNION of the colonies, however necessary, I apprehend is not to be brought about by the means that have hitherto been used for that purpose. A governor of one colony, who happens from some circumstance in his own government to see the necessity of such a union, writes his sentiments of

the matter to the other governors, and desires them to recommend it to their respective assemblies. They accordingly
lay the letters before those assemblies and perhaps recommend the proposal in general words. But governors are
often on ill terms with their assemblies, and seldom are the
men that have the most influence among them. . . .

Now if you were to pick out half a dozen men of good
understanding and address, and furnish them with a reasonable scheme and proper instructions, and send them in the
nature of ambassadors to the other colonies, where they
might apply particularly to all the leading men and by
proper management get them to engage in promoting the
scheme; where, by being present, they would have the opportunity of pressing the affair in both public and private,
obviating difficulties as they arise, answering objections as
soon as they are made, before they spread and gather
strength in the minds of the people, etc., etc.; I imagine such
an union might thereby be made and established. . . . A
voluntary union entered into by the colonies themselves, I
think, would be preferable to one imposed by Parliament;
for it would be perhaps not much more difficult to procure, and more easy to alter and improve as circumstances
should require and experience direct.

In his inimitable manner, Franklin continued to outline every
detail of the proposed union. There was to be a grand council
with membership proportioned among the colonies based upon
their contributions to the common treasury; a governor-general,
a military man, appointed and paid by the King; a defense fund
to be raised by a tax on liquor. The plan was discussed in the
Albany congress.

MANY OBJECTIONS and difficulties were started, but at
length they were all overcome, and the plan was unanimously agreed to, and copies ordered to be transmitted to

the Board of Trade and to the assemblies of the several provinces. Its fate was singular; the assemblies did not adopt it, as they all thought there was too much *prerogative* in it, and in England it was judged to have too much of the *democratic*. . . . Another scheme was formed, supposed to answer the same purpose better, whereby the governors of the provinces, with some members of their respective councils, were to meet and order the raising of troops, building of forts, etc., and to draw on the treasury of Great Britain for the expense, which was afterward to be refunded by an act of Parliament laying a tax on America.

Franklin had, as usual, pushed his plan in the columns of the *Gazette* and in this connection had published (and had probably drawn) the first cartoon in America. It was a picture of a snake cut into eight pieces, marked with the initials of New England, New York, New Jersey, Pennsylvania, Maryland, Virginia, North Carolina and South Carolina. It was captioned "Join or Die."

The revised plan was shown to Franklin by Governor Shirley of Massachusetts. In three letters to the governor, Franklin delineated, twenty-one years before the fighting started, the causes of the American Revolution.

December 18, 1754

SIR: I mentioned it yesterday to your excellency as my opinion that excluding the people of the colonies from all share in the choice of the grand council would probably give extreme dissatisfaction, as well as the taxing of them by act of Parliament, where they have no representation. . . .

First, they would say . . . that the Parliament of England is at a great distance, subject to be misinformed and misled by such governors and councils, whose united interests might possibly secure them against the effect of any complaint from hence.

That it is supposed an undoubted right of Englishmen not to be taxed but by their own consent, given through their representatives.

That the colonies have no representatives in Parliament.

That to propose taxing them by Parliament, and refuse them the liberty of choosing a representative council to meet in the colonies . . . shows a suspicion of their loyalty to the crown, or of their regard for their country, or of their common sense and understanding, which they have not deserved.

That compelling the colonies to pay money without their consent, would be rather like raising contributions in an enemy's country, than taxing of Englishmen for their own public benefit.

That it would be treating them as a conquered people, and not as true British subjects. . . .

That, besides the taxes necessary for the defense of the frontiers, the colonies pay yearly great sums to the mother country unnoticed; for . . . we are restrained in our trade with foreign nations; and where we could be supplied with any manufacture cheaper from them, but must buy the same dearer from Britain, the difference of price is a clear tax to Britain. . . .

Some manufacturers we could make, but are forbidden, and must take them of British merchants; the whole price is a tax paid to Britain. . . .

In short, as we are not suffered to regulate our trade and restrain the importation and consumption of British superfluities, as Britatin can the consumption of foreign superfluities, our whole wealth centers finally amongst the merchants and inhabitants of Britain; and if we make them richer, and enable them better to pay their taxes, it is nearly the same as being taxed ourselves, and equally beneficial to the crown. . . .

These, and such kind of things as these, I apprehend will

be thought and said by the people, if the proposed alteration of the Albany plan should take place. Then the administration of the board of governors and council so
appointed, not having the representative body of the people
to approve and unite its measures, and conciliate the minds
of the people to them, will probably become suspected and
odious, dangerous animosities and feuds will arise between
the governors and governed, and everything go into confusion.

Franklin believed that under his plan, the united colonies
could have defended themselves against the attacks of the French
and their Indian allies. England was unwilling to give them
that much latitude. In his autobiography Franklin says:

THE BRITISH GOVERNMENT, not choosing to permit the union of the colonies as proposed at Albany, and to trust that
union with their defense . . . sent over General Braddock
with two regiments of regular British troops for that purpose. He landed at Alexandria, in Virginia, and thence
marched to Frederictown in Maryland, where he halted for
carriages. Our Assembly, apprehending from some information, that he had conceived violent prejudices against them
. . . wished me to wait upon him, not as from them, but as
postmaster-general, under the guise of proposing to settle
with him the mode of conducting with most celerity and certainty the despatches between him and the governors of the
several provinces. . . .

We found the general at Frederictown, waiting impa-
tiently for the return of those he had sent through the back
parts of Maryland and Virginia to collect wagons. I stayed
with him several days. . . . When I was about to depart, the
returns of wagons to be obtained were brought in, by which
it appeared that they amounted only to twenty-five, and not
all of those were in serviceable condition. . . .

I happened to say I thought it was pity they had not been landed rather in Pennsylvania, as in that country almost every farmer had his wagon. The general eagerly laid hold of my words, and said, "Then you, sir, who are a man of interest there, can probably procure them for us, and I beg you will undertake it."

Franklin published an advertisement in the *Gazette,* offering a price of fifteen shillings per day for a vehicle with four horses and a driver, or two shillings a day for a pack horse with saddle. He then continued to explain why it was to the best interests of the countrymen to provide the transportation.

To THE INHABITANTS of the Counties of Lancaster, York and Cumberland. Friends and Countrymen:

Being occasionally at the camp at Frederic a few days since, I found the general and officers extremely exasperated on account of their not being supplied with horses and carriages, which had been expected from this province. . . .

It was proposed to send an armed force immediately into these countries, to seize as many of the best carriages and horses as should be wanted, and compel as many persons into the service as would be necessary to drive and take care of them.

I apprehended that the progress of British soldiers through these counties on such an occasion, especially considering the temper they are in, and their resentment against us, would be attended with many and great inconveniences to the inhabitants, and therefore more willingly took the trouble of finding first what might be done by fair and equitable means. The people of these back counties have lately complained to the Assembly that a sufficient currency was wanting; you have an opportunity of receiving and dividing among you a very considerable sum; for, if the service of this expedition should continue, as it is more than probable it will, for one hundred and twenty days, the hire of these wagons and horses will amount to upward of thirty thousand pounds, which will be paid you in silver and gold of the King's money.

The service will be light and easy, for the army will scarce march above twelve miles per day, and the wagons and baggage-horses, as they carry those things that are absolutely necessary to the welfare of the army, must march with the army, and no faster; and are, for the army's sake, always placed where they can be most secure, whether in a march or in a camp.

If you are really, as I believe you are, good and loyal subjects to His Majesty, you may now do a most acceptable service, and make it easy to yourselves. . . . The King's business must be done; so many brave troops, come so far for your defense, must not stand idle through your backwardness to do what may be reasonably expected from you; wagons and horses must be had; violent measures will probably be used, and you will be left to seek for a recompense where you can find it, and your case, perhaps, be little pitied or regarded.

I have no particular interest in this affair, as, except the satisfaction of endeavoring to do good, I shall have only my labor for my pains. If this method of obtaining the wagons and the horses is not likely to succeed, I am obliged to send word to the general in fourteen days; and I suppose Sir John St. Clair, the hussar, with a body of soldiers, will immediately enter the province for the purpose, which I shall be sorry to hear, because I am very sincerely and truly your friend and well-wisher,

B. FRANKLIN

Franklin secured the wagons, although he had to put up his own money to pay advances and had to personally guarantee their safe return—his credit was better than King George's with the Pennsylvania farmers.

He tried to dissuade Braddock from his disastrous attack.

IN CONVERSATION with him one day, he was giving me some account of his intended progress. "After taking Fort Duquesne," says he, "I am to proceed to Niagara; and, having taken that, to Frontenac, if the season will allow time; and I suppose it will, for Duquesne can hardly detain me above three or four days; and then I see nothing that can obstruct my march to Niagara." Having therefore revolved in my mind the long line his army must make in their march by a very narrow road, to be cut for them through the woods and bushes, and also what I had read of a former defeat of fifteen hundred French, who invaded the Iroquois country, I had conceived some doubts and some fears for the event of the campaign. But I ventured only to say, "To be sure, sir, if you arrive well before Duquesne, with these fine troops, so well provided with artillery, that place not yet completely fortified, and as we hear with no very strong garrison, can probably make but a short resistance. The only danger I apprehend of obstruction to your march is from ambuscades of Indians, who, by constant practice, are dexterous in laying and executing them. . . ."

He smiled at my ignorance and replied, "These savages may, indeed, be a formidable enemy to your raw American militia, but upon the King's regular and disciplined troops, sir, it is impossible they should make any impression." I was conscious of an impropriety in disputing with a military man in matters of his profession, and said no more. The enemy, however, did not take the advantage of his army which I apprehended . . . but let it advance without interruption till within nine miles of the place; and then . . . attacked its advanced guard by a heavy fire from behind trees and bushes, which was the first intelligence the general had of an enemy's being near him. . . . The officers, being on horseback, were more easily distinguished, picked out as marks, and fell very fast; and the soldiers were crowded together in a huddle, having or hearing no orders, and standing to be shot at till two-thirds of them were killed; and then being seized with a panic, the whole fled with precipitation.

The wagoners took each a horse out of his team and scampered. Their example was immediately followed by others; so that all the wagons, provisions, artillery and stores were left to the enemy. The general, being wounded, was brought off with difficulty. . . . The flyers, not being pursued, arrived at Dunbar's camp, and the panic they brought with them instantly seized him and all his people; and, though he had now above one thousand men, and the enemy who had beaten Braddock did not at most exceed four hundred Indians and French together, instead of proceeding and endeavoring to recover some of the lost honor, he ordered all the stores, ammunition, etc., to be destroyed, that he might have more horses to assist his flight towards the settlements . . . he continued his hasty march through all the country, not thinking himself safe till he arrived at Philadelphia, where the inhabitants could protect him. This whole transaction gave us Americans the first suspicion that our exalted ideas of the prowess of the British regulars had not been well founded. . . .

As soon as the loss of the wagons and horses was generally known, all the owners came upon me for the valuation which I had given bond to pay. Their demands gave me a great deal of trouble . . . and some began to sue me. General Shirley at length relieved me from this terrible situation by appointing commissioners to examine the claims, and ordering payment. They amounted to near

twenty thousand pound, which to pay would have ruined me.

While British regulars skulked in Philadelphia, the Assembly
passed a bill appropriating £60,000 to finance a militia. It was
Franklin's bill and he was chairman of the committee to spend
the money. But more than money was needed. A war party of
Shawnees had wiped out the village of Gnadenhuetten. This
hamlet, seventy-five miles northwest of Philadelphia, was peopled by German Moravians. Somebody had to organize a defense. So, Franklin writes, "While the several companies of the
county and city were forming, and learning their exercise, the
governor prevailed upon me to take charge of our northwest
frontier which was invested by the enemy, and provide for the
defense of the inhabitants by raising troops and building a line
of forts. I undertook this military business, though I did not conceive myself well qualified for it."

On December 18, 1755, the portly philosopher mounted his
horse to lead fifty provincial cavalrymen and three covered
wagons on a six week's campaign against the Indians. Approaching fifty, and with no previous military experience, sedentary
Franklin seemed ill suited for the rigors of wilderness war, but
with his rare gift for both planning and doing, he was the only
man who might organize the outlying Germans to defend their
settlements. His first stop was the Moravian settlement of
Bethlehem, of which he said, "I was surprised to find it in such
a good posture of defense; the destruction of Gnadenhuetten
had made them apprehend danger. The principal buildings were
defended by a stockade; they had purchased a quantity of arms
and ammunition from New York, and had even placed quantities of small paving stones between the windows of their high
stone houses, for their women to throw down upon the heads of
any Indians that should attempt to force into them."

Franklin had no military rank. He said, "He [the governor]
proposed to commission me as a general. I had not so good an

opinion of my military abilities as he professed to have and I believe his professions must have exceeded his real sentiments." But to Moravian Bishop Spangenberg he was a general, and was so styled by the Germans. Actually he was more than a general. The broad powers given him by the governor's commission made him king of the wild frontier.

At Bethlehem, Franklin assembled the militia companies that were reporting for duty from outlying counties, including one commanded by Captain Isaac Wayne, who was accompanied by his eleven-year-old son Anthony—not yet known as "Mad" Anthony Wayne. He posted his men in a most military manner, perhaps with the advice of his son William who was with him and who had served with the British in the attack on Ticonderoga. Being Franklin, he could not resist having some new ideas on military matters. He wrote:

IF DOGS ARE CARRIED out with any party, they should be large, strong and fierce; and every dog led in a slip string, to prevent their tiring themselves by running out and in, and discovering the party by barking at squirrels, etc. Only when the party comes near thick woods and suspicious places, they should turn out a dog or two to search them. In case of meeting a party of the enemy, the dogs are all then to be turned loose and set on. They will be fresher and finer for having previously been confined, and will confound the enemy a good deal, and be very serviceable. This was the Spanish method of guarding their marches.

The northwest frontier of Pennsylvania was protected by the soaring eastern ridge of the Appalachians, pierced only by Lehigh Gap. Bethlehem was at the southern end of the Gap, razed Gnadenhuetten at the northern end. If the Indians got through the Gap in force, the German settlements would be at their mercy. Worse, if the French followed, Philadelphia would be endangered or, if they fortified the Gap, the best route to the west would be closed to the English. The amateur general decided that a fort must be built on the far side of the Gap and, on a day of dismal January rain, he led his small force into the forbidding mountain pass.

Franklin did not know it, but he almost had a very competent young adjutant on that march. A few days before he set out, Governor Morris of Pennsylvania had received a letter from a colonel in Virginia saying that he was disgusted with the inaction there and was thinking of resigning his commission. He said, "If you propose to levy troops and their destination is not a secret, I should be favored were I let into the scheme so that I might act conjunctively." Morris never took advantage of George Washington's offer.

Franklin spent what he considered his fiftieth birthday passing through Lehigh Gap, saying, "I still feel some regard for this sixth of January as my old nominal birthday, although the change in style has carried the real day forward to the seventeenth." The Gregorian calendar, adopted by England in 1752, had robbed him of eleven days. It was a strange way for a philosopher to spend his fiftieth birthday. He said, "We had not marched many miles before it began to rain, and it continued raining all day; there were no habitations on the road to shelter us, till we arrived near night at the house of a German where, and in his barn, we were all huddled together as wet as water could make us. It was well we were not attacked on our march, for our arms were of the most ordinary sort, and our men could not keep the locks of their guns dry."

As the little army left the Gap it was fired on by Indian snipers in the hills—the only time in a long, war-filled life that Benjamin Franklin was under fire.

Franklin apparently learned how to build a fort by reading a book. In the American Philosophical Society is a ponderous tome entitled *Short Treatise on Fortifications and Geometry,* with copious notes in Franklin's handwriting in the margins—

a reprehensible practice to which the good doctor was sadly addicted. Vauban or others of the great military engineers of the day would not have considered it much of a fort, but it served to keep the Indians, who had no artillery, out of eastern Pennsylvania. Franklin described it:

THE NEXT MORNING our fort was planned and marked out, the circumference measuring 455 feet, which would require as many palisades to be made of trees, one with another, of a foot in diameter. Our axes, of which we had seventy, were immediately set to work to cut down trees and, our men being dexterous in the use of them, great despatch was made. . . .

Seeing the trees fall so fast, I had the curiosity to look at my watch when two men began to cut at a pine; in six minutes they had it upon the ground, and I found it of fourteen inches diameter; each pine made three palisades of eighteen feet long, pointed at one end. While these were preparing, our other men dug a trench all around of three feet deep, in which the palisades were to be planted; and the bodies being taken off our wagons, and the fore and hind wheels separated by taking out the pin which united the two parts of the perch, we had ten carriages with two horses each to bring the palisades from the woods to the spot. When they were set up, our carpenters built a platform of boards all around within, about six feet high, for the men to stand on when to fire through the loopholes. We had one swivel-gun, which we mounted on one of the angles, and fired it as soon as fixed, to let the Indians know if any were within hearing, that he had such pieces; and thus our fort (if that name may be given to so miserable a stockade) was finished in a week, though it rained so hard every other day that the men could not well work.

Although this wilderness campaigning was a rugged life for a middle-aged fat man, it apparently was not fraught with too much hardship. In one letter to his wife Franklin wrote, "Our lodging is on deal featherbeds in warm blankets." In another he said, "We have enjoyed your roast beef, and this day began on the roast veal. All agree that they are both the best that ever were of the kind. . . . Your citizens, that have their dinners hot and hot, know nothing of good eating. We find it in much greater perfection when the kitchen is fourscore miles from the dining room."

After building two flanking outposts to the main fort, Franklin's work on the frontier was completed and he set out for Philadelphia via Bethlehem. Here he paused to study the Moravians. War or no war, Franklin's curiosity could not be confined.

WHILE AT BETHLEHEM, I inquired a little into the practice of the Moravians: some of them had accompanied me and all were very kind to me. I found that they worked for a common stock, eat at common tables, and slept in common dormitories, great numbers together. . . .

I inquired concerning Moravian marriages, whether the report was true that they were by lot. I was told that lots were used only in particular cases; that generally, when a young man found himself disposed to marry, he informed the elders of his class, who consulted with the elder ladies that governed the young women. As these elders of the different sexes were well acquainted with the tempers and dispositions of their respective pupils, they could best judge what matches were suitable, and their judgments were generally acquiesced in; but if, for example, it should happen that two or three young women were found to be equally proper for the young man, the lot was then referred to. I objected, if the matches are not made by the mutual choice of the parties, some of them may chance to be very unhappy. "And so they may," answered my informer, "if you let the parties choose for themselves." Which, indeed, I could not deny.

Back in Philadelphia, Franklin was commissioned colonel of the city's militia regiment—the only formal military rank he ever held. After a grand review of the regiment, Franklin says, "They accompanied me to my house, and would salute me with some rounds fired before my door, which shook down and broke several glasses of my electrical apparatus." A crashing termination to Franklin's career as a warrior and a prophecy of the end of his leisured, philosophical way of life.

CHAPTER VI

THE COLONIAL AGENT

❦

Idealist William Penn founded his 26,000,000-acre colony as a religious experiment, a haven from persecution, particularly for the Quakers. His sons, who became the proprietaries when they inherited the charter, were neither idealists nor Quakers. They were, quite simply, money-hungry landlords whose sole interest in the colonial venture was big profits at small costs.

The governor of the province was appointed and instructed by the Penns and paid by the Pennsylvania Assembly. This made his position an impossible one. Laws passed by the Assembly had to be approved by the governor before submission to England. He was instructed by the proprietaries to veto any laws that might lessen their profits. If he disobeyed his orders he might be fired by the Penns. If he obeyed them he might not be paid by the Assembly. Most governors did not last long.

By the middle 1750's Franklin was the leader in the fight between the Assembly and the proprietaries, represented by the governor. He was the only man respected by all the elements in the assembly—the Quakers, the farmers, the small tradesmen and the wealthy merchants. He was the leading politician in Pennsylvania. In 1757 the squabble with the Penns came to a head over the question of the Assembly's right to tax the lands of the proprietaries. It was decided to send somebody to England to try to reason with the Penns and, if necessary, petition the King for relief. Obviously, Franklin was the man for the job, although Thomas Penn, the principal owner, already detested him.

In their letters to England, a succession of governors had blamed him for their troubles with the Assembly. Political opponents, currying favor with the Penns, had told them that Franklin was the ringleader, the troublemaker who was seeking to curtail their feudal income. And a small courtesy from the officers of Franklin's regiment had frightened and infuriated the absentee landlords. Franklin described the incident:

BEING ABOUT TO SET out on a journey to Virginia, the officers of my regiment took it into their heads that it would be proper for them to escort me out of town as far as the Lower Ferry. . . . They came to my door, just between thirty and forty, mounted, and all in their uniforms. . . . I was a good deal chagrined at their appearance, as I could not avoid their accompanying me. What made it worse was, that as soon as we began to move, they drew their swords and rode with them naked all the way. Somebody wrote an account of this to the proprietor, and it gave him great offense. No such honor had been paid him when in the province, nor to any of his governors; and he said it was only proper to princes of the blood royal. . . .

This silly affair, however, greatly increased his rancor against me, which was before not a little, on account of my conduct in the assembly respecting the exemption of his estate from taxation, which I had always opposed very warmly, and not without severe reflections on his meanness and injustice of contending for it. He accused me to the ministry as being the great obstacle to the King's service, preventing by my influence in the House, the proper form of the bills for raising money, and he instanced this parade with my officers as a proof of my having an intention to take the government of the province out of his hands by force.

The enmity of the Penns did not seriously disturb Franklin. He brushed it aside and expressed his opinion of the Penns by writing, "I am not much concerned about that, because if I have offended them by acting right, I can, whenever I please, reverse their displeasure by acting wrong. . . . I have some natural dislike to persons who so far love money as to be unjust for its sake. . . . I am persuaded that I do not oppose their views from pique, disappointment or personal resentment, but, as I think, from a regard for the public good. I may be mistaken in what is that public good, but at least I mean well."

Shortly before Franklin left for England with his son William, he wrote to Collinson that he was disgusted with politics. "I am heartily sick of our present situation. I like neither the governor's conduct nor the Assembly's, and having some share in the confidence of both, I have endeavored to reconcile them, but in vain; and between them they make me very uneasy." He could not know that at the age of fifty-one he was starting his third career—that the remainder of his life would be devoted principally to politics and diplomacy, and that he would spend twenty-five of his remaining thirty-three years on foreign soil. At the time, the oldest of his fellow Founding Fathers, George Washington, was twenty-five; John Adams, twenty-two; Thomas Jefferson, fourteen; James Madison, six; and Alexander Hamilton, six months.

Franklin's negotiations with the Penns were neither pleasant nor wholly successful. In his report of the meeting, he said that he told Thomas Penn that the original charter of the province gave the Assembly—

ALL THE POWERS and the privileges of an assembly according to the rights of free-born subjects of England. . . . "Yes," said he [Penn], "but if my father granted privileges he was not by the royal charter empowered to grant, nothing can be claimed by such grant." I said: "Then if your father had no right to grant the privileges he pretended to grant, and published all over Europe as granted, those who came to settle in the province on the faith of that grant, and in expectation of enjoying the privileges contained in it, were deceived, cheated and betrayed." He answered that they should themselves have looked to that; that the royal charter was no secret; they who came into the province on his father's offer of privileges, if they were deceived, it was their own fault. And that he said with a kind of triumphing, laughing insolence, such as a low jockey might do when a purchaser complained that he had cheated him on a horse. I was astonished to see him thus meanly give up his father's character, and conceived at the moment a more cordial and thorough contempt for him than I ever felt for any man living . . .

The Penns insisted that the complaints of the Assembly be put in writing. When Franklin complied they pigeonholed them for a year and then replied directly to the Assembly, ignoring the waiting minister.

While waiting, Franklin and William settled down in London in an apartment in the home of Mrs. Margaret Stevenson, who, with her eighteen-year-old daughter Mary, ran a boardinghouse at 7 Craven Street. Staying at a boardinghouse would seem to carry out Franklin's precepts of frugality, except that his quarters consisted of a four-room suite where he was attended by two servants whom he had brought from home. He spent much of his time shopping, and a series of letters to Deborah describe the "frugal" presents that he sent to her and daughter Sarah.

I SEND YOU by Captain Budden a large case and a small box. In the large case is another small box containing some English china, viz.: melons and leaves for a dessert of fruit and cream, or the like; a bowl remarkable for the neatness of its figures, made at Bow, near this city; some coffee cups of the same; a Worcester bowl, ordinary. To show the difference of workmanship, there is something from all the China works in England; and one old true china basin mended, of an odd color. The same box contains four silver salt ladles, newest but ugliest fashion. . . . Also two large fine Flanders bedticks, and two pair of large superfine blankets, two fine damask tablecloths and napkins, and forty-three ells of Ghentish sheeting Holland. . . . Also seven yards of printed cotton, blue ground, to make you a gown. I bought it by candlelight and liked it then, but not so well afterward. If you do not fancy it, send it as a present from me to sister Jenny. There is a better gown for you, of flowered tissue, sixteen yards, of Mrs. Stevenson's fancy, cost nine guineas; and I think it a great beauty. There was no more of the sort, or you should have had enough for a negligee or suit. . . .

I hope Sally applies herself closely to her French and music, and that I shall find she has made great proficiency. The harpsichord I was about, and which was to have cost me forty guineas, Mr. Stanley advises me not to buy; and we are looking out for another. . . .

A few months later the indulgent, frugal father sent his Sally a harpsichord that cost forty-two guineas, and in a later letter he says, "I sent my dear girl a newest fashioned hat and cloak, and sundry little things which I hope will get safe to hand. I now send her a pair of buckles made of French paste stones, which are next in luster to diamonds. They cost three guineas and are said to be cheap at that price."

The enforced wait permitted Franklin to renew his scientific speculations. In response to a query he described how he had attempted to treat paralysis with electricity: "My method was to place the patient first in a chair, on an electric stool, and draw a number of large, strong sparks from all parts of the affected limb or side." He claimed that he perceived some temporary benefit from these treatments but that "the patients . . . finding the shocks pretty severe, they became discouraged, went home, and in a short time relapsed; so that I never knew any advantage from electricity in palsies that was permanent. And how far the apparent, temporary advantage might arise from the exercise of the patient's journey, and coming daily to my house, or from the spirits given by the hope of success . . . I will not pretend to say."

During this period he also experimented with cooling by evaporation. He described an experiment which he made with an English chemist:

BY DIPPING first the ball of the thermometer into the ether, it appeared that the ether was precisely of the same temperament with the thermometer, which stood then at 65; for it made no alteration in the height of the little column of mercury. But when the thermometer was taken out of the ether, and the ether with which the ball was wet, began to evaporate, the mercury sank several degrees. The wetting was then repeated by a feather that had been dipped into the ether, when the mercury sunk still lower.

We continued this operation, one of us wetting the ball and another of the company blowing upon it with the bellows to quicken the evaporation, the mercury sinking all the time, till it came down to 7, which is 25 degrees below the freezing point, when we let off. Soon after it passed the freezing point a thin coat of ice began to cover the ball. . . . From this experiment one may see the possibilities of freezing a man to death on a warm summer's day, if he were to stand in a passage through which the wind blew briskly, and to be wet frequently with ether.

One might also see the possibility of electric refrigeration, particularly when combined with another experiment of which he said: "A vessel of water being placed in another somewhat larger, containing spirit, in such a manner that the vessel of water is surrounded with the spirit, and both placed under the receiver of an air pump, on exhausting the air, the spirit evaporating, leaves such a degree of cold as to freeze the water, though the thermometer in the open air stands many degrees above the freezing point."

History is vague about why Franklin stayed in England for five years on his first visit, and most of his writing for the year 1759 has never come to light. During this period he traveled— to Scotland to get a degree from the University of St. Andrews; to Oxford where he was made a Doctor of Civil Laws. In Belgium and Holland he visited scientists and churches, and concluded that all religion need not be as austere as the Puritanism of his youth. He wrote to a friend in Connecticut:

WHEN I TRAVELED in Flanders I thought of your excessively strict observation of Sunday; and that a man could hardly travel on that day among you on his lawful occasions without hazard of punishment; while, where I was, everyone traveled, if he pleased, or diverted himself in any other way; and in the afternoon both high and low went to the play or the opera, where there was plenty of singing, fiddling and dancing. I looked round for God's judgments, but saw no signs of them. The cities were well built and full of inhabitants, the markets full of plenty, the people well favored and well clothed, the fields well tilled, the cattle fat and strong, the fences, houses and windows all in repair . . . which would almost make one think suspect that the Deity is not so angry at that offense as a New England justice.

Young Mary Stevenson, his landlady's daughter, had gone to live with her aunt—perhaps to avoid a match that Franklin was trying to make between her and his son William—and some of Franklin's most interesting scientific observations are in a series of letters to the girl. Mary—or Polly, as Franklin called her—was a most unusual young lady for that era, and had asked Franklin to make natural philosophy the subject of their correspondence, although, Franklin wrote, "Why will you, by the cultivation of your mind, make yourself still more amiable and a more desirable companion for a man of understanding when you are determined, as I hear, to live single? If we enter, as you propose, into moral as well as natural philosophy, I fancy that when I have fully established my authority as a tutor, I shall take upon me to lecture you a little on that chapter of duty."

He wrote her about the importance of entomology as a science, the distillation of salt water, the direction and origin of streams, and a complex observation on tides, for the length of which he apologized by saying, "After writing six folio pages of philosophy to a young girl is it necessary to finish such a letter with a compliment? Is not such a letter of itself a compliment?"

One letter to Polly describes the type of practical, uncomplicated, everyday kind of experiment which marked most of Franklin's scientific research. Polly had apparently asked about the effect of color on heat absorption. Franklin replied:

MY EXPERIMENT was this. I took a number of little square pieces of broadcloth from a tailor's pattern card, of various colors. They were black, deep blue, green, purple, red, yellow, white and other colors, or shades of colors. I laid them all out upon the snow in a bright sunshiny morning. In a few hours (I cannot now be exact as to the time), the black, being warmed most by the sun, was sunk so low as to be below the stroke of the sun's rays; the dark blue almost as low, the lighter blue not quite so much as the dark, the other colors less as they were lighter; and the quite white remained on the surface of the snow, not having entered it at all.

What signifies philosophy that does not apply to some use? May we not learn from hence, that black clothes are not so fit to wear in a hot sunny climate or season as white ones? . . . That soldiers and seamen, who must march and labor in the sun, should in the East or West Indies have a uniform of white? . . .

A century passed after this letter was written before Europeans generally learned to wear white in their tropical colonies.

Another sideline activity of Franklin's during this English sojourn was the invention of a novel and, for a time, very popular musical instrument which he called the armonica, but which everybody else called a harmonica. He described it in a letter to a fellow scientist in Italy.

YOU HAVE DOUBTLESS HEARD the sweet tone that is drawn from a drinking glass by passing a wet finger round its brim. One Mr. Puckeridge, a gentleman from Ireland, was the first who thought of playing tunes formed of those tones. He collected a number of glasses of different sizes, fixed them near each other on a table, and tuned them by putting into them water more or less, as each note required. The tones were brought out by passing his fingers round their brims. . . . Being charmed by the sweetness of its tones and the music he produced from it, I wished only to see the glasses disposed in a more convenient form, and brought together in a narrower compass, so as to admit of a greater number of tones . . . in the following manner.

The glasses are blown as near as possible in the form of hemispheres, having each an open neck or socket in the middle. The thickness of the glass near the brim about a tenth of an inch . . . but thicker as it comes near the neck, which in the largest glasses is about an inch deep. . . . The largest glass is nine inches diameter, and the smallest three inches. Between these two are twenty-three different sizes, differing from each other a quarter of an inch in diameter. To make a single instrument there should be at least six glasses blown of each size; and out of this number one may probably pick thirty-seven glasses. . . .

The glasses being chosen, and every one marked with a diamond the note you intend it for, they are to be tuned by diminishing the thickness of those that are too sharp. This is done by grinding them round from the neck toward the brim, the breadth of one or two inches, as may be required; often trying the glass by a well-tuned harpsichord. . . .

The glasses being thus tuned, you are to be provided with a case for them, and a spindle on which they are to be fixed. My case is about three feet long, eleven inches every way wide within at the biggest end, and five inches at the smallest end. . . . The spindle, which is of hard iron, lies horizontally from end to end of the box within, exactly in the middle, and is made to turn on brass gudgeons at each end. . . .

This instrument is played upon by sitting before the middle of the set of glasses as before the keys of a harpsichord, turning them with the foot, and wetting them now and then with a sponge and clean water. . . . Both hands are used, by which means different parts are played together. Observe that the tones are best drawn out when the glasses turn from the ends of the fingers, not when they turn to them.

The advantages of this instrument are that its tones are incomparably sweet beyond those of any other; that they may be swelled and softened at pleasure by stronger or weaker pressure of the fingers and continued to any length; and that the instrument, being once well tuned, never again wants tuning.

Until about 1800 the armonica was in great vogue throughout

Europe. Gluck, Mozart and Beethoven wrote music for it, Marie Antoinette took lessons on it, and Franklin played it to amuse his London friends. He also played the harp, guitar and violin, although there is no record of when or how he gained his skill as a musician.

It was during this era in England that Franklin laid the foundation for another of his important roles—as propagandist, the first American public relations man. Franklin well knew the power of the press. Many years before, in an *Apology for Printers* which he had written in reply to a criticism of something that appeared in his paper, he said, "The business of printing has chiefly to do with men's opinions; most things that are printed tending to promote some or oppose others." Later he wrote, "The facility with which the same truths may be repeatedly enforced by placing them daily in different lights in newspapers, which are everywhere read, gives a great chance of establishing them. And we now find that it is not only right to strike while the iron is hot, but that it may be very practicable to heat it by continually striking."

Franklin "struck" repeatedly in the English press and with pamphlets from 1757 until the dawn of the Revolution—how frequently we will never know for sure, as most of his writing was done under pseudonymns. Scholars have argued for years as to which pieces of procolonial propaganda were by Franklin and which were not. He announced his purpose in a letter to the Assembly from London, in 1758, in which he said, "One thing . . . to be done before we push our point with Parliament is removing the prejudices that art and accident have spread among the people of this country against us, and obtaining for us the good opinion of the bulk of mankind without doors. This I hope we have it in our power to do by means of a work now nearly ready for the press, calculated to engage the attention of many readers and at the same time efface the bad impression received of us."

The work to which Franklin referred was the *Historical*

Review of the Constitution and Government of Pennsylvania.
Franklin planned this and William assembled much of the
material, but it was actually written by a lawyer named Richard
Jackson, who insisted on remaining anonymous because he was
trying to get elected to Parliament. Franklin was credited with
it—or blamed for it, depending on the point of view—and it did
not endear him to the Penns with such language as "And who
or what are these proprietories? In the province, unsizable subjects and insufficient lords. At home, gentlemen, it is true, but
gentlemen so very private that in the herd of gentry they are
hardly to be found, not in court, not in office, not in Parliament."

As British victory in the war with France became more
likely and the conditions of a peace came under discussion,
Franklin jumped into the debate about the territory to be
secured from France. There were two schools of thought. Some
were for keeping Guadeloupe, others for keeping Canada. The
orthodox attitude toward colonies was to consider them primarily as a source of raw materials—and the sugar and other
tropical agricultural products of the West Indies were far more
important than the furs of frigid Canada. Franklin's contribution to this question was a pamphlet entitled *The Interest of
Great Britain Considered with Regard to Her Colonies.* Some
say that this had an effect on Great Britain's decision to retain
Canada and return the West Indian conquests. Its main interest
is the view that it gives of Franklin the imperialist, and Franklin
the economist. It shows Franklin for what he was up until the
very eve of the Revolution—a colonial Englishman, as well as
an American, trying to show how the welfare of the mother
country lay in the prosperity of the colonies.

The thinking behind *The Interest of Great Britain* went back
to 1751, when Franklin had written another pamphlet entitled
*Observations Concerning the Increase of Mankind, Peopling of
Countries, etc.,* which he now combined with the new pamphlet
on Canada. This earlier pamphlet was the first expression of the

concept of the "frontier theory" which would shape American life for more than a century.

The population pamphlet was occasioned by mercantile restrictions fostered by British iron-makers. In it Franklin sought to prove that the colonies would be no threat to the mother country in manufacturing so long as there was room to absorb the increased population in agriculture. Franklin started out by showing that population increase in America differed from that in Europe as did the country from the city. Population is increased through marriages. "When families can be easily supported more persons marry, and earlier in life. . . . In countries full settled . . . all lands being occupied and improved to the height, those who cannot get land must labor for others who have it; when laborers are plenty their wages are low; by low wages a family is supported with difficulty; this difficulty deters many from marriage."

But, continues Franklin:

LAND BEING THUS PLENTY in America, and so cheap as that a laboring man that understands husbandry can in a short time save money enough to purchase a piece of new land sufficient for a plantation, whereon he may subsist a family, such are not afraid to marry; for if they even look far enough forward to consider how their children, when grown up, are to be provided for, they see that more land is to be had at rates equally easy, all circumstances considered.

Hence marriages in America are more general, and more generally early than in Europe. And if it is reckoned there that there is but one marriage per annum among a hundred persons, perhaps we may here reckon two; and if in Europe they have but four births to a marriage (many of their marriages being late), we may here reckon eight, of which if one half grow up, and our marriages are made, reckoning one with another at twenty years of age, our people must at least be doubled every twenty years.

But notwithstanding this increase, so vast is the territory of North America that it will require many ages to settle it fully; and, till it is fully settled, labor will never be cheap here, where no man continues long a laborer for others, but gets a plantation of his own, no man continues long a journeyman to a trade, but goes among those new settlers and sets up for himself, etc. . . .

The dangers, therefore, of these colonies interfering with their mother country in trades that depend on labor, manufactures, etc., is too remote to require the attention of Great Britain.

But in proportion to the increase of the colonies, a vast demand is growing for British manufactures, a glorious market wholly in the power of Britain, in which foreigners cannot interfere, which will increase in a short time even beyond her power of supplying, though her whole trade should be to her colonies. Therefore Britain should not too much restrain manufactures in her colonies. A wise and good mother will not do it. To distress is to weaken, and weakening the children weakens the whole family.

In this pamphlet Franklin also spelled out the Malthusian theory of the relation of population to the means of subsistence—a half century before Malthus.

THERE IS, in short, no bound to the prolific nature of plants or animals, but what is made by their crowding and interfering with each other's means of subsistence. Was the face of the earth vacant of other plants, it might be gradually sowed and overspread with one kind only; as, for instance, with fennel; and were it empty of other inhabitants, it might in a few ages be replenished from one nation only; as, for instance with Englishmen. Thus there are now supposed to be upward of one million English souls in North America (though it is thought scarce 80,000 have been brought over sea), and yet perhaps there is not one the fewer in Britain, but rather many more, on account of the employment the colonies afford to manufacturers at home. This million doubling, suppose but once in twenty-five years, will, in another century, be more than the people of England, and the greatest number of Englishmen be on this side of the water. What an accession of power to the British Empire by sea as well as land! What increase of trade and navigation! What numbers of ships and seamen! . . . How important an affair then to Britain is the present treaty for settling the bounds between her colonies and the French, and how careful should she be to secure room enough, since on the room depends so much the increase of her people.

It is paradoxical that Franklin, an urbanite who spent his life in the principal cities of the new and the old worlds, should be, like landowner Jefferson, a strong agrarian. It is even more strange to find in the sedate philosopher a burning pioneer spirit. At a time when all responsible colonials envisioned the growth of the colonies in the terms of the old world concept of a perfectly ordered society concentrated between the sea and the mountains—a colonial "tight little isle" like the mother country—Franklin foresaw a dynamic expansion to the west. His was the "Manifest Destiny" theory that molded America in the following century. At one time he dreamed of founding a colony in the west himself. To the Reverend George Whitfield he wrote:

YOU MENTION YOUR frequent wish that you were a chaplain to an American Army. I sometimes wish that you and I were jointly employed by the Crown, to settle a colony on the Ohio. I imagine we could do it effectually, and without putting the nation to much expense. But I fear we shall never be called upon for such service. What a glorious thing it would be, to settle in that fine country a large strong body of religious and industrious people. What a security to the other colonies, and advantage to Britain, by increasing her people, territory, strength, and commerce. Might it not greatly facilitate the introduction of pure religion among the heathen if we could, by such a colony show them a better sample of Christians than they commonly see in our Indian traders, the most vicious and abandoned wretches of our nation? . . .

Franklin subsequently wrote a *Plan for Settling Two Western Colonies in North America* and tried to organize the project and secure a charter when in England, an activity that died in the troubles preceding the Revolution. It was fitting that the first state formed west of the mountains was called Franklin for three years before it became Tennessee.

The Canada pamphlet was written in answer to some "Remarks" on the Guadeloupe-Canada controversy which favored returning Canada to the French because: its retention by Britain would strengthen the mainland colonies and possibly make them a threat to England; it would permit them to extend westward where it was more difficult for the mother country to exert control; it would make them more self-sufficient—they would supply their own needs to the detriment of English manufacturers; England had spent enough in fighting a war "for the benefit of the colonies."

Franklin replied that the colonies were not separate entities; upon their security rested the safety of the Empire—"Our North American colonies are to be considered as the *frontier of the British empire* on that side. The frontier of any dominion being attacked, it becomes not merely 'the cause' of the people immediately attacked, the inhabitants of that frontier, but properly 'the cause' of the whole body. Where the frontier people owe and pay obedience, there they have a right to look for protection. No political proposition is better established than this." In refuting the other points, Franklin said,

IN SHORT, according to this writer, our present colonies are large enough and numerous enough; and the French ought to be left in North America to prevent their increase, lest they become not only useless, but dangerous to Britain. I agree with the gentleman that, with Canada in our possession, our people in America will increase amazingly . . . but . . . I am far from entertaining, on that account, any fears of their becoming either useless or dangerous to us; and I look on those fears to be merely imaginary and without any probable foundation. . . .

The Remarker thinks that our people in America, "finding no check from Canada, would extend themselves almost without bounds into the inland parts, and increase infinitely from all causes." The very reason he assigns for their so extending, and which is indeed the true one (their being "invited to it by the pleasantness, fertility and plenty of the country"), may satisfy us that this extension will continue to proceed as long as there remains any pleasant, fertile country within their reach. And if we even suppose them confined by the waters of the Mississippi westward, and by those of St. Lawrence and the Lakes to the northward, yet still we shall leave them room enough to increase, even in the matter of settling now practiced there, till they amount to perhaps a hundred millions of souls. This must take some centuries to fulfill; and in the meantime this nation must necessarily supply them with the manufactures they consume; because the new settlers will be employed in agriculture. . . .

Thus our trade must, till that country becomes as fully peopled as England (that is, for centuries to come), be continually increasing, and with it our naval power; because the ocean is between us and them, and our ships and seamen must increase as the trade increases. . . .

Thus much as to the apprehension of our colonies becoming useless to us. I shall next consider the other supposition, that their growth may render them *dangerous*. Of this, I own, I have not the least conception, when I consider that we have already fourteen separate governments on the maritime coast of the continent; and if we extend our settlements, shall probably have as many more behind them on the inland side. Those we now have are not only under different governors, but have different forms of government, different laws, different interests, and some of them different religious persuasions and different manners.

Their jealousy of each other is so great, that however necessary a union of the colonies has long been, for their common defense and security against their enemies, and how sensible soever each colony has been of that necessity, yet they have never been able to effect such a union among themselves, nor even to agree in requesting the mother country to establish it for them. Nothing but the immediate command of the Crown has been able to produce even the imperfect union but lately seen there, of the forces of some colonies. If they could not agree to unite for the defense against the French and Indians who were perpetually harassing their settlements, burning their villages, and murdering their people, can it reasonably be supposed there is any danger of their uniting against their own nation, which protects and encourages them, with which they have so many connections and ties of blood, interest and affection, and which it is well known they all love more than they love one another?

In short, there are so many causes that must operate to prevent it, that I will venture to say a union amongst them for such a purpose is not merely improbable, it is impossible. . . . When I say such a union is impossible, I mean

without the most grievous tyranny and oppression. People who have property in a country which they may lose, and privileges which they may endanger, are generally disposed to be quiet, and even to bear much, rather than to hazard all. While the government is mild and just, while important civil and religious rights are secure, such subjects will be dutiful and obedient. *The waves do not rise but when the winds blow.*

On the subject of Canada, Franklin again expressed his position as an imperialist in a letter in which he said, "No one can more sincerely rejoice than I do on the reduction of Canada; and this is not merely as I am a colonist, but as I am a Briton. I have long been of the opinion that the foundations of the future grandeur and stability of the British Empire lie in America; and though, like other foundations, they are low and little seen, they are, nevertheless, broad and strong enough to support the greatest political structure human wisdom ever yet erected."

As the year 1762 dawned, Franklin wavered between returning to America and making his home permanently in England. In one letter he wrote, "I feel here like a thing out of its place, and useless because it is out of its place. How then can I any longer be happy in England?" A few days later he wrote, "The attraction of reason is at present on the other side of the water, but that of inclination will be for this side. You know which usually prevails. I shall probably make but this one vibration and settle here forever. Nothing can prevent it if I can, as I hope, prevail with Mrs. F. to accompany me." Fortunately for America, Deborah had an unreasoning fear of an ocean crossing and refused to accompany her husband to Europe.

Franklin finally sailed for America, saying, "I am going from the old world to the new, and I feel like those who are leaving this world for the next; grief at the parting, fear at the passage;

hope of the future." There were many in England who grieved at his departure. Lord Hume wrote: "America has sent us many good things, gold, silver, sugar, tobacco, indigo, etc.; but you are the first philosopher, and indeed the first great man of letters for whom we are beholden to her."

CHAPTER VII

THE MAN OF REASON

ॐ

The time of Franklin is often called the "Age of Reason" and Franklin was the personification of the time. In describing his political career, a French contemporary wrote, "In a word, his politics were those of a man who believed in the power of reason and the reality of virtue." And a German writer of the time said, "Reason and virtue, made possible through reason alone, consequently again reason and nothing but reason, is the magic with which Benjamin Franklin conquered heaven and earth."

But in the late 1760's and the early years of the following decade, Franklin the politician did not conquer heaven and earth. It was a difficult time for the man of reason. He was caught between two forces of unreason—the bullheaded British King and his kept Parliament on the one hand and the cantankerous colonial radicals on the other. He sought to stem the storm with reason—a program for an ever-expanding union of the colonies as a semiautonomous part of the British Empire, largely self-governing. Ties of blood would bring harmony, ties of commerce would bring mutual prosperity.

This was too much for the conservative, shortsighted English

with their eighteenth-century concept of colonialism under which colonies were mere sources of profit through supplying cheap raw materials and consuming the mother country's manufactures. It was too little for the American hotheads in whose minds the first glimmer of independence was gleaming.

On the one hand Franklin was the first great American citizen. On the other he was the last great American imperialist. He spent the years leading up to the Revolution trying to conform these views; was still trying almost up to the day that the farmers at the bridge at Concord fired the shot heard round the world. During his last ten-year sojourn in England, he devoted all his skill as a writer, a propagandist and a diplomat in trying to convince the English that something like a dominion status was the solution for the problems in America—that the beginning of the British Commonwealth of Nations must replace the British Empire. He did not succeed. What he anticipated was not fully established for England until India became a free member of the Commonwealth in 1949.

In 1764 it became obvious to Franklin, now speaker of the Assembly, that Pennsylvania must be freed from the rule of the avaricious, shortsighted Penns. He believed that the problems of the province in its relation with the mother country would be solved if Pennsylvania became a crown colony. Franklin's greatest blind spot as a prophet was his faith in George III. He wrote to his friend Strahan in London, "You now fear for our virtuous young King that the faction forming will overpower him and render his reign uncomfortable. On the contrary, I am of the opinion that his virtue and the consciousness of his sincere intentions to make his people happy will give him firmness and steadiness in his measures and in the support of the honest friends he has chosen to serve him; and when that firmness is fully perceived, faction will dissolve and be dissipated like a morning fog before the rising sun, leaving the rest of the day clear with a sky serene and cloudless." He could not know that German George was already a little bit crazy.

As the first step to unite the people behind the plan to petition the crown to take over the colony, Franklin wrote *Cool Thoughts on the Present Situation of Our Public Affairs,* which attacked the basic idea of the proprietary form of government, and showed how Massachusetts, New Hampshire, New Jersey and the Carolinas had benefited when they became crown colonies. He sought to allay the fears of the Presbyterians that royal government would mean an established church and an Anglican Bishop. Then he concluded:

IN FINE, it does not appear to me that this change of government can possibly hurt us; and I see many advantages that may flow from it. The expression *change of government* seems, indeed, to be too extensive, and is apt to give the idea of a general and total change in our laws and Constitution. It is rather and only a change of *governor;* that is, instead of self-interested proprietaries, a gracious King! His Majesty, who has no views but for the good of the people, will thenceforth appoint the governor who, unshackled by proprietory instructions, will be at liberty to join with the Assembly in enacting wholesome laws. . . .

In November, 1764, the Assembly borrowed £1,100 to send Franklin back to London to present the petition to the King. He accepted only £500, left the partly finished house that he was building and a wife whom he would never see again, and sailed for England with a dramatic exit line: "I am now to take leave (perhaps at last leave) of the country I love and in which I have spent the greatest part of my life. . . . I wish every kind of prosperity to my friends; and I forgive my enemies." There seems no reason for this emotional farewell speech. Franklin expected to be gone a few months, had no idea that his exile would last more than ten years.

When he arrived in England scant attention was paid to the petition. A much larger issue was forming—the proposed Stamp

Act. Although it was presented to the Privy Council, the petition was never acted on—after the Revolution, Pennsylvania gave the Penns £130,000 for their lands in the state.

Franklin made one of his few political mistakes in his position on the Stamp Act. He opposed it, but not vigorously. He did not feel that the way a tax was levied was important—what was important was the principle involved, the right of Parliament to levy direct taxes without the consent of the colonial assemblies. He made this clear away back in 1754 in his letters to Governor Shirley. He proposed to try to change the principle and, in the meantime, live with the Stamp Act and compensate for it by gaining the right to establish a colonial paper currency. To a lawyer in Philadelphia he wrote mildly, "The Stamp Act, notwithstanding all the opposition we have been able to give it, will pass. Every step in the law, every newspaper, advertisement and almanac is severely taxed. If this should, as I imagine it will, occasion less law and less printing, it will fall particularly hard on us lawyers and printers."

On the face of it the Stamp Act did not seem like a very onerous law. A stamp for a bill of lading was to cost fourpence; for a half-sheet newspaper one halfpenny; for a pamphlet one shilling; for an almanac twopence; for a pack of cards one shilling; for a college degree two pounds—and so on, through fifty-five items. Franklin was amazed and disturbed at the violent reaction back home. When Patrick Henry's ringing words reached his ears in London, he wrote to Pennsylvania:

THE RASHNESS OF the Assembly in Virginia is amazing. I hope, however, that ours will keep within the bounds of prudence and moderation; for that is the only way to lighten or get clear of our burdens. As to the Stamp Act, though we propose doing our endeavor to get it repealed, yet the success is uncertain. . . . A firm loyalty to the Crown and faithful adherence to the government of this nation, which it is the safety as well as the honor of the colonies to

be connected with, will always be the wisest course for you and I to take, whatever may be the madness of the populace or their blind leaders, who can only bring themselves and country into trouble and draw on greater burdens by acts of rebellious tendency.

Franklin saw the Stamp Act as one trick in a game of cards. His attitude was, "You can't win 'em all." He was out to win the game, and this called for calm, reasonable diplomacy on several fronts. The local assemblies saw the act as a complete denial of their prerogatives, and felt that their right to approve direct taxation was fundamental and sacred. Sparked by the newly formed Sons of Liberty, riots raged from New Hampshire to South Carolina. The Revolution had started and Franklin, taken by surprise, was on the firing line. He agreed thoroughly with the principle that motivated the outbreak in America—and as thoroughly disagreed with the tactics.

He set about working for the repeal of the odious Act. At first he went underground. There was one faction which he could cultivate in terms of self-interest: the merchants, manufacturers and shippers who were suffering by colonial reprisals against British goods. Although they had not much weight in Parliament, they were represented—and they did have an effect on public opinion. Franklin outlined his campaign in terse notes which show that he still thought the principle of representation more important than the repeal of the Act.

INTERNAL TAX. Freemen to be taxed by their representatives. People of America fond of liberty. Suppose themselves to enjoy much of it. Will think all lost. They fear the example. 'Tis raising contributions on them (they will say) as in a conquered country. Right they should contribute, but they will do as much as they can afford voluntarily if properly called on. At present they love Britain . . . are fond of British people, British customs, modes, books, manufac-

tures. A disgust of all these will ensue. Trade will suffer more than the tax profits. They will grow obstinately frugal. . . . The disgust occasioned by this tax will sow the seeds and lay the foundation of future disunion, misery, etc. . . . It is depriving subjects of the only means in their power to show their loyalty to their sovereign. Would the Commons like to have the Lords lay all the taxes on them, though they were to lay them ever so justly and equitably? People will make less conscience of smuggling.

It is not wise to do it. Everything one has a right to do is not best to be done. More money will be got by voluntary grant. People will give from affection rather more than they can spare.

Under Franklin's guidance the merchants trading in North America formed a committee and petitioned Parliament for the repeal of the Act. The Commons agreed to hear witnesses and Franklin made a day-long appearance before the House as the principal advocate for repeal. His clear, straightforward answers to every question won wide acclaim throughout England and the colonies. Few knew that this was really the first rigged quiz show. Franklin had provided the members who were favorable to the merchants with a line of questioning that would permit him to develop a complete, cogent presentation of the evils of the type of taxation that was represented by the Stamp Act. He was not only the star of the show, he was also the producer and stage manager.

To start, he had one friendly member set the stage with questions that would remind the house that the colonies were already paying heavy taxes.

Q. Do the Americans pay any considerable taxes among themselves?

A. Certainly many, and very heavy taxes.

Q. Are not all the people very able to pay those taxes?

A. No. The frontier counties, all along the continent, having been frequently ravaged by the enemy and greatly impoverished, are able to pay very little tax. And therefore, in consideration of their distresses, our late tax laws do expressly favor those counties, excusing the sufferers; and I suppose the same is done in other governments.

Another merchant's man gave him an opportunity to point out the impossibility of administering the act.

Q. Are you not concerned in the management of the post office in America?

A. Yes. I am Deputy Postmaster-General of North America.

Q. Don't you think the distribution of stamps by post to all the inhabitants very practicable, if there was no opposition?

A. The posts only go along the sea coasts; they do not, except in a few instances, go back into the country; and if they did, sending for stamps by post would occasion an expense of postage amounting, in many cases, to much more than that of the stamps themselves. . . .

Q. From the thinness of the back settlements, would not the Stamp Act be extremely inconvenient to the inhabitants, if executed?

A. To be sure it would; as many of the inhabitants could not get stamps when they had occasion for them without taking long journeys and spending perhaps three or four pounds that the Crown might get sixpence.

Opposition members sought to upset Franklin's carefully rigged exposition, but none of them had the facts at their finger tips as did Franklin. He made some of his most telling points in answer to questions from inimical members.

A. Yes, I have heard of such resolutions.

Q. What will be the opinion of the Americans on those resolutions?

A. They will think them unconstitutional and unjust.

Q. Was it an opinion in America before 1763 that the Parliament had no right to lay taxes and duties there?

A. I never heard of any objection to the right of laying duties to regulate commerce; but a right to lay internal taxes was never supposed to be in Parliament, as we are not represented there.

Q. On what do you found your opinion that the people in America made any such distinction?

A. I know that whenever the subject has occurred in conversation where I have been present, it has appeared to be the opinion of everyone that we could not be taxed by a Parliament where we were not represented. But the payment of duties laid by an act of Parliament, as regulations of commerce, was never disputed.

Q. You say the colonies have always submitted to external taxes and object to the right of Parliament only in laying internal taxes. Now can you show that there is any kind of difference between the two taxes to the colony on which they may be laid?

A. I think the difference is very great. An external tax is a duty laid on commodities imported; that duty is added to the first cost and other charges on the commodity, and when it is offered for sale, makes a part of the price. If the people do not like it at that price, they refuse it; they are not obliged to pay it. But an internal tax is forced from the people without their consent, if not laid by their own representatives. The Stamp Act says we shall have no commerce, make no exchange of property with each other, neither purchase nor grant nor recover debts; we shall neither marry nor make our wills, unless we pay such and such sums; and thus it is intended to extort our money from us or ruin us by the consequences of refusing to pay it.

Q. But supposing the external tax or duty to be laid on the necessaries of life imported into your colony, will not that be the same thing in its effects as an internal tax?

A. I do not know a single article imported into the northern colonies but what they can either do without or make themselves. . . .

Q. Can anything less than a military force carry the Stamp Act into execution?

A. I do not see how a military force can be applied to that purpose.

Q. Why may it not?

A. Suppose a military force sent into America, they will find nobody in arms; what then are they to do? They cannot force a man to take stamps who chooses to do without them. They will not find a rebellion; they may indeed make one.

Q. If the act is not repealed, what do you think will be the consequences?

A. The total loss of the great respect and the affection the people of America bear to this country, and of all the commerce that depends on that respect and affection. . . .

Q. Supposing the Stamp Act continued and enforced, do you imagine that ill-humor will induce the Americans to give as much for worse manufactures of their own, and use them, preferably to better of ours?

A. Yes, I think so. People will pay as freely to gratify one passion as another, their resentment as their pride.

Franklin was a writer, not an orator. The next two friendly questions brought from him the nearest thing to a speech that he ever made in his long public career.

Q. But if the legislature should think fit to ascertain its right to lay taxes, by an act laying a small tax contrary to their opinion, would they submit to pay the tax?

A. The proceedings of the people in America have been considered too much together. The proceedings of the assemblies have been very different from those of the mobs, and should be distinguished, as having no connection with each other. The assemblies have only peaceably resolved what they take to be their rights; they have taken no measures for opposition by force; they have not built a fort, raised a man, or provided a grain of ammunition, in order to such opposition. The ringleaders of riots they think ought to be punished; they would punish them themselves if they could. . . . But as to an internal tax, how small soever, laid by the legislature here on the people there, while they have no representatives in this legislature, I think it will never be submitted to. They will oppose it to the last. They do not consider it at all necessary for you to raise money on them by your taxes; because they are, and always have been, ready to raise money by taxes among themselves and to grant large sums, equal to their abilities, upon requisition from the Crown. . . . America has been greatly misrepresented and abused here, in papers and pamphlets and speeches, as ungrateful and unreasonable and unjust; in having put this nation to immense expense for their defense and refusing to bear any part of that expense. The colonies raised, paid and clothed near 25,000 men during the last war; a number equal to those sent from Britain, and far beyond their proportion; they went deeply into debt in doing this, and all their taxes and estates are mortgaged for many years to come for discharging that debt. Government here was at that time very sensible of this. The colonies were recommended to Parliament. Every year the King sent down to this House a written message to this purpose: that His Majesty, being highly sensible of the zeal and vigor with which his faithful subjects in North America had exerted themselves in defense of His Majesty's just rights and possessions, recommended it to this House to take the same into consideration and enable him to give them a proper compensation. You will find those messages on your own journals every year of the war to the very last; and you did accordingly give £200,000 annually to the Crown, to be distributed in such compensation to the colonies.

This is the strongest of all proofs that the colonies, far from being unwilling to bear a share in the burden, did exceed their proportion; for if they had done less, or had only equaled their proportion, there would have been no room or reason for compensation. Indeed, the sums reimbursed them were by no means adequate to the expense they incurred beyond their proportion; but they never murmured at that; they esteemed their sovereign's approbation of their zeal and fidelity, and the approbation of this House, far beyond any other kind of compensation.

Q. But suppose Great Britain should be engaged in a war in Europe, would North America contribute to the support of it?

A. I do think they would as far as their circumstances would permit. They consider themselves as a part of the British Empire, and as having one common interest with it; they may be looked on here as foreigners, but they do not consider themselves as such. They are zealous for the honor and prosperity of this nation; and, while they are well used, will always be ready to support it, as far as their little power goes. . . . They make no distinction of wars, as to their duty of assisting them. I know the last war is commonly spoke of here as entered into for the defense, or for the sake, of the people in America. I think it is quite misunderstood. It began about the limits between Canada and Nova Scotia; about territories to which the Crown indeed laid claim but which were not claimed by any British colony; none of the lands had been granted to any colonist; we had therefore no particular concern or interest in that dispute. . . .

The trade with the Indians, though carried on in America, is not an American interest. The people of America are chiefly farmers and planters; scarce anything that they raise or produce is an article of commerce with the Indians. The Indian trade is a British interest. It is carried on with British manufacturers for the profit of British manufacturers and merchants; therefore, the war, as it commenced for the defense of territories of the Crown the property of no American, and for the defense of a trade purely British, was really a British war; and yet the people of America made no scruple of contributing their utmost toward carrying it on and bringing it to a happy conclusion.

The session ended, simply, with a telling reminder to manufacturers, merchants and labor of the effect of the Stamp Act on business and employment.

Q. What used to be the pride of the Americans?
A. To indulge in the fashions and manufactures of Great Britain.
Q. What is now their pride?
A. To wear their old clothes over again till they can make new ones.

Franklin appeared before Commons on February 13, 1765. On March 8, the Stamp Act was repealed. Back home, Franklin had fallen from favor because of his weak opposition to the act. Now he became a popular hero when he was credited for its repeal—and it is true that no one but Franklin could have made the telling argument before the House. For the moment his oil had calmed the troubled waters—but he was not happy about it. There was a joker in the repeal bill. To save face Parliament had tacked on an amendment that they had the right to enact laws for the colonies "in all cases whatsoever." This was the principle that Franklin was fighting—and repeal had not changed it.

During the lull of the next few years Franklin continued his propaganda and, briefly, relaxed. He practiced his frugality by sending more presents home. He wrote to Deborah: "As the Stamp Act is at length repealed, I am willing you should have a new gown, which you may suppose I did not send sooner as I knew you would not like to be finer than your neighbors unless in a gown of your own spinning. Had the trade between the two countries totally ceased, it was a comfort to me to recollect that I had once been clothed from head to foot in woolen and linen of my wife's manufacture, that I was never prouder of any dress in my life, and that she and her daughter might do it again if it was necessary. . . ."

He traveled. Although he made no significant experiments during this period, he met and exchanged views with many scientists throughout Europe. He visited Baron Munchausen but, unfortunately, did not elaborate or record any of his famous tall stories. He wrote chatty letters to Polly Stevenson. An interesting example of Franklin's insatiable curiosity—of the reasoning from effect back to cause which he applied to everything—was his speculation on the manner in which French women applied rouge.

As TO ROUGE, they don't pretend to imitate nature in laying it on. There is no gradual diminution of the color, from the full bloom in the middle of the cheek to the faint tint near the sides, nor does it show differently in different faces. I have not had the honor of being at any lady's toilet to see how it is laid on, but I fancy I can tell you how it is or may be done. Cut a hole of three inches diameter in a piece of paper; place it on the side of your face in such a manner as that the top of the hole may be just under your eye; then with a brush dipped in the color paint face and paper together; so when the paper is taken off there will remain a round patch of red exactly the form of the hole. This is the mode, from the actresses on the stage upward through all the ranks of ladies to the princesses of the blood; but it stops there, the Queen not using it, having in the serenity, complacence and benignity that shine so eminently in—or rather through—her countenance, sufficient beauty, though now an old woman, to do extremely well without it.

In France Franklin came under the spell of the physiocrats, who were laying the foundation for the science of economics as he had laid it for the science of electricity. His previous random views in this area took an ordered form under physiocratic doctrine. It influenced him when he wrote *Positions to be Examined Concerning National Wealth:*

ALL FOOD OR SUBSISTENCE for mankind arises from the earth or waters.

Necessities of life, that are not food, and all other conveniences, have their values estimated by the proportion of food consumed while we are employed procuring them.

A small people, with a large territory, may subsist on the productions of nature, with no other labor than that of gathering the vegetables and catching the animals.

A large people, with a small territory, finds these insufficient and, to subsist, must labor the earth to make it produce greater quantities of vegetable food suitable for the nourishment of men and of the animals they intend to eat.

From this labor arises a great increase of vegetable and animal food, and of materials for clothing, as flax, wool, silk, etc. The superfluity of these is wealth. With this wealth we pay for the labor employed in building our houses, cities, etc., which are therefore only subsistence metamorphosed.

Manufactures are only another shape into which so much provisions and subsistence are turned, as were equal in value to the manufactures produced. This appears from hence, that the manufacturer [workman] does not, in fact, obtain from the employer, for his labor, *more* than a mere subsistence, including raiment, fuel and shelter; all which derive their value from the provisions consumed in producing them. . . .

Thus the advantage of having manufactures in a country does not consist, as is commonly supposed, in their highly advancing the value of rough materials of which they are formed; since, though six pennyworth of flax may be worth twenty shillings when worked into lace, yet the very cause of its being worth twenty shillings is that, besides the flax, it has cost nineteen shillings and sixpence to the manufacturer. But the advantage of manufactures is that under their shape provisions may be more easily carried to a foreign market; and, by their means, our traders may more easily cheat strangers. Few, where it is not made, are judges of the value of lace. The importer may demand forty, and perhaps get thirty shillings for what cost him but twenty.

Finally, there seems to be three ways for a nation to acquire wealth. The first is by war, as the Romans did, in plundering their conquered neighbors. This is robbery. The second by commerce, which is generally cheating. The third by agriculture, the only honest way, wherein man receives a real increase of the seed thrown into the ground, in a kind of continued miracle, wrought by the hand of God in his favor as a reward for his innocent life and his virtuous industry.

In contrasting the situation of "a small people with a large territory" and a "large people with a small territory" he had established the fundamental basic difference between the mother country and the colonies—a difference which could not be reconciled by politics or diplomacy, although he did not yet realize this.

England before there was a United States or the post of Ambassador.

But he had other, more far reaching, worries. Irresponsible Charles Townshend had become Britain's Chancellor of the Exchequer and had introduced acts for taxes on several products, including glass, paper and tea, with the stipulation that the revenue was to be used to pay the salaries of British officials in the colonies who had, previously, been paid by the Assemblies. This was, in effect, the same kind of direct tax as the Stamp Act. Also, New York had rebelled at the Quartering Act and Townshend proposed to dissolve the New York Assembly. Franklin summarized the situation in a letter to Lord Kames.

I APPREHEND some late incidents are likely to revive the contest between the two countries. I fear it will be a mischievous one. It becomes a matter of great importance that clear ideas should be formed on solid principles, both in Britain and America, of the true political relation between them, and the mutual duties belonging to that relation. . . .

I am fully persuaded with you that a consolidating union, by a fair and equal representation of all parts of this empire in Parliament, is the only firm basis on which its political grandeur and prosperity may be founded. . . . The time has been when the colonies might have been pleased with it: they are now indifferent about it; and if it is much longer delayed, they will refuse it. But the pride of this people cannot bear the thought of it, and therefore it will be delayed. Every man in England seems to consider himself as a piece of a sovereign over America; seems to jostle himself into the throne with the King, and talks about "our subjects in the colonies." The Parliament cannot well and wisely make laws suited to the colonies without being properly and truly informed of their circumstances, abilities, tempers, etc. This it cannot be, without representatives from thence; and yet it is fond of this power and adverse to the only means of acquiring the necessary knowledge for exercising it; which is desiring to be omnipotent without being omniscient.

It is a common but mistaken notion here that the colonies were planted at the expense of Parliament, and that therefore the Parliament has a right to tax them, etc. The truth is they were planted at the expense of private adventurers, who went over there to settle with the leave of the King, given by charter. On receiving this leave and these charters, the adventurers voluntarily engaged to remain the King's subjects, though in a foreign country; a country which had not been conquered by either the King or Parliament, but was possessed by a free people.

Upon the whole, I have lived so great a part of my life in Britain, and have formed so many friendships in it, that I love it and sincerely wish its prosperity; and therefore wish to see that union, on which alone I think it can be secured and established. As to America, the advantages of such a union to her are not so apparent. She may suffer at present from the arbitrary power of this country; she may suffer for a while in a separation from it; but these are secondary evils that she will outgrow. . . . America, an immense territory, favored by nature with all advantages of climate, soil, great navigable rivers and lakes, etc., must become a great country, populous and mighty; and will, in less time than is generally conceived, be able to shake off any shackles that may be imposed on her, and perhaps place them on the imposers. In the meantime, every act of oppression will sour their tempers, lessen greatly, if not annihilate, the profits of your commerce with them, and hasten their final revolt; for the seeds of liberty are universally found there and nothing can eradicate them.

Franklin had given up hope that Parliament would see the light. In a letter to his son he went farther to the left than even fiery Samuel Adams by questioning the English legislature's

right to make any laws governing the colonies. "The more I
have thought and read on the subject the more I find myself
confirmed in the opinion that no middle ground can be maintained. . . . Something might be made of either of the extremes:
that Parliament has the right to make all laws for us, or that
it has power to make no laws for us; and I think that the
arguments for the latter are more numerous and weighty than
those of the former."

Franklin next submitted to the *London Chronicle* a lengthy
dissertation titled *Causes of the American Discontents before
1768,* which carried the subhead "The waves never rise but
when the wind blows." After reiterating the grievances that he
had previously set forth, he continued:

BUT NOT ONLY the interest of a particular body of merchants, the interest of any small body of British tradesmen
or artificers has been found, they say, to outweigh that of all
the King's subjects in the colonies. There cannot be a
stronger natural right than that of a man's making the best
profit he can of the natural produce of his lands, providing
that he does not thereby hurt the state in general. Iron is
to be found everywhere in America and beaver furs are the
natural produce of that country; hats, nails and steel are
wanted there as well as here. It is of no importance to the
common welfare of the empire whether a subject of the
King's gets his living by making hats on this or that side of
the water. Yet the hatters of England have prevailed to obtain an act in their own favor, restraining that manufacture
in America, in order to oblige the Americans to send their
beaver to England to be manufactured and purchase back
the hats, loaded with the charges of a double transportation.
In the same manner have a few nail-makers, and a still
smaller body of steel-makers (perhaps there are not half a
dozen of these in England) prevailed totally to forbid, by
an act of Parliament, the erecting of slitting mills or steel

furnaces in America, that the Americans may be obliged to take all the nails for their buildings and steel for their tools from these artificers under the same disadvantages. . . .

Thus they get all our money from us by trade and every profit we can anywhere make by our fisheries, our produce or our commerce centers finally with them, but this does not signify. It is time then to take care of ourselves by the best means in our power. Let us unite in solemn resolutions and engagements with and to each other, that we will give these new officers as little trouble as possible by not consuming the British manufactures on which they are to levy the duties. Let us agree to consume no more of their expensive gewgaws. Let us live frugally and let us manufacture industriously what we can for ourselves. Thus we shall be able honorably to discharge the debts we already owe them, and after that we may be able to keep some money in our country, not only for the uses of our internal commerce, but for the service of our gracious sovereign, whenever he shall have occasion for it and think proper to require it of us in the old *constitutional* manner. For, notwithstanding the reproaches thrown out against us in their public papers and pamphlets, notwithstanding we have been reviled in their senate as rebels and traitors, we are truly a loyal people. Scotland has its rebellions, and England its plots against the present royal family; but America is untainted by these crimes. There is in it scarce a man, there is not a single native of our country, who is not firmly attached to the King by principle and affection.

But a new kind of loyalty seems to be required of us, a loyalty to Parliament; a loyalty that is to extend, it is said, to a surrender of all our properties whenever a House of Commons (in which there is not a single member of our choosing) shall think fit to grant them away without our consent; and to a patient suffering the loss of our privileges as Englishmen if we cannot submit to make such surrender.

Franklin's hopes for the acceptance of his commonwealth plan were fading. He still thought it best, and had faith in the Crown, but he was not reflecting the attitude back home when he said "There is scarce a man . . . who is not . . . attached to the King." Those who were called "rebels and traitors" by Parliament, were being styled Patriots by an ever-increasing number of Americans. Of the reception of his views at home and abroad, Franklin said, "I do not find that I have gained any point, in either country, except that of rendering myself suspected of my impartiality; in England of being too much an American, and in America of being too much an Englishman." And, in another letter, "As to my own sentiments, I am weary of suggesting them to so many different inattentive heads, though I must continue to do it while I stay among them."

Franklin wanted to go home. The British ministry desperately wanted to get rid of him, or at least to muzzle him. He was threatened with the loss of his post office appointment unless he went home and worked at it—and at the same time was tentatively offered a more profitable post in England if, inferentially, he would stop exposing and exploiting the government's mistakes in dealing with the colonies.

The situation eased temporarily when the Townshend Acts were repealed, except for a tax on tea retained by order of the King to save face, confirm Parliament's right to tax, and to please the powerful East India Company. Again, Franklin was not satisfied with the compromise. He thought it "was bad policy when they attempted to heal our differences by repealing part of the duties only; as it is bad surgery to leave splinters in a wound which must prevent its healing or in time occasion it to open afresh." The same day that the repeal bill was presented to Commons, British soldiers fired into a crowd in Boston and killed four men. The Boston Massacre far outweighed the compromise repeal in the colonial newspapers. Franklin saw the handwriting of disunion on the wall.

THE RESENTMENT of the people will, at times and on particular incidents, burst into outrages and violence . . . and this naturally draws down severity and acts of further oppression from hence. The more the people are dissatisfied the more rigor will be thought necessary; severe punishments will be inflicted to terrify; rights and privileges will be abolished; greater force will then be required to secure execution and submission; the expense will become enormous; it will then be thought proper, by fresh exactions, to make the people defray it; thence the British nation and government will become odious, and subjection to it will be deemed no longer tolerable; war ensues, and the bloody struggle will end in absolute slavery to America or ruin to Britain by the loss of her colonies: the latter most probable, from America's growing strength and magnitude. . . .

I do not pretend to the gift of prophecy. History shows that by these steps great empires have crumbled heretofore; and the late transactions we have so much cause to complain of show that we are in the same train, and that without a greater share of prudence and wisdom than we have seen both sides to be possessed of we shall probably come to the same conclusions.

During the early 1770's Franklin had some time for travel, made some experiments and wrote observations and speculations in several fields. He compiled *Letters on Philosophical Subjects* to be added to a new edition of his *Experiments and Observations on Electricity*. These letters, many of which had been written years before, touched on smallpox, population, whirlwinds, geology, evaporation, salt mines, modern music, the origin of storms, sound, tides, heat and the effect of oil on water. He sent seeds of European plants to a botanist in America—we have Franklin to thank, if that is the proper word, for kohlrabi. He wrote a long treatise on the cultivation of silkworms in America, which he considered a fine idea because

"The food for the worms which produce the silk is in the air, and the ground under the trees may still produce grass or some other vegetable good for man or beast." He speculated, from fossils of mastodons found in Ohio, that "the earth had anciently been in another position, and the climates differently placed from what they are at present." He made a pioneer diagnosis of lead poisoning, and wrote a most interesting letter on the common cold:

I HOPE THAT after having discovered the benefit of fresh and cool air applied to the sick, people will begin to suspect that possibly it may do no harm to the well. . . . I have long been satisfied from observation that besides the general colds now termed influenzas (which may possibly spread by contagion as well as by a particular quality of the air) people often catch cold from one another when shut up together in close rooms, coaches, etc., and when sitting near and conversing so as to breathe in each other's transpiration; the disorder being in a certain state. I think, too, that it is the frowzy, corrupt air from animal substances and the perspired matter from our bodies which, being long confined in beds not lately used and clothes not lately worn and books long shut up in close rooms, obtains that kind of putridity which occasions the colds observed upon sleeping in, wearing and turning over such bedclothes and books; and not their coldness or dampness. From these causes, but more from full living with too little exercise, proceed in my opinion most of the disorders which for about one hundred and fifty years past the English have called colds. . . . Traveling in our severe winters, I have suffered cold sometimes to an extremity only short of freezing, but this did not make me catch cold. And, for moisture, I have been in the river every evening two or three hours for a fortnight together, when one would suppose I might imbibe enough of it to take cold if humidity could give it; but no such effect ever followed. The way to avoid colds was to eat and drink temperately, take enough exercise, and breathe as much fresh air as possible.

At a time when no one had ever heard of germs, Franklin guessed almost as much as present-day medical science knows about the causes of colds.

In 1771 he visited for a week at the home of Bishop Jonathan Shipley, whose five young daughters idolized the old philosopher, and started to write his autobiography in the form of a letter to his son. This was the only book that he ever attempted, and it was never finished. He worked on it for a week in 1771, again, briefly, in 1784. He was dictating a third section in the last days of his life. Death left the story in the middle of his second stay in London and the book in the middle of a sentence.

He wrote another unfinished piece about this time entitled *A Scheme for a New Alphabet and Reformed Mode of Spelling.* In this he proposed to change the alphabet so that each word could be spelled as it sounded. Each letter would always have the same sound and there would be no superfluous letters in a word. To do this he suggested dropping the letters *c, j, q, w, x* and *y,* which he considered unnecessary, and substituting six other letters for sounds for which there are now no letters, including *th, sh* and *ng.*

Today, experts agree that Franklin's proposal is fundamentally sound, although not complete. Had he pushed for the adoption of his revolutionary idea at a time when America was in a mood to revolt against all things English, including the outmoded spelling of the language, he might have saved generations of young Americans untold hours of struggling to master the archaic and arbitrary spelling.

But there were more pressing concerns to engage the attention of the unofficial ambassador in the early 1770's. American resistance was stiffening. The British ministry could not understand the desire for political freedom in the colonies, or all the

talk about "rights." They saw in the colonial unrest only a
desire to avoid paying a just share of the Empire's expenses—
and they thought that, somehow, Franklin was responsible for
the boycott and the mobs. He was the voice of the Americans in
England, the man who kept hammering home the unpalatable
story of colonial rights. Then he added satire to reason with two
stinging essays, *Rules by Which a Great Empire May Be Reduced to a Small One* and *An Edict of the King of Prussia.*

Rules was addressed "to all ministers who have the management of extensive dominions which, from their very greatness
have become troublesome to govern." He cited twenty ways in
which this trouble could be avoided by acts that would dis-
member the empire—such as "That the possibility of this
separation may always exist, take special care the provinces are
never incorporated with the mother country; that they do not
enjoy the same common rights, the same privileges in commerce; and that they are governed by severer laws, all of your
enacting, without allowing them any share in the choice of the
legislators."

He advised that, if the colonies had added to the strength of
the mother country by aiding her in war and commerce, "Forget
it all, or resent it all, as if they had done you an injury. . . .
However peaceably your colonies have submitted to your
government, shown their affection to your interests, and patiently
borne their grievances, you are to suppose them always inclined
to revolt, and treat them accordingly. Quarter troops among
them, who by their insolence may provoke the rising of mobs,
and by their bullets and bayonets suppress them. By this means,
like the husband who uses his wife ill from suspicion, you may in
time convert your suspicions into realities."

Since provinces must have governors and judges, Franklin
suggested that for the former they find "prodigals who had
ruined their fortunes, broken gamesters or stockjobbers . . . for
they will probably be rapacious and provoke the people by their
extortions." Also, when the people complain of injustice "punish

such suitors with long delay, enormous expense, and a final judgment in favor of the oppressor."

IF WHEN YOU ARE engaged in war, your colonies should vie in liberal aids of men and money against the common enemy, upon your simple requisition, and give far beyond their abilities, reflect that a penny taken from them by your power is more honorable to you than a pound presented by their benevolence; despise therefore their voluntary grants, and resolve to harass them with novel taxes. . . .

Possibly, indeed, some of them might still comfort themselves, and say: "Though we have no property, we have yet something left that is valuable; we have constitutional liberty, both of person and of conscience. . . ." To annihilate this comfort, begin by laws to perplex their commerce with infinite regulations, impossible to be remembered and observed; ordain seizures of their property for every failure; take away the trial of such property by jury, and give it to arbitrary judges of your own appointing, and of the lowest characters in the country, whose salaries and emoluments are to arise out of the duties or condemnations. . . .

To make your taxes more odious, and more likely to procure resistance, send from the capital a board of officers to superintend the collection, composed of the most indiscreet, ill-bred and insolent you can find. Let these have large salaries out of the extorted revenue, and live in open, grating luxury upon the sweat and blood of the industrious. . . .

Send armies into their country under pretense of protecting the inhabitants; but instead of garrisoning the forts on their frontiers with those troops to prevent incursions, demolish those forts and order the troops into the heart of the country, that the savages may be encouraged to attack the frontiers, and that the troops may be protected by the inhabitants. This will seem to proceed from your ill will or your ignorance, and contribute further to produce and strengthen an opinion among them that you are no longer fit to govern them. . . .

Rules was addressed, with irony and insult, to British ministers who had treated Franklin with contempt. In his *Edict* hoax, he showed how ridiculous was the Crown's claim to absolute monarchy over America by saying that England had been settled by German colonists and that, therefore, Prussia could apply to Britain the same laws that England applied to America.

FREDERICK, by grace of God, King of Prussia, etc., etc., etc., to all present and to come, health. . . . We, of our . . . authority royal, have made and issued this present Edict, viz.:
Whereas it is well known to all the world, that the first German settlements made in the island of Britain were by colonies of people subject to our renowned ducal ancestors, and drawn from their dominions . . . and that the said colonies have flourished under the protection of our august house for ages past; have never been emancipated therefrom; and yet have hitherto yielded little profit to the same . . . and whereas it is just and expedient that a revenue should be raised from the said colonies in Britain . . . and that those who are descendants of our ancient subjects, and thence still owe us due obedience, should contribute to the replenishing of our royal coffers (as they must have done, had their ancestors remained in the territories now to us appertaining); we do therefore hereby ordain and command that, from and after the date of these presents, there shall be levied and paid to our officers of the customs . . . a duty of 4½ per cent *ad valorem,* for the use of us and our successors. . . .

And whereas there hath been from time to time discovered in the said island of Great Britain, by our colonists there, many mines or beds of iron-stone; and sundry subjects of our ancient dominion, skillful in converting the said stone into metal, have in time past transported themselves thither, carrying with them and communicating that art; and the inhabitants of the said island, presuming that they had a natural right to make the best use they could of the natural productions of their country for their own benefit, have . . . built furnaces for smelting the said stone into iron . . . thereby endangering a diminution of the said manufacture in our ancient dominion; we do therefore further hereby ordain that, from and after the date hereof, no mill or other engine for slitting or rolling of iron, or any plating-forge to work with a tilt-hammer, or any furnace for making steel, shall be erected or continued in the said island of Great Britain. But we are nevertheless graciously pleased to permit the inhabitants of the said island to transport their iron into Prussia, there to be manufactured, and to them returned; they paying our Prussian subjects for the workmanship. . . .

We do not, however, think fit to extend this our indulgence to the article of wool; but, meaning to encourage, not only the manufacturing of woolen cloth, but also the raising of wool, in our ancient dominions, and to prevent both, as much as may be, in our said island, we do hereby absolutely forbid the transportation of wool from thence, even to the mother country, Prussia; and, that those islanders may be further and more effectually restrained in making any advantage of their own wool in the way of manufacture, we command that none shall be carried out of the country into another. . . . Nevertheless, our loving subjects there are hereby permitted (if they think proper) to use all their wool as manure for the improvement of their land.

And whereas the art and mystery of making *hats* hath arrived at great perfection in Prussia, and the making of hats by our remoter subjects ought to be as much as possible restrained; and forasmuch as the islanders before mentioned, being in possession of wool, beaver and other furs, having presumptuously conceived they had a right to make some advantage thereof, by manufacturing the same into hats, to the prejudice of our domestic manufacture, we do therefore hereby strictly command and ordain, that no hats or felts whatsoever . . . shall be . . . conveyed out of one county in the said island into another county, or to any other place whatsoever, by any person or persons whatsoever. . . . But, lest the said islanders should suffer inconveniency by the want of hats, we are further graciously pleased to permit them to send their beaver furs to Prussia; and we also permit hats made thereof to be exported from Prussia to Britain. . . .

And lastly, being willing further to favor our said colonies in Britain, we do hereby also ordain and command, that all the *thieves,* highway and street robbers, housebreakers, forgerers, murderers . . . and villains of every denomination, who have forfeited their lives to the law of Prussia, but whom we, in our great clemency, do not think fit here to hang, shall be emptied out of our jails into the said island of Great Britain, for the better peopling of that country.

We flatter ourselves that these our royal regulations and commands will be thought just and reasonable by our much-favored colonists in England; the said regulations being copied from their statutes . . . or from resolutions of both Houses, entered into for the good government of their own colonies in Ireland and America. . . .

By the King in his Council,

RECHTMÄSSIG, *Sec.*

There were those who took Franklin's *Edict* seriously and looked for Frederick to come marching to the shore of the Channel with an army. Most sophisticates found it amusing, and it was an immediate best seller.

At the same time that Franklin was pointing out to the

English the probable disastrous consequences of their conduct, he was calling for moderation back home. "I trust that the general prudence of our countrymen will see that by our growing strength we advance fast to a situation in which our claims must be allowed; that by a premature struggle we may be crippled and kept down another age; that as between friends every affront is not worth a duel, between nations every injury is not worth a war, so between the governed and the governing every mistake in government, every encroachment on rights, is not worth a rebellion."

He had despaired of convincing Parliament through reason and he was starting to waver in his faith in the King. In a letter to his son he said, "Between you and I, the later measures have been, I suspect, very much the King's own and he has in some cases a great share of what his friends call firmness."

But there was still hope for a peaceful settlement, he thought, with the aid of a growing group in England which favored conciliation.

THE FRIENDS OF LIBERTY here [he wrote] wish we may long preserve it on our side of the water, that they may find it there if adverse events should destroy it here. They are therefore anxious and afraid lest we should hazard it by premature attempts in its favor. . . . With regard to the sentiment of people in general here, concerning America, I must say that we have among them many friends and well-wishers. The dissenters are all for us, and many of the merchants and manufacturers. There seems to be, even among the country gentlemen, a general sense of our growing importance, a disapprobation of the harsh measures with which we have been treated, and a wish that some means may be found of perfect reconciliation. A few members of Parliament in both houses, and perhaps some in high office, have in a degree the same idea; but none of these seem willing, as yet, to be active in our favor, lest adversaries should take advantage and charge it upon them as betraying the interests of the nation."

Then, in December, 1773, occurred two incidents which ended all Franklin's hopes of effecting a reasonable reconciliation. One was the piece of delinquency which has become famed as the Boston Tea Party, which Franklin called "an act of violent injustice" and which resulted in the closing of the port of Boston. "I suppose," wrote Franklin, "we never had since we were a people so few friends in Britain. . . . I cannot but hope that the affair of the tea will have been considered in the Assembly before this time and satisfaction proposed if not made; for such a step will remove much of the prejudice now entertained against us, and put us again on a fair footing in contending for our old privileges as occasion may arise." Ultimately, in his last effort to prevent war, Franklin offered to pay for the tea himself.

The other incident was the affair of the Hutchinson letters. Thomas Hutchinson was the American Tory governor of Massachusetts. In 1768–69 he had written some letters to a member of the ministry advocating the measures of which the colonists were complaining. They called for a firm hand to keep the colony in order—even force, if necessary; recommended that Crown officers be independent of the Assembly; and said, "There must be an abridgment of what are called English liberties."

When these letters fell into Franklin's hands he was shocked at what he considered Hutchinson's treason to the colony. He sent them to the Massachusetts Committee of Correspondence, saying:

ON THIS OCCASION I think fit to acquaint you that there has lately fallen into my hands part of a correspondence that I have reason to believe laid the foundation of most if not all our present grievances. I am not at liberty to tell through

what channel I received it; and I have engaged that it shall
not be printed, nor copies taken of the whole or any part of
it; but I am allowed to let it be seen by some men of worth
in the province, for their satisfaction only. In confidence of
your preserving inviolably my engagement, I send you en-
closed the original letters. . . . For my own part, I cannot
but acknowledge that my resentment against this country
for its arbitrary measures in governing us, conducted by the
late minister, has, since my conviction by these papers that
those measures were projected, advised, and called for by
men of character among ourselves . . . been considerably
abated. I think they must have the same effect with you; but
I am not, as I have said, at liberty to make the letters public.
I can only allow them to be seen by yourself, by the other
gentlemen of the Committee of Correspondence, with a few
other such gentlemen as you may think fit to show them to.

Franklin was sworn to secrecy as to the source of the letters.
He could only say that "a gentleman of character and distinction" had come to him and said that the sending of troops to
Boston and "all the other grievances we complained of took
their rise not from government here but were projected . . .
solicited and obtained by some of the most responsible among
the Americans themselves, as necessary for the welfare of that
country. As I could not readily assent to the probability of this
he undertook to convince me and, he hoped, through me (as
their agent here) my countrymen. Accordingly he called on me
some days after and produced to me these very letters."

Franklin did not try to keep his part in this transaction secret.
His reason for stipulating that the letters be handled with discretion was that their publication might "occasion some riot or
mischievous consequence." Samuel Adams promptly read them
to the Assembly. They were copied and printed and the Assembly petitioned the King to remove Hutchinson.

The publication of the letters caused a scandal in London. It was believed that they had been addressed to a Thomas Whately, then dead. His brother, William, accused a man named Temple of stealing them. The two men first fought the matter out in the newspapers and then in a duel, in which Whately was wounded. At this point Franklin stepped in to publish in the *Public Advertiser* a statement saying, "I alone am the person who obtained and transmitted to Boston the letters in question. Mr. W. could not communicate them because they were never in his possession and, for the same reason, they could not be taken from him by Mr. T." Franklin still refused to say where he had obtained the letters, and this was to prove his downfall.

The petition to remove Hutchinson was to be heard by a committee of the Privy Council. It was a foregone conclusion that they would deny the petition—particularly since the hearing took place a few days after the news of the tea incident reached London. But here was the long-sought opportunity to get rid of the annoying colonial agent. Franklin wrote, "I heard from all quarters that the ministry and the courtiers were highly enraged with me for transmitting those letters. I was called an incendiary, and the papers were filled with invectives against me. Hints were given me that there was some thought of apprehending me, seizing my papers, and sending me to Newgate. I was well informed that a resolution was taken to deprive me of my place; it was only thought best to defer it till after the hearing; I suppose because I was there to be so blackened that nobody would think it injustice."

"Blackened" was a mild word for the vilification and abuse that was heaped on Franklin at the hearing by Alexander Wedderburn, counsel for Hutchinson. "I hope, my Lords, you will mark and brand this man for the honor of this country, or Europe, and of mankind. . . . He has forfeited all the respect of societies and men." According to Wedderburn, the "innocent, well-meaning farmers which comprise the bulk of the Assembly" were merely dupes of Franklin's, who was not an agent for the Assembly but "a first mover and prime conductor of it for his own . . . the actor and secret spring . . . the inventor and first planner of the whole contrivance. . . . My Lords, Dr. Franklin's mind may have been so possessed with the idea of a Great American Republic that he may easily slide into the language of the minister of a foreign, independent state . . . [who might] bribe a villain to steal or betray any state papers. . . . But Dr. Franklin, whatever he might teach the people of Boston, while he is here, at least, is a subject; and if a subject injure a subject he is answerable to the law." Franklin, according to Wedderburn, had staged the whole thing because he wanted to be governor himself and he and his friends wished "to erect themselves into a tyranny greater than the Roman."

Franklin stood quietly beside the fireplace in the hearing room listening to this tirade. He could not, or would not, defend himself. He was there, presumably, merely to deliver the petition of the Assembly. The hearing, which had turned into a trial, or, rather, a persecution of Franklin, was supposedly to act on the petition. As an afterthought the committee decided to report to the Privy Council that the petition "is founded upon resolutions formed upon false and erroneous allegations; and that the same is groundless, vexatious and scandalous and calculated only for the seditious purposes of keeping up a spirit of clamor and discontent in the said province." The day after the hearing Franklin received an order removing him as deputy postmaster of the colonies—a step that had obviously been decided on and prepared before the hearing.

Franklin never publicly replied to Wedderburn's abuse. Shortly after the hearing he wrote a *Tract Relative to the Affair of Hutchinson's Letters,* but it was not published until after his death. In it he explained the reason for his reticence. "Such censures I have generally passed over in silence, conceiving, when they were just, that I ought rather to amend than defend; and when they were undeserved that a little time would justify me. Splashes of dirt thrown upon my character I suffered while fresh to remain. I did not choose to spread by endeavoring to remove them, but relied on that vulgar adage that they would rub off when they were dry."

Now completely out of favor with the ministry, Franklin wanted to return to America, but the deliberations of the First Continental Congress raised a slight hope for peaceful settlement. He wrote to Cushing, Speaker of the Massachusetts Assembly, "I have been advised by our friends to stay till the result of your congress should arrive. The coolness, temper and firmness of the American proceedings; the unanimity of all the colonies . . . and the patience with which those injuries are at present borne, without the least appearance of submission, have a good deal surprised and disappointed our enemies; and the tone of public conversation, which has been violently against us, begins evidently to turn. . . ."

In Franklin's mind the only hope lay in complete boycott of British goods, practiced by all the colonies, which would induce the commercial class to exert pressure on the King and ministry. Parliament would do as they were told, for, said Franklin, "As most of the members are bribing or purchasing to get in, there is little doubt of selling their votes to the minister for the time being to reimburse themselves. Luxury introduces necessity even among those that make the most splendid figures here; this brings most of the Commons as well as the Lords to market; and if America would save for three or four years the money she spends in fashions and fineries and fopperies of this country, she might buy the whole Parliament, minister and all."

One of the most interesting and little-known documents on prerevolution diplomacy is the secret history of Franklin's last year in London, entitled *An Account of the Negotiations in London for Effecting a Reconciliation Between Great Britain and the American Colonies*. This was in the form of a letter to his son dated March 22, 1775, although it could not have been entirely written on that date—in printed form it runs 112 pages. It tells the story of the last desperate efforts to avert the crisis of revolution.

This secret diplomacy started with a chess game. In his letter Franklin says:

BEING AT THE Royal Society, Mr. Raper, one of our members, told me there was a certain lady who had a desire of playing with me at chess, fancying she could beat me, and had requested him to bring me to her. It was, he said, a lady with whose acquaintance he was sure I should be pleased, a sister of Lord Howe, and he hoped I would not refuse the challenge. . . . I named the Friday following. He called accordingly. I went with him, played a few games with the lady, whom I found of very sensible conversation and pleasing behavior, which induced me to agree most readily to an appointment for another meeting a few days afterward; though I had not the least apprehension that any political business could have any connection with this new acquaintance.

The next move came from two Quakers named Barclay and Fothergill. Barclay, a rich banker, had close friends in the ministry and Fothergill was physician to Lord Dartmouth, Secretary of State for America. Franklin's letter continues:

ON THE THURSDAY preceding this chess party, Mr. David Barclay called on me to have some discourse concerning the meeting of merchants to petition Parliament. When that was over, he spoke of the dangerous situation of American affairs, the hazard that a civil war might be brought on by the present measures, and the great merit that person would have who could contrive some means of preventing so terrible a calamity, and bring about a reconciliation. He was then pleased to add that he was persuaded, from my knowledge of both countries, my character and influence in one of them, and my abilities in business, no man had so much in his power as myself. I naturally answered that I should

be very happy if I could in any degree be instrumental in
so good a work, but that I saw no prospect of it; for, though
I was sure the Americans were always willing and ready to
agree on any equitable terms, yet I thought an accommodation impracticable, unless both sides wished it; and, by what
I could judge from the proceedings of the ministry, I did
not believe they had the least disposition toward it. . . . Mr.
Barclay apprehended I judged too harshly of the ministers;
he was persuaded they were not all of that temper, and he
fancied they would be very glad to get out of their present
embarrassment on any terms, only saving the honor and
dignity of the government.

This conversation was followed by a meeting between the
two Quakers and Franklin in which they asked him to draw up
a plan for reconciliation. Franklin was reluctant to do so, feeling that it would be useless because "there did not exist the
least disposition in the ministry to an accommodation." Fothergill said that Franklin might be mistaken; "that, whatever might
be the violence of some, he had reason, *good reason,* to believe
others were differently disposed, and that if I would draw a
plan, which we three upon considering should judge reasonable,
it might be made good use of."

Meanwhile there was another "chess party with the agreeable
Mrs. Howe."

AFTER PLAYING AS LONG as we liked, we fell into a little
chat, partly on a mathematical problem, and partly about
the new Parliament, then just met, when she said: "And
what is to be done with this dispute between Great Britain
and the colonies? I hope we are not to have a civil war."
"They should kiss and be friends," said I, "what can they
do better? Quarreling can be of service to neither, but is
ruin to both." "I have often said," replied she, "that I wished
government would employ you to settle the dispute for

them; I am sure nobody could do it so well. Do not you think that the thing is practicable?" "Undoubtedly, madam, if the parties are disposed to reconciliation; for the two countries have really no clashing interests to differ about. It is rather a matter of punctilio, which two or three reasonable people might settle in half an hour. I thank you for the good opinion you are pleased to express of me; but the ministers will never think of employinrg me in that good work; for they choose rather to abuse me." "Aye," said she, "they have behaved shamefully to you. And indeed some of them are now ashamed of it themselves."

Franklin drew up a plan entitled *Hints for Conversation upon the Subject of Terms That Might Probably Produce a Durable Union Between Britain and the Colonies*. There were seventeen points, of which the most significant were:

The tea destroyed to be paid for.

The tea-duty act to be repealed and all money so far collected under it to be returned to the colonies.

All acts restraining manufactures in the colonies to be repealed.

No troops to enter or be quartered in any colony but with the consent of the legislature.

Castle William [in Boston harbor] to be restored to the Province of Massachusetts Bay and no fortress built by the Crown in any province.

All governors to be paid by the Assemblies of each province.

All powers of internal legislation in the colonies to be disclaimed by Parliament.

Barclay and Fothergill maintained that some elements in this plan would never be accepted, but Franklin would agree to few changes. He did permit a change to the effect that acts restricting manufacture would be "reconsidered" instead of "repealed," and other minor revisions. There was nothing new about Franklin's plan—he had been saying for years that this was the only course through which the colonies could fill their proper place in an expanding British Empire. It was not an offer to compromise.

The Quakers asked permission to show the plan to "certain persons." Franklin said, "I had drawn the paper at their request and it was now theirs to do with it what they pleased . . . but it was my opinion, if they wished any attention paid to the propositions, it would be better not to mention me; the ministry having, as I conceived, a prejudice against me and everything that came from me. . . . For my own part, I kept this whole proceeding a profound secret; but I soon after discovered that it had taken air by some other means."

The "other means" came to light at the next chess session. "Visiting Mrs. Howe, she told me as soon as I came in, that her brother, Lord Howe, wished to be acquainted with me; that he was a very good man, and she was sure we should like each other. I said I had always heard a good character of Lord Howe, and should be proud of the honor of being known to him. 'He is but just by,' said she; 'will you give me leave to send for him?' 'By all means, madam, if you think proper.' She rang for a servant, wrote a note, and Lord Howe came in a few minutes."

The chess game had been "cover" to bring Howe and Franklin together. Although Lord Howe had no post in the ministry, he did have great influence and wanted to act as a secret go-between to affect a reconciliation.

HIS LORDSHIP TOLD ME he could now assure me, of a certainty, that there was a sincere disposition in Lord North and Lord Dartmouth to accommodate the differences with America, and to listen favorably to any proposition that might have a probable tendency to answer that salutary purpose. . . . Mrs. Howe said: "I wish, brother, you were to be sent thither on such a service; I should like that much better than General Howe's going to command the army there." "I think, madame," said I, "they ought to provide for General Howe some more honorable employment." Lord Howe here took out of his pocket a paper, and offering it to me said, smiling: "If it is not an unfair question, may I ask whether you know anything of this paper?" Upon looking at it, I saw it was a copy, in David Barclay's hand, of the *Hints* before recited; and said that I had seen it; adding, a little after, that since I perceived his lordship was acquainted with a transaction, my concern in which I had understood was to have been kept secret, I should make no difficulty in owning to him that I had been consulted on the subject, and had drawn up that paper. He said that he was rather sorry to find the sentiments expressed in it were mine, as it gave him less hopes of promoting, by my assistance, the wished-for reconciliation; since he had reason to think there was no likelihood of the admission of those propositions. He hoped, however, that I would reconsider the subject, and form some plan that would be acceptable here.

Howe went on to say that Franklin's services would be of great value to England and that he "might with reason expect any reward in the power of government to bestow." Franklin recognized this bait for a bribe and commented to his son, "This, to me, was what the French vulgarly call 'spitting in the soup.' " It was evident that the ministers thought that Franklin had discretionary powers from the colonies to make a "deal" and, based on their own moral standards, they could not understand a man who could not be bought.

While this was going on, Franklin received a petition to the King from the Continental Congress covering essentially the same points as his plan. When it was brought before the Parliament, it "came down," Franklin said, "among a great heap of letters . . . newspapers, pamphlets, handbills, etc. . . . and was laid on the table before them, undistinguished by any particular recommendation of it to the notice of either House."

The behind-the-scenes negotiations went on and became more mysterious. The Quakers had submitted Franklin's plan to at least two ministers, who considered his conditions too stiff. The bribery offers became more specific—they still thought that Franklin could, if he would, modify the petition from Congress to make it more acceptable to the King's party. Then William Pitt entered the scene with a compromise plan of his own on which he sought Franklin's approval. Franklin said that if the plan "was not so perfect as might be wished, it would at least serve as a basis for a treaty, and in the meantime prevent further mischiefs."

The next day Franklin, at Pitt's request, was present in the House of Lords when the Plan was presented.

LORD CHATHAM, [William Pitt] in a most excellent speech, introduced, explained and supported his plan. When he sat down, Lord Dartmouth rose, and very properly said it contained matter of such weight and magnitude as to require much consideration; and he therefore hoped the noble earl did not expect their lordships to decide upon it by immediate vote, but would be willing it should lie upon the table for consideration. Lord Chatham answered readily that he expected nothing more.

But Lord Sandwich rose, and in a petulant, vehement speech, opposed its being received at all, and gave his opinion that it ought to be immediately rejected, with the contempt it deserved; that he could never believe it to be the production of any British peer; that it appeared to him rather the work of some American; and turning his face toward me, who was leaning on the bar, said he fancied he had in his eye the person who drew it up, one of the bitterest and most mischievous enemies this country had ever known. This drew the eyes of many lords upon me, but as I had no inducement to take it to myself, I kept my countenance as immovable as if my features had been made of wood. . . .

Lord Chatham, in his reply to Lord Sandwich, took notice of his liberal insinuation that the plan was not the
person's who proposed it; declared that it was entirely his
own . . . but he made no scruple to declare that if he were
the first minister of this country, and had the care of settling
this momentous business, he should not be ashamed of publicly calling to his assistance a person so perfectly acquainted
with the whole of American affairs as the gentleman alluded
to, and so injuriously reflected on; one, he was pleased to
say, whom all Europe held in high estimation for his knowledge and wisdom, and ranked with our Boyles and Newtons;
who was an honor, not to the English nation only, but to
human nature! I found it harder to stand this extravagant
compliment than the preceding equally extravagant abuse;
but kept as well as I could an unconcerned countenance, as
not conceiving it to relate to me.

Parliament's refusal even to consider a plan proposed by the
eminent Pitt gave Franklin "an exceeding mean opinion of their
abilities, and made their claim of sovereignty over three millions
of virtuous, sensible people in America seem the greatest of
absurdities, since they appeared to have scarce discretion
enough to govern a herd of swine. Hereditary legislators!
thought I. There would be more propriety, because less hazard
of mischief, in having (as in some university of Germany)
hereditary professors of mathematics!"

There were some further meetings with the Quakers and with
Lord Howe, but Franklin's temper was finally growing short.
Nothing had come of the secret diplomacy except two games
of chess with the agreeable Mrs. Howe. His long held imperial-
istic hopes had faded—he was ripe for the idea of independence,
saw little merit in union when he wrote, "When I consider the
extreme corruption prevalent among all orders of men in this
old, rotten state, and the glorious public virtue so predominant
in our rising country, I cannot but apprehend more mischief

than benefit from a closer union. I fear they will drag us after them in all the plundering wars which their desperate circumstances, injustice and rapacity may prompt them to undertake. . . . However, I would try anything, and bear anything that can be borne with safety to our just liberties, rather than engage in a war with such relations, unless compelled to it by dire necessity in our own defense."

During the chess-playing interlude, Deborah Franklin had died, alone except for Sarah, although William had posted hastily from his new position as Governor of New Jersey to arrive breathlessly at the funeral. When the news reached Franklin he resolved to return to America. There was no further hope from negotiations, although he spent most of the day with Edmund Burke three days before the latter made his great and unavailing speech for reconciliation—which he made on the day Franklin sailed. When the Minute Men repulsed the British at Concord, Franklin was taking the temperature of the Gulf Stream as part of the preparation for a paper on the subject that he would write ten years later.

He went to London as a monarchist, believing firmly in imperialism. He returned as a democrat, about to believe in independence. The cause of his conversion may be summarized in a single sentence that he wrote. "It seems I am too much of an American."

CHAPTER IX

LIFE BEGINS AT SEVENTY

❦

When Franklin returned to Philadelphia his seventieth birthday was approaching. Revolution is a young man's game and the old doctor might well have been ready for retirement. Instead, the next year and a half was, perhaps, the busiest period in his life.

He took his place in the Pennsylvania Assembly and was appointed to the Committee of Safety to plan the defense of the province. He was made a member—the oldest—of the Continental Congress and was promptly appointed Postmaster General to organize a new American post office. To Priestley, in England, he wrote, "My time was never more fully employed. In the morning at six I am at the Committee of Safety, which Committee holds till near nine, when I am at the Congress, and that sits till four in the afternoon. . . . It will never be credited in Britain that men can be as diligent with us from zeal for the public good, as with you for thousands per annum. Such is the difference between uncorrupted new states and corrupted old ones."

He labored on Congressional committees to draft a final petition to the King; to draw up a declaration for Washington on taking command; to provide for making saltpeter; to arrange for printing money—which Franklin designed. He supervised construction of log and iron obstructions in the channel of the Delaware as part of Philadelphia's defense—which later gave his friend Admiral Lord Howe considerable trouble. He designed and had made a pike to oppose the British bayonet and wrote to General Charles Lee his thoughts on some archaic weapons:

WE HAVE GOT a large quantity of saltpeter, one hundred and twenty tons, and thirty more expected. Powder-mills are now wanting. I believe we must set to work and make it by hand. But I still wish, with you, that pikes could be introduced, and I would add bows and arrows. These were good weapons, not wisely laid aside:

1st. Because a man may shoot as truly with a bow as with a common musket.

2dly. He can discharge four arrows in the time of charging and discharging one bullet.

3dly. His object is not taken from his view by the smoke of his own side.

4thly. A flight of arrows seen coming upon them, terrifies and disturbs the enemies' attention to their business.

5thly. An arrow sticking in any part of a man puts him *hors de combat* till it is extracted.

6thly. Bows and arrows are more easily provided everywhere than muskets and ammunition.

On the personal side he had a sad disappointment when he met with his son to try to induce him to resign as Governor of New Jersey. William, a confirmed Tory, refused. Father and son were on opposing sides during the war, much of which William spent in a Connecticut prison.

Franklin drew up and presented to Congress, in July, 1775, the first concrete plan for a confederation of the colonies. It proposed that "The name of this Confederacy shall henceforth

be *The United Colonies of North America*," and continued for
twelve brief articles which set forth the purpose of the Confederacy: "common defense against enemies . . . security of
liberty and properties . . . safety of persons and families . . .
mutual and general welfare." Each colony was to "retain as
much as it may think fit of its present laws." There was to be a
Congress with members elected annually which should have
the power to determine "on war and peace; the entering into
alliances and sending ambassadors; the settling of disputes
between colony and colony. . . . All charges of wars, and all
general expenses to be incurred for the common welfare shall
be defrayed out of a common treasury."

There is no record of what action was taken on this first proposal for a United States. It was probably debated briefly and
referred to committee, where it died. A more complete plan of
confederation was adopted by Congress in 1777 and accepted
by all of the states in 1781. Franklin's proposal did not mention
independence—Congress was not yet ready for that. But independence was implicit in it. Colonies do not make alliances and
send ambassadors. Nine months after Franklin submitted his
confederation plan—in April, 1776—he was still in the minority
in Congress in favoring union and independence. He wrote to
Josiah Quincy:

YOU ASK: "When is the Continental Congress by general
consent going to be formed into a supreme legislature; alliances, defensive and offensive, formed; our ports opened
and a formidable naval force established at the public
charge?" I can only answer, at present, that nothing seems
to be wanting but that "general consent." The novelty of
the thing deters some; the doubt of success, others; the vain
hope of conciliation, many. But our enemies take continually every proper measure to remove these obstacles, and
their endeavors are attended with success, since every day
furnishes us with new causes for increased enmity, and new

reasons for wishing an eternal separation, so that there is a rapid increase in the formerly small party who were for an independent government.

The old man was not allowed merely to sit on committee and quietly draft proposals. He was sent to Massachusetts to confer with Washington after the latter took command; on a long, cold journey to Montreal, which Montgomery had captured, to try to induce the Canadian French to join with the American colonies—a hopeless task because the Catholic French had already been thoroughly alienated by Puritan-minded Americans.

Franklin wrote little during this period—he had little time. He did write, shortly after his return to America, one of his few unfriendly letters which showed how deeply he felt about British injustice and the American cause. One of his best friends in England was William Strahan. A fellow printer, Strahan had tried hard to coax Deborah to come to England, years before, in the hope that Franklin would stay there, and the two fathers had discussed the possibility of a marriage between William and Strahan's daughter. Franklin's many letters to Strahan had always started "Dear Friend" or "Dear Straney." Now he addressed him as:

MR. STRAHAN: You are a member of Parliament, and one of that majority which has doomed my country to destruction. You have begun to burn our towns, and murder our people. Look upon your hands; they are stained with the blood of your relations! You and I were long friends; you are now my enemy, and I am,

Yours,

B. FRANKLIN

Written in the heat of emotion the letter was never sent. Years later the old men were still good friends.

Franklin wrote to others in England describing events in America. To Edmund Burke he said, "You will see by the papers that General Gage . . . drew the sword and began the war. His troops made a most vigorous retreat—twenty miles in three hours—scarcely to be paralleled in history; the feeble Americans, who pelted them all the way, could scarce keep up with them." To Priestley he wrote: "Britain, at the expense of three million, has killed one hundred and fifty Yankees this campaign, which is twenty thousand pounds a head; and at Bunker's Hill she gained a mile of ground, half of which she lost again by our taking the post on Ploughed Hill. During this same time sixty thousand children have been born in America. From these data his mathematical head will easily calculate the time and expense necessary to kill us all and conquer our whole territory."

Franklin took little part in the debates on the floor of Congress. He was no orator. "I was," he said, "but a bad speaker, never eloquent, subject to much hesitation in my choice of words, hardly correct in language, and yet I generally carried my points." He had several times caused Poor Richard to express his low opinion of wordy and bombastic speechmaking: "Here comes the orator, with his flood of words and his drop of reason"; "The worst wheel on the cart makes the most noise"; and "He that speaks much, is much mistaken."

Thomas Jefferson said, of Franklin in Congress, "I served with General Washington in the legislature of Virginia before the Revolution and, during it, with Dr. Franklin in Congress. I never heard either of them speak for ten minutes at a time, nor to any but the main point which was to decide the question. They laid their shoulders to the great points, knowing that the little ones would follow of themselves." John Adams saw it differently. He said that Franklin in Congress was seen, "from day to day, sitting in silence, a great part of the time asleep in his chair."

Young lawyer Adams was always envious of old Doctor

Franklin. He said, of himself, that he was "constantly proposing measures, supporting those I approved when moved by others, opposing such as I disapproved, discussing and arguing on every question." Yet when the speechmaking was over, Franklin was appointed to most of the important committees that did the work, Adams to few. Later, the second President sarcastically said that when the history of the Revolution was written the essence of the whole thing would be "that Dr. Franklin's electrical rod smote the earth and out sprang General Washington. That Franklin electrified him with his rod—and thenceforward these two conducted all the policy, negotiations, legislatures and war."

One of Franklin's most important prewar appointments was to the Committee of Secret Correspondence—the first American State Department. To Priestley he wrote, early in July, 1775, "We have not yet applied to any foreign power for assistance, nor offered our commerce for their friendship. Perhaps we never may, yet it is natural to think of it, if we are pressed." Congress soon thought of looking abroad for help. The Correspondence Committee was to establish contacts abroad with those who might be friendly to the American cause. Most of this work fell to Franklin. It is not much of an exaggeration to say that he was the only one who knew anybody in Europe, and he knew hundreds of scientists, philosophers, artists, musicians, publishers, politicians and even royalty.

He induced the Committee to appoint his friend Charles Dumas as an American agent in Holland and wrote to him regarding the colonies' position and their needs.

It GIVES US GREAT PLEASURE to learn from you that *"Toute l'Europe nous souhaite le plus heureux succès pour la maintien de nos libertés."* But we wish to know whether any one of them, from principles of humanity, is disposed magnanimously to step in for the relief of an oppressed people; or whether if, as it seems likely to happen, we should be obliged to break off all connection with Britain, and declare ourselves an independent people, there is any state or power in Europe who would be willing to enter into an alliance with us for the benefit of our commerce, which amounted before the war to near seven million sterling per annum, and must continually increase, as our people increase most rapidly. . . . The Committee of Congress . . . have directed me to request of you that, as you are situated at the Hague, where ambassadors from all the courts reside, you would make use of the opportunity that situation affords you of discovering, if possible, the disposition of the several courts with respect to such assistance or alliance, if we should apply for the one or propose the other. . . .

When Richard Henry Lee offered his resolution in Congress that "these united colonies are, and of right ought to be, free and independent states," Franklin was sick in bed. He had been returned but a short time from Canada and was suffering from gout, which, he wrote to Washington, "has kept me from Congress and company ever since you left us, so that I know little of what has passed except that a declaration of independence is preparing." Sick or well, Congress had appointed him to a committee to draft the Declaration, along with Thomas Jefferson, John Adams, Roger Sherman and Robert Livingston.

Apparently Livingston and Sherman had little to do with the Declaration except to agree with the others that Jefferson should write the first draft. Legend puts a statement in Jefferson's mouth to the effect that Franklin would have been selected to write it except that they could not trust him not to put a joke in it, but there is no serious authority for this. His actual contributions to Jefferson's draft were minor and in the nature of the same kind of changes to "point it up" that he made in Poor Richard's maxims. As an instance, Jefferson's draft said, "We hold these truths to be sacred and undeniable." Franklin changed it to "We hold these truths to be self-evident."

Franklin's most memorable contributions to the Declaration are the only two light and humorous stories connected with the solemn occasion. Jefferson told one. When Congress was tearing his precious document apart, he recalled:

I WAS SITTING BY Dr. Franklin, who perceived that I was not insensible to these mutilations. "I have made it a rule," said he, "whenever in my power, to avoid becoming the draftsman of papers to be reviewed by a public body. I took my lesson from an incident which I will relate to you. When I was a journeyman printer one of my companions, an apprentice hatter, having served his time was about to open shop for himself. His first concern was to have a handsome signboard with a proper inscription. He composed it in these words: 'John Thompson, hatter, makes and sells hats for ready money,' with a figure of a hat subjoined. But he thought he would submit it to his friends for their amendments. The first he showed it to thought the word 'hatter' tautologous, because followed by the words 'makes hats' which show he was a hatter. It was struck out. The next observed that the word 'makes' might as well be omitted, because customers would not care who made the hats. If good and to their mind, they would buy, by whomever made. He struck it out. A third said he thought the words 'for ready money' were useless, as it was not the custom of the place to sell on credit. Everyone who purchased expected to pay. They were parted with and the inscription now stood: 'John Thompson sells hat.' 'Sells hats?' says his next friend. 'Why, nobody will expect you to give them away. What then is the use of that word?' It was stricken out; and 'hats' followed it, the rather as there was one painted on the board. So his inscription was reduced ultimately to 'John Thompson' with the figure of a hat subjoined."

The other anecdote is widely known. As John Hancock signed

his name he is supposed to have said, "We must be unanimous; there must be no pulling different ways; we must all hang together." Franklin's alleged reply was, "Yes, we must indeed all hang together or most assuredly we will all hang separately." While this anecdote sounds like Franklin, and has become part of our historical tradition, there is no contemporary evidence that he said it.

Franklin was also on the committee, with Jefferson and Adams, to design the shield of the United States. Of their original design the only thing retained by Congress was the Eye of Providence which now gleams balefully from the back of every dollar bill—and the slogan "E Pluribus Unum." Nobody knows which of the committee members contributed these.

After the loss of the Battle of Long Island, and when Washington was driven from New York, Congress looked longingly to France. In September, 1776, Franklin, together with Jefferson and Silas Deane, were secretly appointed commissioners to treat with the French. Deane was already in Paris. Jefferson declined to go because of his wife's illness and was, unfortunately, replaced by Arthur Lee.

When Franklin landed in France he dropped into the middle of a melodramatic plot that was already afoot to give aid to the colonies. An adventurer named Caron de Beaumarchais had induced French Foreign Minister Charles Gravier, Comte de Vergennes and, through him, the French King, to set up a secret source of military supplies under the guise of a fictitious Spanish trading firm to be called Roderigue Hortalez and Company. France and Spain had agreed to give Beaumarchais one million francs each for the purchase of arms which were being collected from French arsenals and shipped to Haiti and Martinique where the Americans could pick them up.

By the time Franklin arrived Silas Deane was wrapped up in this scheme with Beaumarchais and would continue to handle it. Arthur Lee, who had come over from London, was sulking because Deane would not let him know what was going on, and because everyone immediately turned to Franklin and ignored him. Vergennes, although always interested in anything that would weaken England, had cooled down somewhat when news of Washington's defeat at Long Island reached France. He did not want to be on the losing side.

Franklin also found himself in the middle of a nest of spies. The English had an excellent intelligence service in France, headed by a double agent named Edward Bancroft, an American confidant of Deane's who later worked for the American commission and kept the English advised of every move that was made. Although Franklin trusted Bancroft, he knew that he was surrounded by spies. This did not disturb him much. He wrote:

AS IT IS IMPOSSIBLE to discover in every case the falsity of pretended friends who would know our affairs, and more so to prevent being watched by spies when interested people may think proper to place them for that purpose, I have long observed one rule which prevents any inconvenience from such practices. It is simply this—to be concerned in no affairs that I would blush to have made public, and to do nothing but what spies may see and welcome. When a man's actions are just and honorable, the more they are known, the more his reputation is increased and established. If I was sure, therefore, that my *valet de place* was a spy, as probably he is, I think I should not discharge him for that, if in other respects I liked him.

When the wily doctor stepped ashore in France he saw that there was a part to be played—a role that he could act with relish and skill. The author of "Bonhomme Richard" was visualized by most of France as a simple, benign, homely philosopher and moralist, a kindly, gentle Quaker. If that was what they wanted, that is what Franklin would give them. He was no Quaker, but if the French thought that he was and admired him for it, he saw no reason to dissuade them. The shrewd sage could very well play the backwoods philosopher if that was what was expected of him—particularly since the character admirably served his purpose.

He dressed the part. When he came ashore he had been wearing a fur hat—it was cold on the Atlantic in November. The French took this to be the symbol of the simple American philosopher, so Franklin continued to wear it—or at least carry it—even in the salons of Paris. He wrote to a friend: "Figure me in your mind as jolly as formerly and as strong and hearty, only a few years older; very plainly dressed, wearing my thin gray straight hair that peeps out under my only coiffure, a fine fur cap which comes down to my forehead almost to my spectacles. Think how this must appear among the powdered heads of Paris." In the dossier of the French police is this description: "Dr. Franklin, who lately arrived in this country from the English colonies, is very much run after and feted, not only by his fellow savants, but by all who can get hold of him; for he is difficult to be approached and lives in a seclusion which is supposed to be at the instance of the government. This Quaker wears the full costume of his sect. He has an agreeable physiognomy; spectacles always on his eyes; but little hair—a fur cap is always on his head. He wears no powder; tidy in his dress; very white linen. His only defense is a walking stick. If he sees our ministers it is at Paris, at night, and in the greatest secrecy."

Franklin started his diplomacy on several fronts. His personal popularity was important. Through it French public opinion and the weight of the intellectuals could be brought to bear in favor of the Americans. He sought to play on the "balance of power" situation in Europe. The power pendulum had been swinging toward England for some time, particularly after the French defeat in the Seven Years War. Franklin hammered away at the meaning of this to France and Spain, saying that he had come overseas to—

PROCURE THOSE AIDS from European powers, for enabling us to defend our freedom and independence, which it is certainly their interest to grant; as by that means the great and rapidly growing trade of America will be open to them all, and not a monopoly to Great Britain, as heretofore; a monopoly that, if she is suffered again to possess, will be such an increase of her strength by sea, and if she can reduce us again to submission, she will have thereby so great an addition to her strength by land, as will, together, make her the most formidable power the world has yet seen; and, from her natural pride and insolence in prosperity, of all others the most intolerable.

And, to the French people, he talked about liberty and freedom, already becoming magic words in Gallic dreams:

ALL EUROPE is on our side of the question, as far as applause and good wishes can carry them. Those who live under arbitrary power do nevertheless approve of liberty, and wish for it; they almost despair of recovering it in Europe; they read the translations of our separate colony constitutions with rapture; and there are such numbers everywhere, who talk of removing to America, with their families and fortunes, as soon as peace and our independence shall be established, that it is generally believed we shall have a prodigious addition of strength, wealth and arts from the emigration of Europe; and it is thought that to lessen or prevent such emigrations, the tyrannies established there must relax, and allow more liberty to their people. Hence it is a common observation here that our cause is the cause of all mankind, and that we are fighting for their liberty in defending our own. It is a glorious task assigned us by Providence, which has, I trust, given us spirit and virtue equal to it, and will at last crown it with success.

Franklin again employed satire to fan the universal disgust with England's use of German mercenaries against the colonists, by publishing a hoax entitled *The Sale of Hessians*. The Duke of Brunswick and the Princes of Hesse Cassel and Waldeck were being paid slightly over seven pounds a man, plus an annual subsidy, for each of the more than 17,000 soldiers with which they supplied England—all of whom have since, mistakenly, been called "Hessians," regardless of whether or not they came from Hesse. In addition, the German rulers received a bonus for each man killed—three wounded to equal one dead. Franklin wrote, and had published, a letter from a mythical Count de Schaumbergh to an equally fictitious Baron Hohendorf, who supposedly commanded the mercenaries in America.

I HAVE LEARNED with unspeakable pleasure the courage our troops exhibited at Trenton, and you cannot imagine my joy on being told that of the 1,950 Hessians engaged in the fight, but 345 escaped. There were just 1,605 men killed, and I cannot sufficiently commend your prudence in sending an exact list of the dead to my minister in London. This precaution was the more necessary, as the report sent to the English ministry does not give but 1,455 dead. This would make 483,450 florins instead of the 643,500 which I am entitled to demand under our convention. You will comprehend the prejudice which such an error would work in my finances, and I do not doubt you will take the necessary pains to prove that Lord North's list is false and yours correct.

The court of London objects that there were a hundred wounded who ought not to be included in the list, nor paid for as dead; but I trust you will not overlook my instructions to you on quitting Cassel, and that you will not have tried by human succor to recall to life the unfortunates whose days could not be lengthened but by the loss of a leg or an arm.

One of Franklin's minor, but annoying problems was the demand on his time for introductions and recommendations. To Europe, he was "Mr. America," and every merchant who would trade with the colonies, every officer who sought a commission, came to Franklin. He wrote to a friend:

YOU CAN HAVE no conception how I am harassed. All my friends are sought out and teased to tease me. Great officers of all ranks, in all departments; ladies, great and small, besides professed solicitors, worry me from morning to night. The noise of every coach now that enters my court terrifies me. I am afraid to accept an invitation to dine abroad, being almost sure of meeting with some officer or officer's friend, who, as soon as I am put in good humor by a glass or two of champagne, begins his attack upon me. Luckily I do not often in my sleep dream of these vexatious situations, or I should be afraid of what are now my only hours of comfort. If, therefore, you have the least remaining kindness for me, if you would not help to drive me out of France, for God's sake, my dear friend, let this, your twenty-third application, be your last.

Sometimes he could not avoid recommending an officer to Washington—if, for instance, the man was sent to him by Vergennes. To the Commander-in-Chief he wrote, "It is with regret that I give letters of introduction to foreign officers, fearing that you may be troubled with more than you can provide for, or employ to their and your own satisfaction. When particular cases seem to have a claim to such letters I hope you will excuse my taking the liberty."

Franklin seemed to sense that one "particular case" was a man named Steuben—an out-of-work German captain who had served on the staff of Frederick the Great. In a letter to Washington, Franklin said, "The gentleman who will have the honor of waiting upon you is the Baron von Steuben, lately a lieutenant-general in the King of Prussia's service. . . . He is recommended to us by two of the best judges of military merit in this country, M. de Vergennes and M. de St. Germain." Without Franklin's promotion from captain to lieutenant-general, combined with the dropping of important French names, Steuben might never have had the opportunity to reorganize and train the misfit American army at Valley Forge and bring them up to a state of discipline matching the British.

Lafayette was already with Washington, who had virtually adopted the young nobleman, but Franklin became involved in helping to take care of him. He wrote to the general:

SIR: The Marquis de Lafayette, a young nobleman of great expectations and exceedingly beloved here, is by this time probably with you. . . . His friends here have sent him over about £ 500 sterling; and have proposed sending him more; but on reflection, knowing the extreme generosity of his disposition, and fearing that some of his necessitous and artful countrymen may impose on his goodness, they wish to put his money into the hands of some discreet friend, who may supply him from time to time, and by that means knowing his expenses, may take occasion to advise him, if necessary, with a friendly affection, and secure him from too much imposition. They accordingly have desired us to name such a person to them. We have not been able to think of one so capable, and so suitable from the influence of situation, to perform that kind of office, as General Washington, under whose eye the gentleman will probably be. We beg, therefore in his behalf, what his friends out of respect would not take the liberty of asking, that your Excellency would be pleased to furnish him with what money he may want in moderation, and take his drafts payable to us for the sums paid him, which we shall receive here and apply to the public service. We also join with his family in their earnest request that you would favor him with your counsels, which you may be assured will be an act of benevolence gratefully remembered and acknowledged, by a number of very worthy persons here who interest themselves extremely in the welfare of that amiable young nobleman.

The last half of 1777 was the low point for the colonies. The commissioners in France received little news from Congress. The British fleet had virtually isolated Franklin in France. Vergennes had told the King, as early as July, that something more than secret aid was necessary for the Americans, but the King was reluctant to risk war with England unless Spain would come in, and Spain, although she wanted to hurt England, was not anxious to see the English colonies in the new world achieve independence—it might give the Spanish colonies ideas. When Burgoyne took Fort Ticonderoga in July, Vergennes stalled on an appeal from the commissioners for an alliance, and when the news of Howe's capture of Philadelphia reached France in November, he became more evasive. Then, on the morning of December 4, 1777, a messenger arrived from Boston with the news of the defeat of Burgoyne at Saratoga.

Franklin rushed the news to Vergennes. The latter immediately suggested that the envoys renew their proposal for an alliance. Franklin drew up a new draft and, on December 8, his grandson Temple delivered it to the French foreign office. There were secret night meetings between the commissioners and Vergennes, at which the Frenchman said that they must wait for word from Spain—Louis XVI would not act except in concert with his neighbor.

Meanwhile Paul Wentworth, head of British intelligence, appeared in Paris to propose a truce and open negotiations for a reconciliation. Franklin at first refused to see him, but Silas Deane had several meetings with him—which Franklin reported to Vergennes. When word came that Spain would not sign the treaty, Franklin sent for Wentworth. A rumor promptly swept through Paris that Britain and the colonies were about to make

peace and that the Americans would then join the British in con-
quering the French and Spanish colonies in the West Indies.
When Vergennes informed the King that Franklin was talking to
Wentworth, His Majesty promptly decided to approve the alliance independently of Spain.

Franklin left no record of his talk with Wentworth. The
latter reported it in full, saying that he pointed out to Franklin
that England was offering everything that he had ever asked for.
Franklin said "that any of the different opinions he had given
would have done at the time they were given" but the picture
had since changed. According to Wentworth, "he worked himself up into a passion of resentment. . . . I never knew him so
eccentric. Nobody says less, generally, and keeps a point more
closely in view, but he was diffuse and unmethodical today."
Apparently, it never occurred to Wentworth that Franklin was
playing with him and stalling for time. Some historians speculate
that Franklin, through Whig friends in England, had engineered
Wentworth's visit solely to put pressure on the French for
prompt action.

Franklin wrote to America—

ON THE SUCCESS of our negotiations here, in the completion
of the two treaties with his most Christian Majesty; the one
of amity and commerce, on the plan of that proposed by
Congress, with some good additions; the other of alliance for
mutual defense, in which the most Christian King agrees to
make a common cause with the United States, if England
attempts to obstruct the commerce of his subjects with them;
and guarantees to the United States their liberty, sovereignty and independence, absolute and unlimited, with all
the possessions they now have, or may have, at the conclusion of the war; and the States in return guarantee to him
his possessions in the West Indies. The great principle in
both treaties is a perfect equality and reciprocity; no advantage to be demanded by France, or privileges in commerce,

which the States may not grant to any and every other nation.

In short the King has treated us generously and magnanimously; taken no advantage of our present difficulties, to exact terms which we would not willingly grant, when established in prosperity and power. I may add that he has acted wisely, in wishing the friendship contracted by these treaties may be durable, which probably might not be if a contrary conduct had taken place.

When the treaties were to be signed, on February 5, 1778, Franklin showed up wearing an old blue velvet suit. The signing was delayed a day by the illness of the French representative and, the next day, Franklin again wore the ancient garment. Silas Deane asked him why. "To give it a little revenge," said Franklin. "I wore this coat on the day Wedderburn abused me at Whitehall." The English saw this as a sign that Franklin was holding a grudge. Franklin undoubtedly did it more in amusement than anger.

With the signing of the French treaties the English Parliament promptly passed two bills recognizing the Continental Congress and offering the colonies everything they had ever asked for, short of outright independence. There was a race across the Atlantic between a British frigate carrying copies of the bills and a French ship carrying the treaties. The English won. While some members of Congress were advocating consideration of the English proposal, the French ship arrived with the treaties, which were ratified two days later. Franklin's diplomacy had done more than Washington's army to assure the ultimate victory.

One man who was very unhappy about the part that Franklin had played was George III. He wrote a very unkingly letter in which he said:

THE MANY INSTANCES of the inimical conduct of Franklin toward this country makes me aware that hatred to this

country is the constant object of his mind and therefore I
trust that, fearing the rebellion, colonies may accept the
generous offers I am enabled by Parliament to make them
by the Commissioners now to be sent to America; that his
chief aim in what he has thrown out is to prevent their going,
or to draw out of administration an inclination to go further
lengths than the act of Parliament will authorize. That information from him may prevent America from concluding
with the Commissioners.

Yet I think it so desirable to end the war with that country,
to be enabled, with redoubled ardor, to avenge the faithless
and insolent conduct of France, that I think it may be
proper to keep open the channel of intercourse with that
insidious man.

CHAPTER X

THE IDOL OF FRANCE

❧

DEAR SALLY: . . . The clay medallion of me you say you gave to Mr. Hopkinson was the first of the kind made in France. A variety of others have been made since of different sizes; some to be set in the lids of snuff boxes, and some so small as to be worn in rings; and the numbers sold are incredible. These, with the pictures, busts, and prints (of which copies upon copies are spread everywhere), have made your father's face as well known as that of the moon, so that he durst not do anything that would oblige him to run away, as his phiz would discover him wherever he should venture to show it. It is said by learned etymologists that the name *doll,* for the images children play with, is derived from the word IDOL. From the number of *dolls* now made of him, he may be truly said, in that sense, to be *i-doll-ized* in this country.

So Franklin wrote to his daughter in 1779—and other sources indicate that his statement was not an exaggeration. It seemed that no well-ordered home in France was complete without a portrait of the American sage over the fireplace. There is an

anecdote that Louis XVI became so fed up with hearing the
Comtesse de Polignac sing the praises of the great American,
that he presented her with a chamber pot decorated with Franklin's picture. French intellectuals had long honored him as a
scientist. The French bourgeoisie revered him as the wise author
of *Bonhomme Richard*. Now French society made a pet of the
rustic philosopher, as they insisted on considering Franklin.

His natural wit, charm, good nature and good manners had
much to do with this. In the eyes of Catholic France he was,
perhaps, the only civilized American at a time when almost all
Americans hated and feared Catholics and considered all French
immoral. Franklin was at home anywhere—in the salons of
society, the Assembly of the savants, at the table of the diplo-
mats.

Franklin's personal popularity was, literally, worth millions
to the United States. Vergennes favored all-out aid to the colonies, not because he loved America but because he hated England and saw a strong Britain as a dangerous threat to France.
But Vergennes needed support. Turgot, French Minister of
Finance, begrudged every franc that bought guns for the rebels.
And it was unnatural for France's young King to support a
rebellion against a fellow monarch. Although Louis XVI was
more interested in boar hunting and tinkering with locks than
in international politics, he was the head of the most absolute
monarchy in Europe.

The love of the French for Franklin did not extend to his
fellow commissioners. In most of the negotiations, Deane was
off at the side, still dealing with Beaumarchais. Lee rubbed
Vergennes, and almost everybody else, the wrong way. He was
convinced that Deane was dishonest and that Franklin was
"concerned in the plunder, and that in time we shall collect the
proof." His letters to Congress caused the recall of Deane—
against whom there was never any proof of dishonesty. He wrote
repeatedly to Franklin demanding accounts, which Deane had

handled. When Franklin did not answer him, he wrote a particularly strong letter, saying "I trust, sir, that you will think with me that I have a right to know your reasons for treating me thus. If you have anything to accuse me of, avow it, and I will answer you. If you have not, why do you act so inconsistently with your duty to the public and so injuriously to me? . . . Is this the example you, in your superior wisdom think proper to set, of order, decorum, confidence and justice?"

This elicited from Franklin the angriest letter that he ever wrote:

IT IS TRUE THAT I omitted answering some of your letters. I do not like to answer angry letters. I am old, cannot have long to live, and have much to do and have no time for altercation. If I have often received and borne your magisterial snubbings and rebukes without reply, ascribe it to the right causes: my concern for the honor and success of our mission which would be hurt by our quarreling, my love of peace, my respect for your good qualities, and my pity for your sick mind, which is forever tormenting itself with its jealousies, suspicions and fancies that others mean you ill, wrong you, or fail in their respect of you. If you do not cure yourself in this temper it will end in insanity, of which it is a symptomatic forerunner, as I have seen in several instances. God preserve you from so terrible an evil; and for His sake pray suffer me to live in quiet.

It is probable that Franklin never sent this letter. He wrote another two days later which, while it was far from friendly, did not call Lee crazy. Lee was justified in the belief that things were being kept from him. Vergennes thought that the leak to the British was through Lee, and insisted that dealings with Franklin be kept from his fellow commissioners. The situation among the envoys improved somewhat when John Adams arrived to replace Deane.

Adams wrote a description of Franklin, the idol of France. "Franklin's reputation," he said, "was more universal than that of Leibniz or Newton, Frederick or Voltaire, and his character more beloved and esteemed than any or all of them. . . . His name was familiar to government and people, to kings, courtiers, nobility, clergy and philosophers, as well as plebeians, to such a degree that there was scarcely a peasant or a citizen, a *valet de chambre*, coachman or footman, a lady's chambermaid or a scullion in a kitchen who was not familiar with it and who did not consider him a friend to humankind. . . . When they spoke of him they seemed to think he was to restore the golden age."

Despite this, Adams did not like Franklin. He thought that he was too easygoing, too subservient to the French. Adams was more inclined to demand that which Franklin politely requested. Franklin got what he asked for. Adams did not get what he demanded. In describing the old doctor's tactics, Adams said, "He loves his ease, hates to offend, and seldom gives any opinion till obliged to do it. . . . Although he has as determined a soul as any man, yet it is his constant policy never to say yes or no decidedly but when he cannot avoid it." In his criticism, Adams did not realize that he was describing a master diplomat.

One of Adams' first official acts in Paris was to advise Congress that American affairs could be better handled by one commissioner than by three. Lee had already suggested this, adding that he was the man for the job. Geraud, French ambassador to the United States, assured Congress that Lee would not be acceptable. Congress appointed Franklin sole Minister Plenipotentiary to the French Court in September, 1778.

For Franklin, the remaining war years were busy but pleasant. He had taken a small house on the estate of a nobleman at Passy, a suburb of Paris, where he lived comfortably. To Margaret Stevenson, his longtime English landlady, he wrote:

YOU WISH TO KNOW how I live. It is in a fine house, situated in a neat village, on high ground, half a mile from Paris, with a large garden to walk in. I have abundance of aquaintance, dine abroad six days in seven. Sundays I reserve to dine at home, with such Americans as pass this way, and I then have my grandson Ben, with some other American children from the school.

If being treated with all the politeness of France, and the apparent respect and esteem of all ranks, from the highest to the lowest, can make a man happy, I ought to be so. Indeed, I have nothing to complain of, but a little too much business, and the want of that order and economy in my family, which reigned in it when under your prudent direction.

The ambassador whose watchword was frugality lived well. Dinner consisted of a roast, followed by game or fowl, with two vegetables, two sweets, fruit, cheese, bonbons, ices and wine. The inventory of the wine cellar showed 1,040 bottles in 1779. John Adams said that he lived extravagantly, and John's wife Abigail thought that the rented coach and uniformed coachman was a needless expense. Although Franklin himself said, later, that frugality was "a virtue I could never acquire in myself," he undoubtedly lived more economically than any other ambassador to the French court.

He had time for some letter writing—to persons as diverse as eleven-year-old John Quincy Adams and General George Washington. Franklin was at his most charming with children, who adored the old man. He received many letters from French schoolchildren, merely to wish him well. Young John Quincy addressed him as "Dear Friend" despite a difference in age of more than sixty years, and Franklin called the future President "Dear Master Johnny." In reply to Washington's letter of commendation for Lafayette, Franklin wrote—when the Marquis finally showed it to him—

SIR: I have received but lately the letter your Excellency did me the honor of writing to me in recommendation of the Marquis de Lafayette. His modesty detained it long in his own hands. We became acquainted, however, from the time of his arrival at Paris; and his zeal for the honor of our country, his activity in our affairs here, and his firm attachment to our cause and to you, impressed me with the same regard and esteem for him that your Excellency's letter would have done, had it been immediaely delivered to me.

Should peace arrive after another campaign or two, and afford us a little leisure, I should be happy to see your Excellency in Europe, and to accompany you, if my age and strength should permit, in visiting some of its ancient and most famous kingdoms. You would, on this side of the sea, enjoy the great reputation you have acquired, pure and free from those little shades that the jealousy and envy of a man's countrymen and contemporaries are ever endeavoring to cast over living merit. Here you would know and enjoy what posterity will say of Washington. For a thousand leagues have nearly the same effect with a thousand years. The feeble voice of those groveling passions cannot extend so far either in time or distance. At present I enjoy that pleasure for you; as I frequently hear the old generals of this martial country, who study the maps of America, and mark upon them all your operations, speak with sincere approbation and great applause of your conduct; and join in giving you the character of one of the greatest captains of the age.

I must soon quit this scene, but you may live to see our country flourish, as it will amazingly and rapidly after the war is over; like a field of young Indian corn, which long fair weather and sunshine had enfeebled and discolored, and which in that weak state, by a thunder-gust of violent wind, hail and rain, seemed to be threatened with absolute destruction; yet the storm being past, it recovers fresh verdure, shoots up with double vigor, and delights the eye, not of its owner only, but of every observing traveler.

He wrote one of his frequent letters to daughter Sarah, lecturing her on frugality. Although Sarah's son Benjamin was with Franklin in Europe, he never seemed to realize that his darling Sally had grown up. He wrote, "I was charmed with the account you gave me of your industry, the tablecloths of your own spinning, etc.; but the latter part of the paragraph, that you had sent for linen from France, because weaving and flax were grown dear, alas, that dissolved the charm; and your sending for long black pins, and lace, and feathers! disgusted me as much as if you had put salt into my strawberries. The spinning, I see, is laid aside, and you are to be dressed for the ball! You seem not to know, my dear daughter, that of all the dear things in this world, idleness is the dearest, except mischief. . . ."

Although, during the years before the peace treaty, Franklin did not have much time for scientific experiments, he did keep up his correspondence with fellow scientists in Europe, including England. In 1779 his *Political, Miscellaneous and Philosophical Pieces* was published in England with a title page that called him "The Minister Plenipotentiary at the Court of Paris for the United States of America"—at a time when Great Britain did not recognize the existence of such a country. His conjectures concerning the cause of the Aurora Borealis were published in both England and France in 1778. In this speculation he said, in part:

AIR HEATED by any means becomes rarefied and specifically lighter than other air in the same situation not heated.

Air being thus made lighter rises, and the neighboring cooler, heavier air takes its place. . . .

The air heated between the tropics is continually rising,

its place is supplied by northerly and southerly winds which come from the cooler regions. . . .

The great quantity of vapor rising between the tropics forms clouds, which contain much electricity.

Some of them fall in rain before they come to the polar region. . . .

Water, though naturally a good conductor, will not conduct well when frozen into ice by a common degree of cold; not at all where the cold is extreme. . . .

The great cake of ice that eternally covers those regions may be too hard frozen to permit the electricity, descending with the snow, to enter the earth.

It will therefore be accumulated upon that ice.

The atmosphere, being heavier in the polar regions than in the equatorial, will there be lower . . . consequently the distance to the vacuum above the atmosphere will be less at the poles than elsewhere. . . .

The vacuum above is a good conductor.

May not then the great quantity of electricity brought into the polar regions by the clouds, which are condensed there and fall into snow, which electricity would enter the earth but cannot penetrate the ice; may it not, I say . . . break through that low atmosphere and run along in the vacuum over the air toward the equator, diverging as the degrees of longitude enlarge, strongly visible where densest, and becoming less visible as it more diverges; till it finds a passage to the earth in more temperate climates, or is mingled with their upper air?

If such an operaton of nature were really performed, would it not give all of the appearances of an *aurora borealis?*

Although Franklin had little time for experiments, he encouraged others to keep up the search for truth in nature. To Priestley he wrote, "The rapid progress true science now makes occasions my regretting sometimes that I was born too soon. It is impossible to imagine the height to which may be carried, in a thousand years, the power of man over matter. . . . O that mortal science were in as fair a way of improvement, that men would cease to be wolves to one another, and that human beings would at length learn what they now improperly call humanity."

The beginning of Franklin's physical decline started late in 1780, although early that year he had shown no evidence of it when he wrote to a friend and physician in Philadelphia, saying: "For my own part, I do not find that I grow any older. Being arrived at seventy, and considering that by traveling farther in the same road I should probably be led to the grave, I stopped short, turned about, and walked back again: which having done these four years, you may now call me sixty-six. Advise those old friends of ours to follow my example; keep up your spirits, and that will keep up your bodies; you will no more stoop under the weight of age than if you had swallowed a handspike."

By the end of this year he was laid low with a six weeks' attack of gout, a painful and annoying ailment that never fully left him. But his malady could not repress his unfailing humor. When pain kept him awake, he wrote his *Dialog Between Franklin and the Gout,* dating it "Midnight, 22 October, 1780."

Franklin: Eh! oh! eh! What have I done to merit these cruel sufferings?

Gout: Many things: you have ate and drank too freely, and too much indulged those legs of yours in their indolence.

Franklin: Who is it that accuses me?

Gout: It is I, even I, the Gout.

Franklin: What! My enemy in person?

Gout: No, not your enemy.

Franklin: I repeat it, my enemy; for you would not only torment my body to death, but ruin my good name; you reproach me as a glutton and a tippler; now all the world, that knows me, will allow that I am neither the one nor the other.

Gout: The world may think as it pleases; it is always very complaisant to itself, and sometimes to its friends; but I very well know that the quantity of meat and drink proper for a man who takes a reasonable degree of exercise, would be too much for another who never takes any. . . . Let us examine your course of life. While the mornings are long, and you have leisure to go abroad, what do you do? Why, instead of gaining an appetite for breakfast, by salutary exercise, you amuse yourself with books, pamphlets or newspapers, which commonly are not worth the reading. Yet you eat an inordinate breakfast, four dishes of tea, with cream, and one or two buttered toasts, with slices of hung beef, which I fancy are not things the most easily digested. Immediately afterward you sit down to write at your desk, or converse with persons who apply to you on business. Thus the time passes till one, without any kind of bodily exercise. But all this I could pardon, in regard, as you say to your sedentary condition. But what is your practice after dinner? Walking in the beautiful gardens of those friends with whom you have dined would be the choice of men of sense; yours is to be fixed down to chess, where you are found engaged for two or three hours! . . . Wrapt in the speculations of this wretched game, you destroy your constitution. What can be expected from such a course of living, but a body replete with stagnant humors, ready to fall a prey to all kinds of dangerous maladies, if I, the Gout, did not occasionally bring you relief by agitating those humors, and so purifying or dissipating them?

Franklin: Oh! eh! oh! Ohhh! As much instruction as you please, Madam Gout, and as many reproaches; but pray, Madam, a truce with your corrections! . . . It is not fair to say I take no exercise, when I do very often, going out to dine and returning in my carriage. . . .

Gout: Flatter yourself then no longer, that half an hour's airing in your carriage deserves the name of exercise. Providence has appointed few to roll in carriages, while he has given to all a pair of legs, which are machines infinitely more commodious and serviceable. Be grateful, then, and make a proper use of yours. . . .

Franklin: Your reasonings grow very tiresome.

Gout: I stand corrected. I will be silent and continue my office; take that, and that.

Franklin: Oh! Ohh! Talk on, I pray you.

Gout: No, no; I have a good number of twinges for you tonight; and you may be sure of some more tomorrow.

Franklin: What, with such a fever! I shall go distracted. Oh! eh! Can no one bear it for me?

Gout: Ask that of your horses; they have served you faithfully. . . . I have here a list of offenses against your own health distinctly written, and can justify every stroke inflicted on you.

Franklin: Read it then.

Gout: Do you remember how often you have promised yourself, the following morning, a walk in the grove of Boulogne, in the garden de la Muette, or in your own garden, and have violated your promise, alleging, at one time, it was too cold, at another, too warm, too windy, too moist, or what else you pleased; when in truth it was too nothing, but your insuperable love of ease? . . . You know M. Brillon's gardens and what fine walks they contain; you know the handsome flight of a hundred steps, which lead from the terrace above to the lawn below. . . . What an opportunity was here for you to have had exercise. . . . Did you embrace it, and how often?

Franklin: I cannot immediately answer that question.

Gout: I will do it for you: Not once.

Franklin: Not once?

Gout: Even so. . . . On the contrary, you call for tea and the chessboard; and lo! you are occupied in your seat till nine o'clock, and that besides two hours' play after dinner; and then instead of walking home, which would have bestirred you a little, you step into your carriage. . . .

Franklin: Ah! how tiresome you are! . . . Oh! oh!—for Heaven's sake leave me! and I promise faithfully never more to play at chess, but to take exercise daily, and live temperately.

Gout: I know you too well. You promise fair, but after a few months of good health, you will return to your old habits; your fine promises will be forgotten like the forms of the last year's clouds. Let us then finish the account, and I will go. But I leave you with an assurance of visiting you again at a proper time and place; for my object is your good, and you are sensible now that I am your real friend.

Franklin was involved in every aspect of Franco-American affairs, even those in which he had no experience. A projected invasion of England, with Lafayette handling the landing force and John Paul Jones in command of the fleet, is supposed to have originated with the French Marquis, but a letter from Franklin to Layfayette indicates that, if he did not propose it, he certainly helped plan it.

The joint expedition was overruled by the King and Jones set out alone with a squadron headed by a converted merchantman, *Le Duc de Duras,* which he had renamed the *Bonhomme Richard* in honor of Franklin. When he left for the cruise which ended in the epic battle with the *Serapis,* Jones carried orders from Franklin which read, in part: "You are to bring to France all the English seamen you may happen to take prisoners, in order to complete the good work you have already made such progress in, of delivering by an exchange the rest of our countrymen now languishing in the jails of Great Britain."

The old doctor seemed to be more distressed by what he considered British inhumanities in conducting the war than by political differences. If war there must be, let it be a humane one. When Edmund Burke wrote him relative to Burgoyne's parole, he replied, "Since the foolish part of mankind will make wars from time to time to settle with each other, not having sense enough otherwise to settle their differences, it certainly becomes the wiser part, who cannot prevent those wars, to alleviate as much as possible the calamities attending them." He thought that "unarmed trading ships, as well as fishermen and farmers, should be respected, as working for the common benefit of mankind, and never be interrupted in their operations, even by national enemies; but let only those fight with one another whose trade it is, and who are armed and paid for that purpose." To implement such a doctrine, he issued an annual safe conduct to British ships carrying supplies to the Moravian colony in Labrador, and gave this famous passport for Captain Cook:

To All Captains and Commanders of Armed Ships Acting by Commission from the Congress of the United States of America, Now in War with Great Britain.

Gentlemen: A ship having been fitted out from England before the commencement of this war, to make discoveries of new countries in unknown seas, under the conduct of that most celebrated navigator, Captain Cook; an undertaking truly laudable in itself, as the increase of geographical knowledge facilitates the communication between distant nations, in the exchange of useful products and manufactures, and the extension of arts, whereby the common enjoyments of human life are multiplied and augmented, and science of other kinds increased to the benefit of mankind in general; this is, therefore, most earnestly to recommend to every one of you that, in case the said ship, which is now expected to be soon in the European seas on her return, should happen to fall into your hands, you would not consider her as an enemy, nor suffer any plunder to be made of the effects contained in her, nor obstruct her immediate return to England, by detaining her or sending her into any other part of Europe or to America, but that you would treat the said Captain Cook and his people with all civility and kindness, affording them, as common friends to mankind, all the assistance in your power, which they may happen to stand in need of. In so doing you will not only gratify the generosity of your own disposition, but there is no doubt of your obtaining the approbation of Congress, and of your own American owners. I have the honor to be, etc.

At Passy, near Paris, this tenth day of March, 1779,

B. FRANKLIN
Minister Plenipotentiary from the Congress of the United States to the Court of France

The Royal Academy gave Franklin a gold medal struck in honor of Captain Cook—making the man whom George III considered England's worst enemy the only American to be honored by England for his conduct during the war.

But prisoners and passports, scientists and society were only sidelines with Franklin. His main work was raising money. The economics of the Revolution was unique. Congress had no authority to levy taxes in the states, and the individual states were reluctant to raise money for federal use by taxation—they were not yet sufficiently "united." So, year after year, Congress printed money, of which Franklin said, "The effect of paper currency is not understood on this side of the water. And indeed the whole is a mystery even to the politicians; how we have been able to continue a war for four years without money, and how we could pay with paper that had no previously fixed fund specifically to redeem it. This currency, as we manage it, is a wonderful machine. It performs its office when we issue it; it pays and clothes troops and provides victuals and ammunition; and when we are obliged to issue a quantity excessive, it pays itself off by depreciation."

The magical paper money might buy wheat and hay and

beef and pork at home, but it was worthless in Europe. Foreign goods must be paid for in hard cash. A trickle of American commodities that got past British cruisers raised a little, but Franklin had to borrow or beg the bulk of the money to finance the Revolution from a French government already hard pressed to pay their own share of war costs. Between 1778 and 1782, he raised 18,000,000 livres.

Although not adverse to diplomatically prying money out of the French, Franklin opposed the frantic scrambling for money around Europe. To Adams, in Holland, he wrote: "I have long been humiliated with the idea of our running from court to court begging for money and friendship, which are the more withheld the more eagerly they are solicited, and would perhaps have been offered if they had not been asked. The supposed necessity is our only excuse. The proverb says: 'God helps those who help themselves.' And the world, too, in this sense, is very godly."

Congress made his work more difficult, and his situation with Vergennes most embarrassing, by instructing him to borrow money for a particular purpose; spending it for something else; and then requesting another loan for the same purpose. Franklin said, "To apply again to this court for money for a particular purpose, which they had already over and over again provided for, was extremely awkward."

But Congress was sure that Dr. Franklin would provide. When they instructed him to borrow they did not wait for the loan to be confirmed, they issued drafts against it which were sent to Franklin for payment until "the drafts of the treasurer of the loans coming very fast upon me, the anxiety I have suffered, and the distress of mind lest I should not be able to pay them, have for a long time been very great indeed." Later, he wrote, "The Congress have drawn on me very considerably for other purposes, which has sometimes greatly embarrassed me, but I have duly accepted and found means to pay their drafts; so that their credit in Europe has been well supported. But, if every agent of Congress in different parts of the world is permitted to run in debt, and draw upon me at pleasure to support his credit, under the idea of its being necessary to do so for the honor of Congress, the difficulty upon me will be too great, and I may in fine be obliged to protest the interest bills. I therefore beg that a stop may be put to such irregular proceedings."

To Jay, in Spain, he wrote: "The storm of bills which I found coming upon us both has terrified and vexed me to such a degree that I have been deprived of sleep, and so much indisposed by continual anxiety as to be almost incapable of writing." To Adams, in Holland, he said: "This has, among other things made me quite sick of my Gideonite office—that of drawing water for the whole congregation of Israel."

In 1780, when military affairs in the southern colonies were at low ebb and Congress had been forced to repudiate the paper currency by another issue which replaced forty old dollars for one new one, Washington wrote to Franklin that America must have either peace or more money. Franklin appealed again to Vergennes. "He assured me of the King's good will to the United States; remarking, however, that being on the spot I must be sensible to the great expense France was actually engaged in, and the difficulty of providing it." The King could not loan the twenty-five million livres that Franklin requested, but, "to give the states a signal proof of his friendship, His Majesty had resolved to grant them the sum of six million, not as a loan, but as a free gift." Franklin claimed that the King stipulated that the money could be drawn on only by Washington. He said that he himself "remarked that it was not the usage with us for the general to draw. . . . But I was told that it was His Majesty's order. . . . It was thought best to put it into the General's hands that it might not get into those of different boards or committees who might think themselves under a necessity of diverting it to other purposes. There was no room to dispute on this point, every donor having the right of qualifying his gifts with such terms as he thinks proper."

It seems strange that locksmith Louis XVI would have been shrewd enough to make such a stipulation. Vergennes or Turgot might have—but the idea may have originated with Franklin's frustration at Congress' financial irresponsibility. He knew that Washington could be trusted not to draw on him for money that was not there.

CHAPTER XI

THE PEACEMAKER

ॐ

To generations of Americans the Revolution ended when Corn-wallis surrendered at Yorktown on October 19, 1781. It did not end for Franklin for another two years. The fighting on land between the British and Americans was over, but the war —which now involved France, Spain and Holland—went on, while Franklin trod the toilsome trail of the peacemaker.

Franklin had talked and written of peace throughout the war. The English dissenters seemed to believe that only Franklin's approval was necessary to end the conflict, and put out constant feelers as to what terms would be acceptable. At about the time the French treaty of alliance was signed, Franklin had been approached with a peace offer from London which he gave to Deane to bring back to America. Later, Franklin wrote to Deane, "The negotiator is gone back, apparently much cha-grined at his little success. I have promised him faithfully that since his propositions could not be accepted they should be buried in oblivion. I therefore earnestly desire that you would put that paper immediately in the fire on receipt of this, without taking or suffering to be taken any copy of it or communicating its contents."

In April, 1778, David Hartley, Whig M.P. and good friend of Franklin's, came to Paris to talk peace and Franklin wrote to Vergennes detailing his position on England's halfway peace overtures:

SIR: Mr. Hartley, a member of Parliament, an old acquaintance of mine, arrived here from London on Sunday last. He is generally in the opposition, especially on American questions, but has some respect for Lord North. In conversation, he expressed the strongest anxiety for peace with America, and appeared extremely desirous to know my sentiments of the terms which might probably be accepted if offered; whether America would not, to obtain peace, grant some superior advantages in trade to Britain, and enter into an alliance, offensive and defensive; whether, if war should be declared against France, we had obliged ourselves by treaty to join with her against England.

My answers have been that the United States were not fond of war, and with the advice of their friends would probably be easily prevailed with to make peace on equitable terms; but we had no terms committed to us to propose, and I did not choose to mention any; that Britain, having injured us heavily by making this unjust war upon us, might think herself well off, if on reparation of those injuries we admitted her to equal advantages with other nations in commerce, but certainly she had no reason to expect superior; that her known fondness for war, and the many instances of her readiness to engage in wars on frivolous occasions, were probably sufficient to cause an immediate rejection of every proposition for an offensive alliance with her; and that, if she made war against France on our account, a peace with us at the same time was impossible; for that, having met with friendship from that generous nation, when we were cruelly oppressed by England, we were under ties stronger than treaties could form, to make common cause; which we should certainly do to the utmost of our power. . . .

I thought it right to give your Excellency an account of these interviews, and to acquaint you with my intention of avoiding such hereafter; as I see but little prospect of utility in them, and think they are very liable to hurtful misrepresentations.

During his Paris visit Hartley formed the impression that Franklin was in personal danger—from what source is not clear. On his return to London, he wrote: "Take care of your own safety; events are uncertain, and men may be capricious." In his voluminous correspondence Franklin never indicated concern for his own safety. In this instance he answered, "I thank you for your kind caution, but having nearly finished a long life, I set but little value on what remains of it. Like a draper, when one chaffers with him for a remnant, I am ready to say: 'As it is only the fag end, I will not differ with you about it; take it for what you please.' Perhaps the best use such an old fellow can be put to, is to make a martyr of him."

Franklin was convinced that no treaty could be made with the British government headed by Lord North and completely subservient to the King. During 1778 and early 1779, he reiterated this in several letters replying to feelers put out by Hartley, and became vehement on the subject in answering a letter in which the English M.P. talked of a proposal that would drive a wedge between America and France.

I HAVE JUST RECEIVED your favor of the twenty-third past, in which you mention that "the alliance between France and America is the great stumbling block in the way of making peace," and you go on to observe that "whatever engagements America may have entered into, they may (at least by consent of parties) be relinquished, for the purpose of removing so material an obstacle to any general treaty of free and unengaged parties," adding that "if the parties could meet for the sake of peace upon free and open ground, you should think that a very fair proposition to be offered to the people of England, and an equitable proposition in itself."

The long, steady and kind regard you have shown for the welfare of America, by the whole tenor of your conduct in parliament, satisfies me that this proposition never took its rise with you, but has been suggested from some other quarter; and that your excess of humanity, your love of peace, and your fears for us that the destruction we are threatened with will certainly be effected, have thrown a mist before your eyes, which hinders you from seeing the malignity and mischief of it. We know that your King hates Whigs and Presbyterians; that he thirsts for our blood, of which he has already drunk large drafts; that his servile unprincipled ministers are ready to execute the wickedest of his orders, and his venal parliament equally ready to vote them just. Not the smallest appearance of a reason can be imagined capable of inducing us to think of relinquishing a solid alliance with one of the most amiable, as well as most powerful princes of Europe, for the expectation of unknown terms of peace, to be afterward offered to us by such a government; a government that has already shamefully broke all the compacts it ever made with us! . . . Had Lord North been the author of such a proposition, all the world would have said it was insidious, and meant only to deceive and divide us from our friends, and then to ruin us; supposing our fears might be strong enough to procure an acceptance of it; but thanks to God that is not the case! We have long since settled all the account in our own minds. We know the worst you can do to us, if you have your wish, is to confiscate our estates and take our lives, to rob and murder us; and this you have seen we are ready to hazard, rather than come again under your detested government.

In February, 1780, John Adams returned to Paris at the suggestion of Vergennes, to explore the possibilities of peace. This mission was to be kept secret, supposedly even from Franklin. But not much went on in Paris that the old doctor did not know. Within a few days of Adams' arrival, he wrote to Hartley:

IF CONGRESS HAVE therefore entrusted to others rather than to me, the negotiations for peace, when such shall be set on foot, as has been reported, it is perhaps because they may have heard of a very singular opinion of mine, that there hardly ever existed such a thing as a bad peace or a good war, and that I might therefore easily be induced to make improper concessions. But at the same time they and you may be assured that I should think the destruction of our whole country, and the extirpation of our whole people, preferable to the infamy of abandoning our allies.

As neither you nor I are at present authorized to treat of peace, it seems to little purpose to make or consider propositions relating to it. I have had so many such put into my hands, that I am tired of them.

Franklin carefully ignored the dealings between Adams and Vergennes, which did not last long because Adams' manner so annoyed the French minister. Adams blamed Franklin for this and became fully convinced that he was more interested in gaining the aims of France than those of America. After the failure of his mission, Adams went on to Holland and Franklin wrote to Samuel Huntington, president of Congress, a letter which indicated his opinion of Adams as a diplomat and implied his resentment at the negotiations attempted behind his back:

MR. ADAMS HAS GIVEN offense to the court here by some sentiments and expressions contained in several of his letters written to the Count de Vergennes. I mention this with reluctance, though perhaps it would have been my duty to acquaint you with such a circumstance, even if it were not required of me by the minister himself. He has sent me copies of the correspondence, desiring I would communicate them to Congress; and I send them herewith. Mr. Adams did not show me his letters before he sent them. . . . He thinks, as he tells me himself, that America has been too free in expressions of gratitude to France; for that she is more obliged to us than we to her; and that we should show spirit in our applications. I apprehend that he mistakes his ground, and that this court is to be treated with decency and delicacy. The King, a young and virtuous prince, has, I am persuaded, a pleasure in reflecting on the generous benevolence of the action in assisting an oppressed people, and proposes it as a part of the glory of his reign. I think it right to increase this pleasure by our thankful acknowledgments, and that such an expression of gratitude is not only our duty, but our interest. A different conduct seems to me what is not only improper and unbecoming, but what may be hurtful to us. Mr. Adams, on the other hand, who, at the same time, means our welfare and interest as much as I, or any man, can do, seems to think a little apparent stoutness, and a greater air of independence and boldness in our demands, will procure us more ample assistance. It is for Congress to judge and regulate their affairs accordingly.

M. de Vergennes, who appears much offended, told me yesterday, that he would enter into no further discussions with Mr. Adams, nor answer any more of his letters. . . . It is my intention, while I stay here, to procure what advantages I can for our country, by endeavoring to please this court; and I wish I could prevent anything being said by any of our countrymen here that may have a contrary effect, and increase an opinion lately showing itself in Paris, that we seek a difference, and with a view of reconciling ourselves with England. Some of them have of late been very indiscreet in their conversations.

This abortive mission of Adams', combined with Franklin's frustration at Congress' unreasonable demands for money and the continuing efforts of Arthur Lee and his associates to undervalue him, probably prompted his resignation, which he tendered to the president of Congress in March, 1781—buried in the middle of a letter dealing with other matters:

I MUST NOW BEG LEAVE to say something relating to myself, a subject with which I have not often troubled the Congress. I have passed my seventy-fifth year, and I find that the long and severe fit of the gout which I had last winter, has shaken me exceedingly, and I am yet far from having recovered the bodily strength I before enjoyed. I do not know that my mental faculties are impaired—perhaps I shall be the last to discover that; but I am sensible of great diminution in my activity, a quality I think particularly necessary in your minister for the court. I am afraid, therefore, that your affairs may some time or other suffer by my deficiency. I find also, that the business is too heavy for me, and too confining. . . .

I have been engaged in public affairs, and enjoyed public confidence, in some shape or other, during the long term of fifty years, and honor sufficient to satisfy any reasonable ambition; and I have no other [thought?] left but that of repose, which I hope the Congress will grant me, by sending some person to supply my place. At the same time, I beg they may be assured that it is not any the least doubt of their success in the glorious cause, nor any disgust received in their service, that induces me to decline it, but purely and simply the reasons above mentioned.

It is probable that this resignation was a political move, that he neither hoped nor expected that it would be accepted. In any event, when Congress immediately refused to release him, he expressed pleasure rather than disappointment:

THE CONGRESS HAVE done me the honor to refuse accepting my resignation, and insist on my continuing in their service till the peace. I must therefore buckle again to business, and thank God that my health and spirits are of late improved. I fancy it may have been a double mortification to those enemies you have mentioned to me, that I should ask as a favor what they hoped to vex me by taking from me; and that I should nevertheless be continued. But this sort of consideration should never influence our conduct. We ought always to do what appears best to be done, without much regarding what others may think of it. I call this continuance an honor, and I really esteem it to be a greater than my first appointment, when I consider that all the interest of my enemies, united with my own request, were not sufficient to prevent it.

With the defeat of Cornwallis in October, 1781, peace negotiations became more positive—and much more complicated. Franklin was delighted by the victory at Yorktown. He heard of it in a note from Vergennes, which he duplicated with a copying press that he had invented and stayed up all night making copies, to be delivered to friends at dawn. But he was concerned that the United States might relax with victory and with the subsequent fall of the British government headed by Lord North. "Depend upon it," he said, "the King hates us cordially and will be content with nothing short of our extirpation." And, in another letter, "We must not . . . be lulled by these appearances. That nation is changeable. And though somewhat humbled at present, a little success may make them as insolent as ever. I remember that, when I was a boxing boy, it was allowed, even after an adversary said he had enough, to give him a rising blow. Let ours be a douser."

On the allied side, the complexities of peace negotiations were based on several treaties. The Franco-American treaty provided that neither party would make a separate peace. Spain was an ally of France, not of America. The Franco-Spanish treaty also provided that neither party would make a separate peace—as did a treaty with Holland. In effect, the United States could not make peace with England without the agreement of the three foreign countries. And Spain, particularly, had no interest in the aims of England's erstwhile colonies in the new world. Her sole concern was getting Gibraltar back from England. She rather opposed independence for the United States.

The situation in England was equally complex. Logically, Charles Fox should have succeeded Lord North as Prime Minister. Fox favored independence for the colonies, and George III would not ask a man with such opinions to lead the ministry. He offered the post to Lord Shelburne, who did not have sufficient following to form a government. Finally, the Marquis of Rockingham became Prime Minister, but the king would not talk to him, except through Shelburne. Fox became secretary of state for foreign affairs; Shelburne secretary for colonial affairs. Negotiations with France, Spain and Holland were in Fox's department—but, as the United States was not recognized as a foreign country, negotiations with the "colonies" was in Shelburne's.

To complete the confusion, Congress appointed five peace commissioners: Franklin, John Adams, John Jay, Henry Laurens and Thomas Jefferson. Adams was in Holland, Jay in Spain, Laurens a prisoner in the Tower of London—and Jefferson stayed in America. That left Franklin to handle, alone, the first involved steps of the peace negotiations, a task which he faced with mixed emotions. To Adams he wrote, "I have never known a peace made, even the most advantageous, that was not censured as inadequate, and the makers condemned as injudicious or corrupt. 'Blessed are the peacemakers' is, I suppose, to be understood in the other world; for in this they are frequently cursed. Being as yet rather too much attached to this world, I had therefore no ambition to be concerned in fabricating this peace. . . . I esteem it, however, as an honor."

The course of the negotiations for the first three months—from late March until the end of June, 1782—is recorded in detail in Franklin's *Journal of the Negotiations for Peace with Great Britain*. The journal began:

As, SINCE THE CHANGE of the ministry in England, some serious professions have been made of their disposition to peace, and of their readiness to enter into a general treaty for that purpose; and as the concerns and claims of five nations are to be discussed in that treaty, which must therefore be interesting to the present age and to posterity, I am inclined to keep a journal of the proceedings, so far as they come to my knowledge; and, to make it more complete, I will first endeavor to recollect what has already past. Great affairs sometimes take their rise from small circumstances. My good friend and neighbor, Madame Brillon, being at Nice all last winter for her health, with her very amiable family, wrote to me that she had met with some English gentry there, whose acquaintance proved agreeable; among them she named Lord Cholmondely, who, she said, had promised to call on his return to England, and drink tea with us at Passy.

When Lord Cholmondely called he said "that he knew Lord Shelburne had a great regard for me, and that he was sure his lordship would be pleased to hear from me." Franklin wrote a note for Cholmondely to deliver, congratulating Shelburne on "the returning good disposition of your country in favor of America, which appears in the late resolutions of the Commons. I am persuaded it will have good effects. I hope it will tend to produce a general peace, which I am sure that your lordship, with all good men, desires; which I wish to see before I die; and to which I shall, with infinite pleasure, contribute everything in my power."

The way in which Franklin used his wide personal relationships to grace official business is evidenced in the last paragraph of his letter to Shelburne. "Your friends, the Abbé Morellet and Madame Helvétius, are well. You have made the latter very happy by your present of gooseberry bushes, which arrived in five days and in excellent order." The opening note in a world-wide peace overture was also a thank you note for some goose-berry bushes.

Shelburne replied to Franklin's letter by sending a Mr. Oswald to Paris, saying: "He is a pacifical man and conversant in those negotiations which are most interesting to mankind. This has made me prefer him to any . . . person of higher rank. He is fully appraised of my mind, and you may give full credit to everything he assures you of." Oswald also brought a letter from Henry Laurens saying that he was out on parole (he had been captured at sea en route to Holland) and was going to see Adams at The Hague. Laurens pointed out that he could not function as a peace commissioner while he was a prisoner on parole and asked Franklin to try to arrange to have him ex-changed for Cornwallis. Franklin promptly arranged with Shel-burne to have him released unconditionally.

In his first talk with Oswald all Franklin could learn was "that the new ministry sincerely wished for a peace; that they considered the object of the war, to France and America, as obtained; that, if the independence of the United States was agreed to, there was no other point in dispute, and therefore nothing to hinder a pacification; that they were ready to treat of peace, but he intimated that if France should insist upon terms too humiliating to England, they would still continue the war, having yet great strength and many resources left. I let him know that America would not treat but in concert with France."

Franklin took Oswald to Vergennes where, after some spar-ring, "Mr. Oswald seemed to wish to obtain some propositions to carry back with him; but M. de Vergennes said to him, very properly: 'There are four nations engaged in the war against you who cannot, until they have consulted and know each

other's minds, be ready to make propositions. Your court being
without allies and alone, knowing its own mind, can express it
immediately. It is therefore more natural to expect the first
proposition from you!' "

Before Oswald returned to report to Shelburne, he and Franklin had another meeting in which the wily doctor started to lay
the groundwork for American claims beyond independence. He
says, in his *Journal:* "I then remarked that his nation seemed
to desire a reconciliation; that, to obtain this, the party which
had been the aggressor and had cruelly treated the other, should
show some marks of concern for what was past, and some disposition to make reparation; that perhaps there were things
which America might demand by way of reparation, and which
England might yield, and that the effect would be vastly greater
if they appeared to be voluntary, and to spring from returning
good will; that I, therefore, wished England would think of offering something to relieve those who had suffered by its scalping
and burning parties."

At this meeting, Franklin frequently referred to a paper in
his hand. Oswald asked to see it. "After some little delay, I
allowed him to read it; the following is an exact copy":

NOTES FOR CONVERSATION: To make a peace durable, what
may give occasion for future wars should if practicable be
removed.

The territory of the United States, and that of Canada,
by long extended frontiers, touch each other.

The settlers on the frontiers of the American provinces are
generally the most disorderly of the people, who, being far
removed from the eye and control of their respective governments, are more bold in committing offenses against neighbors, and are forever occasioning complaints and furnishing
matter for fresh differences between their states.

By the late debates in Parliament, and public writings, it
appears that Britain desires a reconciliation with the Amer-

icans. It is a sweet word. It means much more than mere peace, and what is heartily to be wished for. Nations make a peace whenever they are both weary of making war. But if one of them has made war upon the other unjustly, and has wantonly and unnecessarily done it great injuries, and refuses reparation, though there may, for the present, be peace, the resentment of those injuries will remain, and will break out again in vengeance when occasions offer. These occasions will be watched for by one side, feared by the other, and the peace will never be secure; nor can any cordiality subsist between them.

Many houses and villages have been burnt in America by the English and their allies, the Indians. I do not know that the Americans will insist on reparation; perhaps they may. But would it not be better for England to offer it? Nothing would have a greater tendency to conciliate, and much of the future commerce and returning intercourse between the two countries may depend on the reconciliation. Would not the advantage of reconciliation by such means be greater than the expense? . . .

Britain possesses Canada. Her chief advantage from that possession consists in the trade for peltry. Her expenses in governing and defending that settlement must be considerable. It might be humiliating to her to give it up on the demand of America. Perhaps America will not demand it; some of her political rulers may consider the fear of such a neighbor as a means of keeping the thirteen States more united among themselves and more attentive to military discipline. But on the mind of the people in general would it not have an excellent effect if Britain should voluntarily offer to give up this province, though on these conditions, that she shall, in all times coming, have and enjoy the right of free trade thither, unencumbered with any duties whatsoever; that so much of the vacant lands there shall be sold, as will raise a sum sufficient to pay for the houses burnt by the British troops and their Indians; and also to indemnify the royalists for the confiscation of their estates?

Oswald wanted to take the *Notes* to Shelburne and Franklin gave him the paper. Later, he regretted this, saying, "I was not pleased with my having hinted a reparation to Tories for their forfeited estates, and I was a little ashamed of my weakness in permitting the paper to go out of my hands."

Oswald returned to Paris to advise Franklin that the British Cabinet Council had "agreed to treat for a general peace, and at Paris; and that the principal points in contemplation are, the allowing of American independence, on condition that England be put into the same situation that she was left in by the peace of 1763." Oswald also reported that Fox was sending a negotiator to deal with the foreign countries. It is indicative of England's opinion of Franklin's importance as the peacemaker that when Fox's man, Mr. Grenville, arrived he went to Franklin—not Vergennes.

Franklin kept the other American commissioners informed of what was going on by letter, and urged them to come to Paris. To Jay in Spain he wrote "to press his coming hither, and, being a little out of humor with that court, I said: 'They have taken four years to consider whether they should treat with us. Give them forty and let us mind our own business.' I sent the letter under cover to a person in Madrid who I hoped would open and read it."

In his *Journal* Franklin mentions that Adams was having some difficulties because the ministers of countries which did not recognize the independence of the United States would not return his visits. He continues: "I had heard here, by good luck, that the same resolution was taken by several of them not to return the visits I should make them (as they supposed) when I was first received here as Minister Plenipotentiary, and disappointed their project by visiting none of them. In my private opinion, the first civility is due from the old resident to the stranger and newcomer. My opinion, indeed, is good for nothing against custom, which I should have obeyed, but for the circumstances, that rendered it more prudent to avoid disputes and affronts, though at the hazard of being thought rude or singular."

Franklin's *Journal* ends abruptly on July 1, 1782. A week later he wrote what was to be the basis of the peace treaty. There is no copy of it in Franklin's hand—it exists in a letter from Oswald to Shelburne, dated July 10, recounting a conversation with Franklin:

HAVING REMINDED HIM of what he in a manner promised on the sixth, he took out a minute and read from it a few hints or articles; some, he said, as necessary for them to insist on; others, which he could not say he had any orders about, or were not absolutely demanded, and yet such as it would be advisable for England to offer for the sake of reconciliation and her future interest, viz.:

"1st. Of the first class, necessary to be granted: independence, full and complete in every sense, to the Thirteen States; and all troops to be withdrawn from thence.

"2dly. A settlement of the boundaries of their colonies and the loyal colonies.

"3dly. A confinement of the boundaries of Canada; at least to what they were before the last act of Parliament, I think in 1744, if not to a still more contracted state, on an ancient footing.

"4thly. A freedom of fishing on the Bank of Newfoundland and elsewhere, as well for fish as whales." I own I wondered he should have thought it necessary to ask for this privilege.

He did not mention the leave of drying fish on shore in Newfoundland, and I said nothing of it. I do not remember any more articles which he said they would insist on, or what he called necessary to them to be granted.

Then, as to the advisable articles, or such as he would,

as a friend, recommend to be offered by England, viz.:

"1st. To indemnify many people who had been ruined by towns burnt and destroyed. . . .

"2dly. Some sort of acknowledgment in some public act of Parliament, or otherwise, of our error in distressing those countries so much as we had done." A few words of that kind, the doctor said, would do more good than people could imagine.

"3dly. Colony ships and trade to be received and have the same privileges in Britain and Ireland as British ships and trade. . . ."

"4thly. Giving up every part of Canada. . . ."

When Franklin gave these terms to Oswald none of the other American commissioners had met the British negotiators. Jay had arrived in Paris a few days before, Adams and Laurens were still in Holland. Jay caused some difficulties by objecting to the wording of Oswald's commission as a negotiator which authorized him to deal with the commissioners of the "said colonies and plantations." Jay insisted that this must be changed to authorize him to deal with the United States of America. Also, he wanted England to acknowledge American independence first and then make a treaty—not to make independence part of the treaty. Franklin, no lawyer, could not see that these points made any difference. The important thing was independence, not how Oswald's commission was worded.

Franklin was in bed most of the summer with the first attack of the bladder stone which would remain to plague him for the rest of his life. Jay made no important progress until Adams arrived on October 26. The latter was, by now, so opposed to Franklin that he was reluctant to call on him. He said that "Franklin's cunning will divide us; to this end he will provoke, he will insinuate, he will intrigue, he will maneuver."

When Adams did bring himself to call on Franklin, he said that he would "without reserve" support the "principles, wisdom and firmness" which Jay had shown. The next day, when the Americans met with Oswald and another English representative, Franklin turned to Jay and Adams and said, "I am of your opinion and will go on with these gentlemen in this business."

The American demands concerning the treaty articles were presented on November 5. The English negotiators stalled until November 29, talking of the need for further authority from Parliament. Then Franklin produced another paper from his pocket and said that if there was to be further delay, it might be well for the Americans to demand payment for all the goods that Gage had seized in Boston and Howe in Philadelphia; for all tobacco, rice, indigo and slaves taken by Arnold and Cornwallis in the south; for all the ships and cargoes captured by the British navy and all the villages and farms burned or destroyed during the war. The English signed without further delay.

This provisional treaty was essentially the same as the final treaty signed September 3, 1783, and both differed only in detail from the four necessary points that Franklin had given to Oswald in July, 1782. Fourteen months of negotiation on the part of the other commissioners succeeded only in gaining America the right to dry fish on the shores of Nova Scotia.

The way in which the negotiations were handled placed an added burden on Franklin. The treaty with France, and the commissioners' instructions from Congress, stipulated that peace negotiations should not be undertaken independent of France. But the provisional treaty was signed without consulting Vergennes. True, it contained a clause that a final treaty would not be signed except in conjunction with a peace between France and England, but the way in which it was done was a technical violation and, to say the least, most impolite. Adams and Jay, particularly Adams, did not trust France, and Franklin, in the minority, had to go along with them. Later, he said of Adams, "He means well for his country, is always an honest man, often a wise one, but sometimes, and in some things, absolutely out of his senses."

The burden of explaining this gauche conduct to Vergennes fell on Franklin at the same time that he had to ask for a loan of another six million livres. He so handled this delicate situation that he kept Vergennes' good will—and got the six million.

As soon as the provisional treaty was signed, Franklin wrote to Congress saying: "I am now entering on my seventy-eighth year; public business has engrossed fifty of them; I wish now to be, for the little time I have left, my own master. If I live to see this peace concluded, I shall beg leave to remind Congress of their promise then to dismiss me. I shall be happy to sing with old Simeon: 'Now lettest thou thy servant depart in peace, for mine eyes have seen salvation.' " It would be more than two years before Congress granted his request, but with the end of the war he had at last some time for leisure.

The week the final treaty was signed, he went to see Paris' first balloon ascension. France had been wild with excitement about balloons since the Montgolfier brothers sent up their first straw-burning hot-air bag the previous June. Franklin estimated that fifty thousand people turned out with him to watch the Paris ascension of a hydrogen-filled globe. It was here that a bystander is supposed to have said, "But what good is it?" and Franklin replied, with his famous epigram *"Eh, à quoi bon l'enfant qui vient de naître?"* (Of what good is a newborn baby?) He wrote to Joseph Banks at the Royal Academy in London that this new device might "pave the way for some discoveries in natural philosophy of which at present we have no conception." Later, to the same scientist, he wrote:

I AM SORRY this experiment is totally neglected in England, where mechanic genius is so strong. . . . Your philosophy seems to be too bashful. In this country we are not so much afraid of being laughed at. If we do a foolish thing, we are the first to laugh at it ourselves. . . . It does not seem to me to be a good reason to decline prosecuting a new experiment which apparently increases the power of man over matter, till we can see to what use that power may be applied. When we have learnt to manage it, we may hope some time or other to find uses for it, as men have done for magnetism and electricity, of which the first experiments were mere matters of amusement.

This experiment is by no means a trifling one. It may be attended with important consequences that no one can foresee. We should not suffer pride to prevent our progress in science.

Beings of a frank and *Sic* nature far superior to ours have not disdained to amuse themselves with making and launching balloons, otherwise we should never have enjoyed the light of those glorious objects that rule our day and night, nor have had the pleasure of riding round the sun ourselves upon the balloon we now inhabit. . . .

Franklin was the first American to take a serious interest in aeronautics. In a sense, he predicted air power, the tactical function of paratroops, and the conflict of navy and air force for their respective shares of armament appropriations when he said that the invention of the balloon might "possibly give a new turn to human affairs. Convincing sovereigns of the folly of wars may perhaps be one effect of it since it will be impractical for the most potent of them to guard his dominions. Five thousand balloons, capable of raising two men each, could not cost more than five ships of the line; and where is the prince who can afford to so cover his country with troops for its defense as that ten thousand men descending from the clouds might not, in many places, do an infinite deal of mischief before a force could be brought together to repel them?"

Now Franklin had time to answer some of the questions that Europe had been asking about America. From his printing press in Passy came, in French and English, his paper containing *Information to Those Who Would Remove to America.*

MANY PERSONS IN EUROPE having by letters expressed to
the writer of this, who is well acquainted with North America, their desire of transporting and establishing themselves
in that country, but who appear to have formed, through
ignorance, mistaken ideas and expectations of what is to
be obtained there, he thinks it may be useful, and prevent
inconvenient, expensive and fruitless removals and voyages
of improper persons, if he gives some clearer and truer
notions of that part of the world than appear to have
hitherto prevailed.

He finds it is imagined by numbers that the inhabitants
of North America are rich, capable of rewarding, and disposed to reward, all sorts of ingenuity; that they are at the
same time ignorant of all the sciences, and, consequently,
that strangers possessing talents in the belles-lettres, fine
arts, etc., must be highly esteemed, and so well paid as to
become easily rich themselves; that there are also abundance
of profitable offices to be disposed of, which the natives are
not qualified to fill; and that, having few persons of family
among them, strangers of birth must be greatly respected,
and of course easily obtain the best of those offices, which
will make all their fortunes; that the governments too, to
encourage emigration from Europe, not only pay the expense of personal transportation, but give lands gratis to
strangers, with Negroes to work them, utensils of husbandry,
and stocks of cattle. These are all wild imaginations; and
those who go to America with expectations founded upon
them will surely find themselves disappointed.

Information continued to point out that, although no Americans were "so miserable as the poor of Europe," few were rich.
There were no patrons of the arts, few government jobs—"no
superfluous ones, as in Europe." There were no military positions, the armies were disbanded. And, Americans were not
exactly illiterate. They had nine colleges, "all furnished with

learned professors." Particularly, one would be unwise to go to
America—

WHO HAS NO other quality to recommend him but his birth.
In Europe it indeed has its value; but it is a quality that
cannot be carried to a worse market than that of America,
where people do not inquire concerning a stranger, "What
is he?" but, "What can he do?". . .

Strangers are welcome, because there is room enough for
them all, and therefore the old inhabitants are not jealous
of them; the laws protect them sufficiently, so that they have
no need of the patronage of great men; and everyone will
enjoy securely the profits of his industry. But, if he does not
bring a fortune with him, he must work and be industrious
to live. . . . In short, America is the land of labor, and by
no means what the English call *Lubberland,* and the French
Pays de Cocagne, where the streets are said to be paved
with half-peck loaves, the houses tiled with pancakes, and
where the fowls fly about ready roasted, crying, *Come,
eat me!*

The type of emigrants who could succeed in America were
farmers or those who would be farmers. "A little money saved
of the good wages they receive there, while they work for others,
enables them to buy the land and begin their plantation, in
which they are assisted by the good will of their neighbors, and
some credit . . . tolerably good workmen in any of those mechanic arts are sure to find employ, and to be well paid for their
work, there being no restraints preventing strangers from exercising any art they understand, nor any permission necessary."

While his press was busy giving information to Europe,
Franklin's pen poured advice and opinion on many minor subjects back to America. He was mildly distressed by accounts of
the formation of the Society of the Cincinnati, an organization of
former army officers, even though his good friend, George

Washington, headed it. Membership was to be hereditary and the old imperialist had become so democratic that the idea of handing down honors to the eldest son shocked him. To his daughter he wrote:

I SHOULD NOT MYSELF, if my advice had been asked, have objected to their wearing their ribands and badges themselves according to their fancy, though I certainly should do the entailing it as an honor on their posterity. For honor, worthily obtained (as that, for example, of our officers), is in its nature a personal thing, and incommunicable to any but those who had some share in obtaining it. Thus among the Chinese, the most ancient, and from long experience, the wisest of nations, honor does not descend but ascends. If a man, from his learning, his wisdom or his valor, is promoted by the Emperor to the rank of Mandarin, his parents are immediately entitled to all the same ceremonies of respect from the people that are established as due to the Mandarin himself; on the supposition that it must have been owing to the education, instruction and good example afforded him by his parents, that he was rendered capable of serving the public.

I wish, therefore, that the founders of the Cincinnati, if they must go on with their project, would direct the badges of their honor to be worn by their fathers and mothers, instead of handing them down to their children. It would be a good precedent, and might have a good effect. It would also be a kind of obedience of the fourth commandment, in which God enjoins us to honor our father and mother, but has nowhere directed us to honor our children.

One aspect of the founding of his country in which Franklin did not have a hand was in the selection of the national emblem. Perhaps that, in part, accounted for his disdain for eagles.

I WISH THE BALD EAGLE had not been chosen as the representative of our country; he is a bird of bad moral character; he does not get his living honestly; you may have seen him perched on some dead tree, where, too lazy to fish for himself, he watches the labor of the fishing-hawk; and when that diligent bird has at length taken a fish, and is bearing it to his nest for the support of his mate and the young ones, the bald eagle pursues him and takes it from him. . . .

I am, on this account, not displeased that the figure is not known as a bald eagle, but looks more like a turkey. For in truth, the turkey is in comparison a much more respectable bird, and withal a true original native of America. . . .

In August, 1784, Franklin replied to the first letter he had received from his son William in many years:

I . . . AM GLAD TO FIND that you desire to revive the affectionate intercourse that formerly existed between us. It will be very agreeable to me; indeed, nothing has ever hurt me so much, and affected me with such keen sensations, as to find myself deserted in my old age by my only son; and not only deserted, but to find him taking up arms against me in a cause wherein my good fame, fortune and life were all at stake. You conceived, you say, that your duty to your King and regard for your country required this. I ought not to blame you for differing with me in public affairs. We are men, all subject to errors. Our opinions are not in our own power; they are formed and governed much by circumstances that are often as inexplicable as they are irresistible. Your situation was such that few would have censured your remaining neuter, though there are natural duties which precede political ones, and cannot be extinguished by them.

This is a disagreeable subject. I drop it; and we will endeavor, as you propose, mutually to forget what has happened relating to it, as well as we can. . . .

This reconciliation never developed into a warm relationship. When Franklin returned to America, William came from London to Southampton to see him. Franklin's only comment in his journal was: "Met my son, who had arrived from London the evening before."

Franklin's correspondence during this period included a continuing exchange of views with scientists throughout Europe, but he was through experimenting. He did contribute one more significant invention—bifocal spectacles—which he created as simply and logically as most of his other scientific and mechanical achievements.

I HAD FORMERLY two pairs of spectacles, which I shifted occasionally, as in traveling I sometimes read, and often wanted to regard the prospects. Finding this change troublesome, and not always sufficiently ready, I had the glasses cut, and half of each kind associated in the same circle. By this means, as I wear my spectacles constantly, I have only to move my eyes up or down, as I want to see distinctly far or near, the proper glasses being always ready. This I find more particularly convenient since my being in France, the glasses that serve me best at table to see what I eat not being the best to see the faces of those on the other side of the table who speak to me; and when one's ears are not well accustomed to the sounds of a language, a sight of the movements in the features of him that speaks helps to explain; so that I understand French better by the help of my spectacles.

On May 2, 1785, Franklin finally received permission from Congress to come home. Thomas Jefferson, always a firm friend of Franklin's, had arrived the previous August to replace him— or, as Jefferson said, to succeed him: nobody could replace him. With Jefferson and Adams, who had come from The Hague, Franklin spent his last months in France drafting treaties of friendship and commerce with European countries, and Franklin wrote the draft of the treaty with the Barbary powers.

The old doctor's journey from Paris to Le Havre was a triumphal procession with many pauses for honors from nobility, clergy, communities, philosophers and friends. Too old and ill to stand the rigors of carriage travel, Franklin rode in a litter loaned by the Queen, slung between two Spanish mules which proceeded at a walk. At Le Havre he boarded the packet for America—and went back to work. During the voyage he wrote more miscellaneous scientific observations than during any similar period in his life.

During each of his eight voyages, covering a period of more than sixty years, Franklin had studied the Gulf Stream. Apparently he was the first to attempt to chart this beneficial current. In 1784 he had written to a friend in the French Academy of Sciences, "I send you a copy of a chart of the Gulf Stream which is little known by European navigators, and yet of great consequence; since in going to America they often get into that stream and unknowingly stem it, whereby the ship is much retarded and the voyage lengthened enormously." Now, on his last voyage, he spent time supervising the lowering of bottles and kegs to test the temperature of the water at various depths.

On this voyage he also wrote his *Maritime Observations*. This was a long "catchall" of opinions, conjectures, suggestions for experiments and advice on myriad subjects relating to ships and the sea. It discussed the construction of Eskimo kayaks, Indian canoes and Pacific proas; the use of watertight compartments, of which Franklin was an early advocate; the rigging of ships; a suggestion for a device to prevent hawsers from breaking; fire and lightning; paddlewheels; collision with ships or icebergs; the use of a floating anchor; the Gulf Stream; lifeboats and suggestions for escaping from wrecks; a better diet for sailors; advice to passengers on what they should bring on shipboard. Midway in this marine encyclopedia Frank apologized for its length and then said, "But the garrulity of an old man has got hold of me and, as I may never have another occasion of writing on this subject, I think I may as well now, once and for all, empty my nautical budget."

During the voyage he also wrote *On the Causes and Cure of Smoky Chimneys* and *A Description of a New Stove for Burning Pit Coal and Consuming All Its Smoke*. He also kept a daily journal. The last entry read:

Wednesday, September 14: With the flood in the morning came a light breeze which brought us above Gloucester Point, in full view of dear old Philadelphia! when we again cast anchor to wait for the health officer, who, having made his visit and finding no sickness, gave us leave to land. My son-in-law came with a boat for us; we landed at Market Street wharf, where we were received by a crowd of people with huzzas, and accompanied with acclamations quite to my door. Found my family well.

God be praised and thanked for all His mercies!

CHAPTER XII

THE LADY'S MAN

In any sophisticated social gathering at which the name of Benjamin Franklin comes up, somebody is almost sure to remark with a leer, "Say, that old boy was quite a man with the ladies," or "Wasn't he the old reprobate?" This concept of the worthy doctor seems to have started many years after his death and to have grown during recent years—there is no reference to it in early writings about him, except for scurrilous political slander regarding his son William's legitimacy.

There is not one iota of evidence in history to justify this image. True, Franklin liked women, and many women adored Franklin. He was closely associated with several, ranging from eleven-year-old Catherine Shipley in England to sixtyish Madame Helvétius in France. He spent much time in their company and some of his most interesting writing is in correspondence with female friends. But there is nothing to indicate that his relations with any of them were other than gallant and intellectual.

It has been said that Franklin was the only great diplomat that America ever produced. Certainly he was America's first man of science. But he had an ability more rare than either of these. He understood women. His manners, his charm and his wit all appealed to the weaker sex; but he had a quality in his relationship with women that went beyond this. At a time when they were emerging from chattlehood, Franklin treated women with a twentieth-century concept of equality—but he tempered this with a gallantry which is virtually unknown in today's war of the sexes. The combination made him irresistible to many intelligent females.

Throughout his life Franklin was a champion of women's rights. One of the first Dogood papers defended women and, when he was in his early teens, his autobiography describes an argument with a friend: "A question was once . . . started between Collins and me of the propriety of educating the female sex in learning and their ability to study. He was of the opinion that it was improper, and that they were naturally unequal to it. I took the contrary side."

Franklin was a lusty man and admitted, in his youth, sexual indiscretions. In writing about his first stay in London he says, "through this dangerous time of youth, and the hazardous situations I was sometimes in among strangers, remote from the eye and advice of my father . . . that hard-to-be-governed passion of youth hurried me frequently into intrigues with low women that fell my way, with some expense and great inconvenience." During this same period he tells about a friend who was living with a little milliner in London and asked Franklin to watch over her when he went away. Franklin said that she was "often in distresses and used to send for me and borrow what I could spare to help her out of them. I grew fond of her company and, being at that time under no religious restraint, and presuming on my importance to her, I attempted familiarities (another erratum) which she repulsed with proper resentment, and acquainted him with my behavior. This made a breach between us." Sadly, on this one occasion in his teens, the first of the Founding Fathers was what was then termed a "cad."

Much has been made of the illegitimacy of William. Every

historian and scholar accepts this as a fact. The only evidence that has been cited is that "everybody knew it," although in law this does not constitute proof. They also make the point that Franklin never denied it, although the sage expressed his attitude toward refuting mud slinging when he refused to answer the charges before the Privy Council.

Because scandal has such popular appeal, books have been written on the subject of "Who was the mother of Franklin's son?" The most malicious version, created by political opponents when Franklin was running for the legislature, has her as a servant girl named Barbara whom Franklin threw out after the birth to die alone and be buried in an unmarked grave. Except for this political libel, history knows nothing of Barbara.

Technically, all three of the Franklin children were illegitimate (another boy, Francis, died of smallpox at age four). Benjamin and Deborah were never legally married. They had been engaged before he first went to London but, when he did not write to her from abroad, she married another man who promptly left her and disappeared. Although he was presumed dead, there was no proof of this, and the Franklin marriage was a common-law one.

But it was a happy one. A thread of affection weaves through all their letters to each other. In his last letter to her, after forty-five years of marriage, Franklin wrote: "It seems but the other day since you and I were ranked among the boys and girls, so swiftly does time fly. We have, however, great reason to be thankful that so much of our lives has passed so happily."

Culturally and intellectually Deborah moved in a different world from her husband. The extent of her literacy is indicated by a typical letter: "Aprill 7 this day is Cumpleet 5 munthes senes you lefte your one House I did reseve a letter from the Capes senes that not one line I due supose that you did write by the packit but that is not arived yit." It is, perhaps, fortunate for America that her fear of an ocean voyage prevented her going to Europe with her husband. Her presence would have been a handicap in cultivating the intelligent and cultured friends which Franklin made for the colonies.

During Franklin's days as a tradesman she was an ideal wife, and a loving one. An insight to this era is contained in the autobiography:

WE HAVE AN ENGLISH PROVERB that says, *He that would thrive must ask his wife*. It was lucky for me that I had one as much disposed to industry and frugality as myself. She assisted me cheerfully in my business, folding and stitching pamphlets, tending shop, purchasing old linen rags for the paper-makers, etc., etc. We kept no idle servants, our furniture of the cheapest. For instance, my breakfast was a long time bread and milk (no tea), and I ate it out of a twopenny earthen porringer, with a pewter spoon. But mark how luxury will enter families, and make a progress, in spite of principle: being called one morning to breakfast, I found it in a China bowl, with a spoon of silver! They had been bought for me without my knowledge by my wife, and had cost her the enormous sum of three-and-twenty shillings, for which she had no other excuse or apology to make, but that she thought her husband deserved a silver spoon and China bowl as well as any of his neighbors.

For the last ten years of her life, when her husband was in England, Deborah managed the affairs of the family in Philadelphia under a power of attorney from Franklin.

The institution of marriage had a strong advocate in Franklin, who said, "The married state is, after all our jokes, the happiest, because conformable to our natures. Man and woman have each of them qualities and tempers in which the other is deficient, and which in union contribute to the common felicity. Single and separate, they are not the complete human beings; they are like the odd halves of scissors: they cannot answer the end of their formation."

Franklin's best-known piece of bawdy writing, couched in the form of a letter to a friend in 1745 but probably for the amusement of the Junto, was *Advice on the Choice of a Mistress*. This started with a hearty recommendation of marriage:

I KNOW OF NO MEDICINE fit to diminish the violent natural inclinations you mention; and if I did, I think I should not communicate it to you. Marriage is the proper remedy. It is the most natural state of man, and therefore the state in which you are most likely to find solid happiness. . . . It is the man and woman united that make the complete human being. Separate, she wants his force of body and strength of reason; he, her softness, sensibility and acute discernment. Together they are more likely to succeed in the world. A single man has not nearly the value he would have in the state of union. He is an incomplete animal. . . . If you get a prudent, healthy wife, your industry in your profession, with her good economy, will be a fortune sufficient.

But if you will not take this counsel and persist in thinking a commerce with the sex inevitable, then I repeat my former advice, that in all your amours you should prefer old women to young ones. . . .

Advice continued with eight amusing reasons for preferring an old mistress. The last reason he gave was the most succinct: "They are so grateful."

Franklin was a family man. The joys and comforts of home life were ever most important to him. In London, Craven Street became his home, and the Stevensons his family. He became, in fact, not a boarder but the head of the household, treating Mrs. Stevenson as a sister and Polly as a daughter. He liked to be surrounded with children. Another Sally Franklin, daughter of a distant English poor relation, came to live at Craven Street, as did Temple, William's young son. Margaret Stevenson and Polly picked out presents to send to Deborah and Sarah, and

Deborah kept the London household supplied with apples, dried peaches, buckwheat flour and cornmeal. After Polly married Dr. Hewson, they came to live at Craven Street. Deborah wrote her husband at length about Sarah's baby, Benny Bache, and Franklin replied with accounts of his godson Billy Hewson. "He was with us a few days last week, grew fond of me, and would not be contented to sit down to breakfast without coming to call 'Pa,' rejoicing when he had got me into my place. When seeing me one day crack one of the Philadelphia biscuits into my tea with the nutcrackers, he took another and tried to do the same with the tea-tongs. It makes me long to be home to play with Ben."

There was nothing on which the great man did not have an opinion, even the raising of babies—although his advice to Polly Hewson was probably written as whimsical humor rather than sound child psychology:

PRAY LET HIM HAVE everything he likes; I think it of great consequence while the features of the countenance are forming; it gives them a pleasant air, and, that being once become natural and fixed by habit, the face is ever after the handsomer for it, and on that much of a person's good fortune and success in life may depend. Had I been crossed as much in my infant likings and inclinations as you know I have been of late years, I should have been, I was going to say, not near so handsome; but as the vanity of that expression would offend other folk's vanity, I change it, out of regard to them, and say, a great deal more homely.

Polly's girl friends formed a circle of young, adoring females around Franklin. He apparently called them his "daughters." He specifically referred to one girl, Judith Osgood, as "my daughter" in a letter. This gave rise among later scandalmongers to tales about Franklin's illegitimate daughter. Judith, a young English girl, was married in 1770. To be Franklin's real daughter, she would have had to have been under thirteen or over forty-four in that year—or be conceived over three thousand miles of ocean.

Franklin's affection for his English family is evidenced in *The Craven Street Gazette,* a parody on the *Court Gazette,* which he wrote to entertain the young people when Mrs. Stevenson and Sally Franklin took a trip. Polly is, variously, the new ministry, lady chamberlain, and lady of the bedchamber. Franklin is the Great Person and Old Fatsides.

THIS MORNING Queen Margaret, accompanied by her first maid of honor, Miss Franklin, set out for Rochester. . . . It is whispered that the new family administration, which took place on her Majesty's departure, promises, like all other new administrations, to govern much better than the old one.

We hear, that the great person (so called from his enormous size), of a certain family in a certain street, is grievously affected at the late changes, and could hardly be comforted this morning, though the new ministry promised him a roasted shoulder of mutton and potatoes for his dinner.

It is said, that the same great person intended to pay his respects to another great personage this day, at St. James's, it being coronation day; hoping thereby to amuse a little his grief; but was prevented by an accident, Queen Margaret, or her maid of honor, having carried off the key of the drawers, so that the lady of the bedchamber could not come at a laced shirt for his Highness. Great clamors were made on this occasion against Her Majesty.

Other accounts say that the shirts were afterward found, though too late, in another place. And some suspect that the wanting a shirt from those drawers was only a ministerial pretense to excuse picking the locks, that the new administration might have everything at its command.

It is confidently asserted that this afternoon, the weather being wet, the great person a little chilly and nobody at home to find fault with the expense of fuel, he was indulged with a fire in his chamber. It seems the design is, to make him contented by degrees with the absence of Queen Margaret. . . .

We have good authority to assure our readers that a Cabinet Council was held this afternoon at tea, the subject of which was a proposal for the reformation of manners, and a more strict observance of the Lord's day. The result was a unanimous resolution, that no meat should be dressed tomorrow; whereby the cook and the first minister will both be at liberty to go to church, the one having nothing to do, and the other no roast to rule. It seems the cold shoulder of mutton, and the apple pie, were thought sufficient for Sunday's dinner. All pious people applaud this measure, and it is thought the new ministry will soon become popular. . . .

Sunday, September 23

It is now found by sad experience, that good resolutions are easier made than executed. Notwithstanding yesterday's solemn order of Council, nobody went to church today. It seems the great person's broad-built bulk lay so long abed that the breakfast was not over till it was too late to dress. At least this is the excuse. In fine, it seems a vain thing to hope reformation from the example of our great folks.

The cook and the minister, however, both took advantage of the order so far, as to save themselves all trouble, and the clause of cold dinner was enforced, though the going to church was dispensed with; just as common working folks observe the commandments. *The seventh day thou shalt rest* they think a sacred injunction; but the other *six days thou shalt labor* is deemed a mere piece of advice, which they may practice when they want bread and are out of credit at the alehouse, and may neglect whenever they have money in their pockets.

Monday, September 24

We are credibly informed, that the great person this day dined with the Club at the Cat and Bagpipes in the City, on cold round of boiled beef. This, it seems, he was under some necessity of doing (though he rather dislikes beef) because truly the ministers were to be all abroad somewhere to dine on hot roast venison. It is thought that, if the Queen had been at home, he would not have been so slighted. And though he shows outwardly no marks of dissatisfaction, it is suspected that he begins to wish for Her Majesty's return.

This even there was high play at Craven Street House. The great person lost money. It is supposed the ministers, as is usually supposed of all ministers, shared the emoluments among them. . . .

We hear that from the time of Her Majesty's leaving Craven Street House to this day, no care is taken to file the newspapers; but they lie about in every room in every window, and on every chair, just where the great person lays them when he reads them. It is impossible government can long go on in such hands. . . .

Another English family which played a part in Franklin's life was that of Jonathan Shipley, Bishop of St. Asaph. His initial contact with Bishop Shipley may have been political, as the cleric became one of the two bishops in the House of Lords to favor the colonies, possibly through Franklin's influence. But his principal admirers in the Shipley household were the five daughters, especially the two youngest, Catherine and Georgiana, aged eleven and fifteen respectively. He met them first in 1771 and continued to correspond with them for the remainder of his life.

Catherine was a gay girl, Georgiana a bookworm. The nature

of his correspondence with the latter may be judged from a portion of a letter that she smuggled to him in France during the war.

PRAY HAVE YOU MET with Smith's *Wealth of Nations?* If not, I venture strongly to recommend it to you. I have read only parts, but propose shortly to read it regularly through. . . . This is the only book that has been published lately worth mentioning, except Gibbon's *History of the Rise and Fall of the Roman Empire.* . . . I have been at length fortunate enough to procure *The Economics,* which I have read with great attention, as indeed everything else I can meet with relative to Socrates, for I fancy I can discover in each trait of that admirable man's character a strong resemblance between him and my much-loved friend —the same clearness of judgment, the same uprightness of intention, and the same superior understanding.

But the most interesting letter in the Shipley correspondence is one written to Mrs. Shipley. Franklin volunteered to escort eleven-year-old Kitty back to school in London. As they rode along in the post chaise they talked, and the old philosopher reported the conversation to her mother in one of the most delightful bread-and-butter letters that a hostess ever received:

London, August 12, 1771

DEAR MADAM: This is just to let you know that we arrived safe and well in Marlborough Street, about six, where I delivered up my charge.

The above seems too short for a letter; so I will lengthen it by a little account of our journey. The first stage we were rather pensive. I tried several topics of conversation, but none of them would hold. But after breakfast we began to recover spirits, and had a good deal of chat. Will you hear some of it?

We talked of her brother, and she wished he was married. And don't you wish your sisters married too? Yes. All but Emily; I would not have her married. Why? Because I can't spare her, I can't part with her. The rest may marry as soon as they please, so they do but get good husbands. We then took upon us to consider . . . what sort of husbands would be fitted for every one of them.

We began with Georgiana. She thought a country gentleman, that loved traveling and would take her with him, that loved books and would hear her read to him; I added, that had a good estate and was a member of Parliament and loved to see an experiment now and then. This she agreed to; so we set him down for Georgiana, and went on to Betsy.

Betsy, says I, seems of a sweet, mild temper, and if we should give her a country squire, and he should happen to be of a rough, passionate turn, and be angry now and then, it might break her heart. O, none of them must be so; for then they would not be good husbands. To make sure of this point, however, for Betsy, shall we give her a bishop? O no, that won't do. They all declare against the Church, and against the Army; not one of them will marry either a clergyman or an officer; that they are resolved upon. What can be their reason for that? Why you know, that when a clergyman or officer dies, the income goes with 'em; and then what is there to maintain the family? There's the point. Then suppose we give her a good, honest, sensible city merchant who will love her dearly and is very rich? I don't know but that may do.

We proceeded to Emily, her dear Emily, I was afraid we should hardly find any thing good enough for Emily; but at last, after first settling that, if she did marry, Kitty was to live a good deal with her; we agreed that as Emily was very handsome we might expect an Earl for her. So haxing fixed her, as I thought, a countess, we went on to Anna Maria.

She, says Kitty, should have a rich man that has a large

family and a great many things to take care of; for she is very good at managing, helps my Mama very much, can look over bills, and order all sorts of family business. Very well; and as there is a grace and dignity in her manner that would become the station, what do you think of giving her a Duke? O no! I'll have the Duke for Emily. You may give the Earl to Anna Maria if you please: but Emily shall have the Duke. I contested this matter for some time; but at length was forced to give up the point, leave Emily in possession of the Duke, and content myself with the Earl for Anna Maria.

And now what shall we do for Kitty? We have forgot her, all this time. Well, and what will you do for her? I suppose that though the rest have resolved against the Army, she may not yet have made so rash a resolution. Yes, but she has; unless, now an old one, an old General that has done fighting, and is rich, such a one as General Rufane; I like him a good deal. You must know I like an old man, indeed I do and somehow or other all the old men take to me; all that come to our house like me better than my other sisters. I go to 'em and ask 'em how they do and they like it mightily; and the maids take notice of it, and say when they see an old man come, there's a friend of yours, Miss Kitty. But then as you like an old General, hadn't you better take him while he's a young officer, and let him grow old on your hands, because then you'll like him better and better every year as he grows older and older. No, that won't do. He must be an old man of seventy or eighty, and take me when I am about thirty. And then, you know, I may be a rich young widow. . . .

Then we chatted on, and she was very entertaining quite to town.

I have now made my letter as much too long as it was at first too short. The Bishop would think it too trifling, therefore don't show it to him. I am afraid too that you will think it so, and have a good mind not to send it. Only it tells you Kitty is well at school and for that I let it go. My love to the whole amiable family, best respects to the Bishop, and one thousand thanks for all your kindnesses, and for the happy days I enjoyed at Twyford. . . .

Fourteen years after her trip in the post chaise with her adored doctor, Kitty and her parents came to Southampton to see him off on his last voyage home. Here she apparently promised to make him a purse if he would write her a "Bagatelle"—a literary trifle. Franklin received the purse and, a year later wrote for Kitty *The Art of Procuring Pleasant Dreams*. It is an amusing commentary on Franklin the humorist and Franklin the seer that some scholars classify this with his other bagatelles, while other erudite editors include it with his serious medical writings.

As a great part of our life is spent in sleep during which we have sometimes pleasant and sometimes painful dreams, it becomes of some consequence to obtain the one kind and avoid the other; for whether real or imaginary, pain is pain and pleasure is pleasure. If we can [not?] sleep without dreaming, it is well that painful dreams are avoided. If while we sleep we can have any pleasing dream, it is, as the French say, *autant de gagne*, so much added to the pleasure of life.

To this end it is, in the first place, necessary to be careful in preserving health, by due exercise and great temperance; for, in sickness, the imagination is disturbed, and disagreeable, sometimes terrible ideas are apt to present themselves. Exercise should precede meals, not immediately follow them; the first promotes, the latter, unless moderate, obstructs digestion. If, after exercise, we feed sparingly, the digestion will be easy and good, the body lightsome, the temper cheerful, and all the animal functions performed agreeably. Sleep, when it follows, will be natural and un-disturbed; while indolence, with full feeding, occasions nightmares and horrors inexpressible; we fall from preci-pices, are assaulted by wild beasts, murderers and demons, and experience every variety of distress. . . .

The piece continues with a long section on fresh air, saying: "Physicians, after having for ages contended that the sick should not be indulged with fresh air, have at length discovered that it may do them good." Few doctors believed this; Franklin was a pioneer in this as in so much else. His opinions on diet and ventilation justify *Pleasant Dreams* as a piece of medical writing.

As an endorsement of his belief in fresh air, Franklin wrote, "It is recorded on Methusalem, who, being the longest liver, may be supposed to have best preserved his health, that he slept always in the open air; for when he had lived five hundred years, an angel said to him: 'Arise, Methusalem, and build thee a house, for thou shalt live yet five hundred years longer.' But Methusalem answered and said, 'If I am to live but five hundred years longer, it is not worth while to build me a house; I will sleep in the air, as I have been used to do.' "

In thanking him for his paper Kitty said, "Where do you read that Methusalem slept in the open air? I have searched the Bible in vain to find it." With tongue in cheek, Franklin was not above quoting the most eminent authority to back up his opinion.

Franklin's relations with the young women in England can best be summarized by the final paragraph of one of his letters to Polly Stevenson: "I cannot conceive that any inconvenience can arise from my loving young ladies, and their believing that I love them. Therefore you may assure your friend Dolly that she judges right. I love all good girls, because they are good, and her for one reason more; because you love her."

His French home in Passy was an all-male establishment.

Temple was now his secretary and Benny Bache had come
over to go to school. Although he and young John Quincy
Adams sometimes came to Sunday dinner, the old man missed
the patter of little feet. After much urging Polly Hewson, now
a widow, brought her three children to stay for a winter. When
they left, Franklin wrote, "You talk of obligations to me when,
in fact, I am the person obliged. I passed a long winter in a
manner that made it appear the shortest I ever passed. . . . My
love to William and Thomas and Eliza, and tell them I miss
their cheerful prattle. Temple being sick and Benjamin in Paris,
I have found it very *triste* breakfasting alone, and sitting alone,
without any tea in the evening."

The women of France made much of Franklin, and the old
sage gloried in it. A companion of Marie Antoinette's described
a fete at which the most beautiful of three hundred women
placed a laurel wreath on his head and kissed him on both
cheeks. John Adams, possibly envious on this score too, said
"at seventy-odd he has neither lost his love for beauty nor his
taste for it." To his niece, Franklin wrote:

YOU MENTION THE KINDNESS of the French ladies to me. I
must explain that matter. This is the civilest nation upon
earth. Your first acquaintances endeavor to find out what
you like, and they tell others. If 'tis understood that you
like mutton, dine where you will you will find mutton. Somebody, it seems, gave out that I loved ladies; and then everybody presented me their ladies (or the ladies presented
themselves) to be embraced; that is, have their necks kissed.
For as to the kissing of lips or cheeks it is not the mode
here; the first is reckoned rude, and the other may rub off
the paint. The French ladies have, however, a thousand
other ways of rendering themselves agreeable; by their various attentions and civilities and their sensible conversation.

The two French women whose names are most intimately

connected with Franklin's were his neighbors, Madame Brillon and Madame Helvétius. The former was apparently in her early thirties, gay, beautiful, and married to an older, philandering husband. Their correspondence, with frequent allusions to sex, gave rise to much of the later lecher image, particularly a reference of Franklin's to a chess game which they played while she was in her bath. The custom of some French ladies of fashion to receive intimate friends while in a covered bathtub was unknown in this country.

In one letter to her Franklin said, "When I was a young man and enjoyed more favors from the sex than at present, I never had the gout. If the ladies of Passy had more of the Christian charity which I have so often recommended to you, in vain, I would not have the gout now." After she had offered to be his confessor, he wrote:

I LAY FAST HOLD on your promise to absolve me of all sins, past, present and future, on the easy and pleasing condition of loving God, America, and my guide above all things. I am in rapture when I think of being absolved of the future. . . . And now I am consulting you upon a case of conscience, I will mention the opinion of a certain father of the Church which I find myself willing to adopt, though I am not sure it is orthodox. It is this: that the most effectual way to get rid of a certain temptation is, as often as it returns, to comply with and satisfy it. Pray instruct me how far I may venture to practice upon this principle?

Madame Brillon's letters describe the two aspects of their relationship. In one she said, "I had a father, the kindest of men, he was my first, and my best friend; I lost him untimely! you have often said to me: *'Could I not take the place of those whom you regret?'* and you told me the custom of certain savages who adopt the prisoners that they capture in war, and make them take the place of the relatives whom they lose; you took in my heart the place of the father whom I so loved, and respected. . . ." In another letter she complained:

MY GOOD PAPA, your visits never cause me any inconvenience, all those around me respect you, love you, and think themselves honored in the friendship you have granted us; I told you that the world criticized the sort of familiarity which existed among us, because I was warned of it; I despise slanderers and am at peace with myself, but that is not enough, one must submit to what is called *propriety* (that word varies in each century, in each country!): to sit less often on your knees. I shall certainly love you none the less, nor will our hearts be more or less pure, but we shall close the mouth of the malicious, and it is no slight thing even for the sage, to make them silent.

Throughout their correspondence they played a word game of love but to all except the most narrow-minded it was obviously a stimulating mental exercise. When winter residence in Paris separated them, Madame Brillon wrote that perhaps Paradise would be better where "we shall be reunited, never to leave each other again. We shall live on roast apples only . . . all parties will be given over to chess . . . every day we shall love one another in order that we may love one another still more the day after; in a word, we shall be completely happy." Franklin picked this up by pointing out that, because of the difference in their ages, he would be in Paradise forty years before her. "However, the idea of an eternity in which I shall be favored with no more than permission to kiss your hands, or sometimes your cheeks . . . is frightful. If you reject me perhaps I shall address myself to Madame d'Hardancourt [her mother] and she will be willing to live with me. . . ."

This aroused Madame Brillon's mock jealousy. She wrote, "I give you my word of honor that I will become your wife in Paradise, on condition, however, that you do not make too many conquests among the heavenly maidens while you are waiting for me. I want a faithful husband when I take one for eternity."

Franklin replied with an amusing treatise on jealousy and infidelity, and a proposal for a personal peace pact between them, paralleling the more important treaty which was then the subject of his serious attention:

WHAT A DIFFERENCE, my dear friend, between you and me: you find in me innumerable faults, while I see only one in you (and perhaps that is the fault of my spectacles). I can sense a kind of greediness in you which causes you to monopolize all my affection; and leaves none for the other lovely ladies of your country. You fancy that it is not possible for my affection (or my love) to be divided without being thereby diminished. You are mistaken; and you forget the trifling manner in which you have treated me. You deny me, and completely disregard, all that might be sensual in our love, permitting me only a few polite and modest kisses such as you might bestow upon some little cousin. All this astonishes me, for why shouldn't I be able to give to others without subtracting from what belongs to you? The sentiments of esteem, admiration, respect and even affection itself can multiply themselves as often as the objects that merit that affection present themselves; and still there remain the same sentiments for the original object of affection, who, consequently, should have no cause to complain of injury. . . .

You see, then, how unjust you are in your demands and in the open war which you declare against me, if I do not comply with them; in fact, it is I who have the greatest reason to complain! My poor little cupid, whom, indeed, you should have cherished, instead of being plump and playful (like those in your elegant pictures), is thin and ready to die of hunger for want of the goodly nourishment which his mother inhumanly refuses him and, moreover, now wants to clip his little wings so that he may not go searching elsewhere! I fancy that neither of us will gain anything in this war; and consequently feeling myself the weakest, I shall make overtures for peace (a thing which, indeed, should be done by the wisest).

For a peace to be durable it is necessary that the terms of the treaty be subject to the strictest principles of justice and reciprocity: in which spirit I have drawn up the following articles:

Article I. There must be peace, friendship, and eternal love between Madame B. and Mr. Franklin.

Article II. In order to keep this peace inviolate, Madame B., for her part, stipulates and agrees that Mr. F. shall visit her whenever she asks him.

Article III. That he shall remain as long as she wishes.

Article IV. That when he is with her, he shall be obliged to take tea, play chess, listen to music or do anything that she might ask of him.

Article V. And that he shall love no other woman but her.

Article VI. The said Mr. Franklin on his part, stipulates and agrees that he will visit Madame B. whenever he pleases.

Article VII. That he will stay as long as he pleases.

Article VIII. That whenever he is with her he will do anything he pleases.

Article IX. And that he will not love any other woman as long as he finds her amiable.

Tell me what you think of these preliminaries? They seem to me to express the point of view and real intention of each party more clearly than most treaties.

I shall insist strongly on the eighth article although without much hope of your consent to carry it out; and on the ninth also, although I despair of ever finding another woman whom I could love with the same tenderness, remaining forever, my dear, dear friend.

Franklin's other neighbor, Madame Helvétius, was the sixtyish widow of a prominent French scientist. In Auteuil, adjacent to Passy, her salon was patronized by men like Voltaire. Franklin was first brought there by Turgot, powerful minister of finance. She had been beautiful. To her, one gallant who lived to be a hundred paid the famous compliment, "Ah, madame, if I were only eighty again." Franklin equaled this by replying, when she chided him for a delayed visit, "Madame, I am waiting till the nights are longer."

Many men admired Madame Helvétius and respected her wit and intellect. Some women held a different view. Abigail Adams left this catty description of the older woman:

SHE ENTERED THE ROOM with a careless, jaunty air; upon seeing ladies who were strangers to her, she bawled out, "Ah! mon Dieu, where is Franklin? Why did you not tell me there were ladies here?" You must suppose her speaking all this in French. "How I look!" said she, taking hold of a chemise made of tiffany, which she had on over a blue lute-string, and which looked as much upon the decay as her beauty, for she was once a handsome woman; her hair was frizzled; over it she had a small straw hat, with a dirty gauze half-handkerchief round it, and a bit of dirtier gauze than ever my maids wore was bowed on behind. She had a black gauze scarf thrown over her shoulders. She ran out of the room; when she returned, the Doctor entered at one door, she at the other; upon which she ran forward to him, caught him by the hand, "*Hélas!* Franklin!"; then gave him a double kiss, one upon each cheek, and another upon his forehead. When we went into the room to dine, she was placed between the Doctor and Mr. Adams. She carried on the chief of the conversation at dinner, frequently locking

her hands into the Doctor's, and sometimes spreading her
arms upon the backs of both of the gentlemen's chairs, then
throwing her arm carelessly upon the Doctor's neck.

I should have been greatly astonished at this conduct,
if the good Doctor had not told me that in this lady I
should see a genuine Frenchwoman, wholly free from af-
fectation, or stiffness of behavior, and one of the best women
in the world. For this I must take the Doctor's word; but I
should have set her down for a very bad one, although sixty
years of age, and a widow. I own I was highly disgusted,
and never wish for an acquaintance with any ladies of this
cast.

Franklin painted a different picture when he wrote her:

I SEE THAT STATESMEN, philosophers, historians, poets, and
men of learning of all sorts are drawn around you, and
seem as willing to attach themselves to you as straws about
a fine piece of amber. . . . I would not attempt to explain
it by the story of the ancient who, being asked why philosophers sought the acquaintance of kings and kings not that
of philosophers, replied that philosophers knew what they
wanted, which was not always the case with kings. Yet thus
far the comparison may go; that we find in your sweet society that charming benevolence, that amiable attention to
oblige, that disposition to please and be pleased, which we
do not always find in the society of one another. It springs
from you; it has its influence on us all; and in your company
we are not only pleased with you but better pleased with
one another and with ourselves.

The old doctor apparently proposed marriage to Madame
Helvétius, but whether seriously or as part of a mock romance
with which they amused themselves is not clear. Madame
Brillon thought it was serious—although the two women were

never jealous of each other. When Franklin left for America they wept together and Madame Brillon blamed Madame Helvétius for letting him go.

The Frenchwoman turned Franklin's proposal down because of her memory of her late husband to whom she kept "upon a table, under a glass" in her bedroom, "a monument . . . over which hung his picture, which was very handsome." Franklin was not brokenhearted. He immediately wrote her a short, gay bagatelle:

MORTIFIED AT THE barbarous resolution pronounced by you so positively yesterday evening, that you would remain single the rest of your life as a compliment due to the memory of your husband, I retired to my chamber. Throwing myself upon my bed, I dreamt that I was dead, and was transported to the Elysian Fields.

I was asked whether I wished to see any persons in particular; to which I replied that I wished to see the philosophers. "There are two who live here at hand in this garden; they are good neighbors, and very friendly toward one another." "Who are they?" "Socrates and Helvétius." "I esteem them both highly; but let me see Helvétius first, because I understand a little French, but not a word of Greek." I was conducted to him; he received me with much courtesy, having known me, he said, by character, sometime past. He asked me a thousand questions relative to the war, the present state of religion, of liberty, of the government in France. "You do not inquire then," said I, "after your dear friend, Madame Helvétius; yet she loves you exceedingly. I was in her company not more than an hour ago." "Ah," said he, "you make me recur to my past happiness, which ought to be forgotten in order to be happy here. For many years I could think of nothing but her, though at length I am consoled. I have taken another wife, the most like her that I could find; she is not indeed altogether so handsome, but she has a great fund of wit and good sense, and her whole study is to please me. She is at this moment gone to fetch the best nectar and ambrosia to regale me; stay here awhile and you will see her." "I perceive," said I, "that your former friend is more faithful to you than you are to her; she has had several good offers, but has refused them all. I will confess to you that I loved her extremely; but she was cruel to me, and rejected me peremptorily for your sake." "I pity you sincerely," said he, "for she is an excellent woman, handsome and amiable. . . ." As he finished these words the new Madame Helvétius entered with the nectar, and I recognized her immediately as my former American friend, Mrs. Franklin! I reclaimed her, but she answered me coldly: "I was a good wife to you for forty-nine years, nearly half a century; let that content you. I have formed a new connection here, which will last to eternity."

Indignant at this refusal of my Eurydice, I immediately resolved to quit those ungrateful shades, and return to this good world again, to behold the sun and you! Here I am; let us *avenge ourselves!*

History has left no picture of a lecher at Passy. The two women and, to a lesser extent, others, were charming companions to an old man whom they admired and adored. There was chess, and music, and poetry and scintillating conversation and, when he left, unhappiness at the loss of a great and good friend. Madame Helvétius wrote: "I see you in your litter, every step taking you farther from us, lost to me and all my friends who love you so much and to whom you leave such long regrets. I am afraid that you are suffering and the journey is tiring you and making your ailment worse. If that is so, come back, dear friend, to us. You will adorn my little retreat. . . . You will increase our happiness and we shall contribute to yours. You cannot doubt this. You could read it in my heart and in the hearts of all my good friends, who are also yours."

And Madame Brillon said:

I HAD SO FULL a heart yesterday in leaving you that I feared for you and myself a grief-stricken moment which could only add to the pain which our separation causes me, without proving to you further the tender and unalterable affection that I have vowed to you for always; every day of my life I shall recall that a great man, a sage, was willing to be my friend, my wishes will follow him everywhere, my heart will regret him incessantly, incessantly I shall say, I passed eight years with Doctor Franklin, they have flown and I shall see him no more! Nothing in the world could console me for this loss, except the thought of the peace and happiness that you are about to find in the bosom of your family.

CHAPTER XIII

THE FIRST FUNNY MAN

❦

Nothing was funny in the early days of colonial America—or, if it was, nobody wrote about it. Today, a sense of humor is considered an outstanding American characteristic, but during the 150 years following the settlement of the colonies there was a remarkable absence of humor. Along with much else, Benjamin Franklin changed this. *Poor Richard's Almanac* was the first jokebook.

Franklin has been called the father of American humor and learned dissertations have related great humorists like Artemus Ward, Mark Twain and Will Rogers to the Founding Father. Mark Twain did not agree. Knowing only Franklin of the *Almanac*—the penny-pinching moralist—Twain did not like him. He amused himself rewriting *Poor Richard* aphorisms— "Never put off till tomorrow what you can do day after tomorrow just as well," and wrote an essay, "The Late Benjamin Franklin," lampooning the great man.

In it he said:

THE SUBJECT of this memoir was of a vicious disposition, and early prostituted his talents to the invention of maxims and aphorisms calculated to inflict suffering on the rising generation of all subsequent ages. His simplest acts, also, were contrived with a view to their being held up for the emulation of boys forever—boys who might otherwise have been happy. . . . With a malevolence which is without parallel in history, he would work all day and then sit up nights, studying algebra by the light of a smoldering fire, so that all other boys would have to do that also, or else have Benjamin Franklin thrown up to them. . . . When I was a child I had to boil soap, notwithstanding my father was wealthy, and I had to get up early and study geometry at breakfast, and peddle my own poetry, and so everything just as Franklin did, in the solemn hope that I would be a Franklin some day. And here I am.

Franklin's sense of humor became evident as soon as he started to write. In those days the flowery, dolorous funeral elegy was very popular. Those that were considered good were widely circulated. One of the Dogood papers of Franklin's early teens contains *A Receipt to Make a New England Funeral Elegy.*

FOR THE SUBJECT OF YOUR ELEGY. Take one of your neighbors who has lately departed this life; it is no great matter at what age the party died, but it will be best if he went away suddenly, being killed, drowned, or froze to death.

Having chosen the person, take all his virtues, excellencies, etc., and if he have not enough, you may borrow some to make up a sufficient quantity: to these add his last words, dying expressions, etc., if they are to be had; mix all these together, and be sure you strain them well. Then season all with a handful or two of melancholy expressions, such as "dreadful," "deadly," "cruel cold death," "unhappy fate," "weeping eyes," etc. Having mixed all these ingredients well, put them into the empty scull of some young Harvard (but in case you have ne'er a one at hand, you may use

your own); there let them ferment for the space of a fortnight, and by that time they will be incorporated into a
body, which take out, and having prepared a sufficient
quantity of double rhymes, such as Power, Flower; Quiver,
Shiver; Grieve us, Leave us; tell you, excel you; expedi-
tions, physicians; fatigue him, intrigue him; etc., you must
spread all upon paper, and if you can procure a scrap of
Latin to put at the end, it will garnish it mightily; then
having affixed your name at the bottom, with a *Moestus
Composuit,* you will have an excellent Elegy.

N.B. This receipt will serve when a female is the subject
of your elegy, provided you borrow a greater quantity of
virtues, excellencies, etc.

To present-day readers, conditioned by television funnymen
and night-club "sick" comics, the jokes with which Franklin
larded the columns of the *Almanac* and the *Gazette* may not
seem funny. But in those days they were the only nonserious
writing current in the colonies. Some samples are: "We hear
from Birmingham in Warwickshire, that a certain tradesman's
wife of that place dying on Tuesday, her husband buried on the
Wednesday, married again on the Thursday, his new wife
brought to bed on the Friday, he hanged himself on the Satur-
day. *A fine week's work, truly."* "I am about courting a girl I
have had but little acquaintance with," he makes a correspond-
ent write. "How shall I come to a knowledge of her faults,
and whether she has the virtues I imagine she has?" "Commend
her among her female acquaintance," advises Franklin.

In another issue he printed a news item that a farmer had
the pewter buttons melted off his waistband by a flash of lightning and added, " 'Tis well nothing else thereabouts was made
of pewter. . . .

"The same day an unhappy man named Sturgis, upon some
difference with his wife, determined to drown himself in the
river; and she (kind wife) went with him, it seems, to see it

faithfully performed and accordingly stood by silent and unconcerned during the whole transaction. He jumped in near Carpenter's Wharf, but was timely taken out again, before what he came about was thoroughly effected, so that they were both obliged to return home as they came and put up for that time with the disappointment."

If he thought it would be amusing, Franklin was not above poking fun at his own convictions. His serious counsels all held up marriage as the best condition of men, yet it was a favorite subject for doggerel in the *Almanac:*

> Wedlock, as old men note, hath likened been,
> Unto a public crowd or common rout;
> Where those that are without would fain get in,
> And those that are within, would fain get out.
> Grief often treads upon the heels of pleasure,
> Married in haste, we oft repent at leisure;
> Some by experience find these words misplaced,
> Married at leisure, they repent in haste.

In one of his letters to Georgiana Shipley, Franklin wrote a comic epitaph to a squirrel. Deborah had sent the girl a squirrel which she named Mungo but called "Skugg"—then a general term for pet squirrels as "Puss" now is for cats. When Mungo was killed by a dog, Franklin wrote:

I LAMENT WITH YOU most sincerely the unfortunate end of poor Mungo. Few squirrels were better accomplished; for he had had a good education, traveled far, and seen much of the world. As he had the honor of being, for his virtues, your favorite, he should not go, like common skuggs, without an elegy or an epitaph. Let us give him one in the monumental style and measure which, being neither prose nor verse, is perhaps the properest for grief; since to use common language would look as if we were not affected, and to make rhymes would seem trifling in sorrow.

EPITAPH

Alas! poor *Mungo!*
Happy wert thou, hadst thou known
Thy own felicity.
Remote from the fierce bald eagle,
Tyrant of thy native woods,
Thou hadst naught to fear from his piercing talons,
Nor from the murdering gun
Of the thoughtless sportsman.
Safe in thy wired castle,
Grimalkin never could annoy thee.
Daily wert thou fed the choicest viands,
By the fair hand of an indulgent mistress;
But, discontented,
Thou wouldst have more freedom.
Too soon, alas, didst thou obtain it;
And wandering,
Thou art fallen by the fangs of wanton, cruel *Ranger!*

Learn hence,
Ye who blindly seek more liberty,
Whether subjects, sons, squirrels or daughters,
That apparent restraint may be real protection;
Yielding peace and plenty
With security.

You see, my dear Miss, how much more decent and
proper this broken style is, than if we were to say, by way
of epitaph,

Here *Skugg*
Lies snug,
As a bug
In a rug.

and yet, perhaps there are people in the world of so little feeling as to think that this would be a good enough epitaph for poor Mungo.

The great contribution of humor to Franklin's writing was the injection of a touch of lightness in his serious writing to drive home a point or to take the curse off pedantry. When he very seriously advised Georgiana Shipley on the importance of understanding the basics before rushing into experiments, he ended by saying: "This prudence of not attempting to give reasons before one is sure of facts, I learned from one of your sex, who, so Selden tells us, being in company with some gentlemen that were viewing and considering something which they called a Chinese shoe, and disputing earnestly about the manner of wearing it, and how it could possibly be put on, put in her word, and said modestly, 'Gentlemen, are you sure it is a shoe? Should not that be settled first?' "

In discussing a political matter that was dragging on interminably, he remarked: "I begin to be a little of the sailor's mind when they were handling a cable out of a store into a ship, and one of 'em said: ' 'Tis a long, heavy cable. I wish we could see the end of it.' 'D—n me,' says another, 'if I believe it has any end; somebody has cut it off.' "

Franklin poked fun at institutions, manners, classes and groups—"Necessity has no law; I know some attorneys of the same"—but he seldom ridiculed another individual, except his country's enemies. He well knew the danger of personal puns or satire, and had Poor Richard advise against such on several occasions: "Thou canst not joke an enemy into a friend, but thou mayest a friend into an enemy," and "Joke went out and brought home his fellow, and they two began to quarrel," or "He makes a foe who makes a jest."

His favorite subject for a jest was himself. Perhaps one important factor in his greatness was that he never took himself too seriously. There was nothing that was so deadly earnest that it could not be helped by humor—recall Jefferson's supposed comment that they would not let Franklin write the Declaration of Independence because they were afraid he would put a joke in it. When Madame Helvétius spurned his suit, he responded with a humorous bagatelle and, on an earlier occasion when he almost killed himself, he ended the description of the occasion with a gag:

BEING ABOUT TO KILL a turkey by the shock from two glass jars, containing as much electrical fire as forty common phials, I inadvertently took the whole through my own arms and body. . . . The company present (whose talking to me and to one another, I suppose, occasioned my inattention to what I was about) say that the flash was very great, and the crack as loud as a pistol; yet, my senses being instantly gone, I neither saw the one nor heard the other; nor did I feel the stroke on my hand. . . . I . . . felt what I know not how well to describe—a universal blow throughout my whole body from head to foot, which seemed within as well as without; after which the first thing I took notice of was a violent, quick shaking of my body, which gradually remitting, my sense as gradually returned.

As soon as he was sufficiently conscious to realize what had happened, he remarked: "Well, I meant to kill a turkey and instead I nearly killed a goose."

Humor was inherent in most of Franklin's hoaxes, as in the *Edict of the King of Prussia.* In some of his propaganda letters to the press in England he used a Baron Munchausen type of tale to make his point. The English press was ever fond of printing misinformation about the colonies, usually to the disadvantage of the Americans. To show the ridiculousness of some newspaper comments on the colonies, Franklin wrote this letter to the press:

DEAR SIR, do not let us suffer ourselves to be amused with such groundless objections. The very tails of the American sheep are so laden with wool, that each has a little car or wagon on four little wheels to support and keep it from trailing on the ground. Would they calk their ships; would they even litter their horses with wool, if it were not both plenty and cheap? . . . And yet all this is as certainly true as the account, said to be from Quebec, in all the papers of last week, that the inhabitants of Canada are making preparations for a cod and whale fishery this "summer in the upper Lakes." Ignorant people may object that the upper Lakes are fresh, and that cod and whales are salt-water fish, but let them know, sir, that cod, like other fish, when attacked by their enemies, fly into any water where they can be safest; that whales, when they have a mind to eat cod, pursue them wherever they fly, and that the grand leap of the whale in the chase up the Falls of Niagara is esteemed by all who have seen it as one of the finest spectacles in nature.

In his day, Franklin was accused of unseemly levity when he made such institutions as the clergy the subject of his light touch. An incident that he described while leading troops against the Indians in Pennsylvania was the type of thing that sometimes got him into hot water.

WE HAD FOR OUR CHAPLAIN a zealous Presbyterian minister, Mr. Beatty, who complained to me that the men did not generally attend his prayers and exhortations. When they enlisted, they were promised, besides pay and provisions, a gill of rum a day, which was punctually served out to them, half in the morning, and the other half in the evening; and I observed they were as punctual in attending to receive it; upon which I said to Mr. Beatty: "It is, perhaps, below the dignity of your profession to act as steward of the rum, but if you were to deal it out and only just after prayers, you would have them all about you." He liked the thought, undertook the office and, with the help of a few hands to measure out the liquor, executed it to satisfaction, and never were prayers more generally and more punctually attended; so that I thought this method preferable to the punishment inflicted by some military laws for nonattendance on divine service.

Some Franklin writing was long criticized for its use of words then considered vulgar. From a letter in which he seriously condemned dueling, comes this paragraph:

FORMERLY, when duels were used to determine lawsuits, from an opinion that Providence would in every instance favor truth and right with victory, they were excusable. At present they decide nothing. A man says something which another tells him is a lie. They fight; but whichever is killed, the point at dispute remains unsettled. To this purpose, they have a pleasant little story here. A gentleman in a coffeehouse desired another to sit farther from him. "Why so?" "Because, sir, you stink." "That is an affront and you must fight me." "I will fight you, if you insist upon it; but I do not see how that will mend the matter. For if you kill me, I shall stink too; and if I kill you, you will stink, if possible, worse than you do at present."

Many of Franklin's humorous writings preached a philosophy or made an argument for something in which he believed. One of the most famous, *The Speech of Polly Baker,* was, according to Franklin, written as a newspaper filler. Yet it deals with, although facetiously, a theme the philosopher frequently treated very seriously: more equality for women.

THE SPEECH OF Miss Polly Baker before a Court of Judicature at Connecticut near Boston in New England; where she was prosecuted the fifth time for having a bastard child: Which influenced the court to dispense with her punishment, and which induced one of her judges to marry her the next day—by whom she had fifteen children.

"May it please the honorable bench to indulge me in a few words; I am a poor, unhappy woman, who have no money to fee lawyers to plead for me, being hard put to it to get a living. . . . This is the fifth time, gentlemen, that I have been dragged before your court on the same account; twice I have paid heavy fines, and twice have been brought to public punishment, for want of money to pay those fines. This may have been agreeable to the laws, and I don't dispute it; but since laws are sometimes unreasonable in themselves, and therefore repealed; and others bear too hard on the subject in particular circumstances, and therefore there is left a power somewhere to dispense with the execution of them; I take the liberty to say that I think this law, by which I am punished, both unreasonable in itself, and particularly severe with regard to me, who have always lived an inoffensive life in the neighborhood where I was born, and defy my enemies (if I have any) to say I ever wronged any man, woman or child. Abstracted from the law, I cannot conceive (may it please your honors) what the nature of my offense is. I have brought five fine children into the world, at the risk of my life. . . . Can it be a crime (in the nature of things, I mean) to add to the King's subjects, in a new country, that really wants people? I own it, I should think it rather a praiseworthy than a punishable action. I have debauched no other woman's husband, nor enticed any other youth; these things I never was charged with; nor has anyone the least cause of complaint against me, unless, perhaps, the ministers of justice, because I have had children without being married, by which they have missed a wedding fee. But can this be a fault of mine? I appeal to your honors. You are pleased to allow I don't

want sense; but I must be stupefied to the last degree, not
to prefer the honorable state of wedlock to the condition
I have lived in. I always was, and still am, willing to enter
into it; and doubt not my behaving well in it, having all the
industry, frugality, fertility and skill in economy appertaining to a good wife's character. I defy anyone to say I ever
refused an offer of the sort; on the contrary, I readily con-
sented to the only proposal of marriage that ever was
made me, which was when I was a virgin, but too easily
confiding in the person's sincerity that made it, I unhappily
lost my honor by trusting to his; for he got me with child,
and then forsook me. . . .

"I should be told, 'tis like, that were there no act of
assembly in the case, the precepts of religion are violated
by my transgressions. If mine is a religious offense, leave it
to religious punishments. You have already excluded me
from the comforts of your church communion. Is not that
sufficient? You believe I have offended heaven, and must
suffer eternal fire: Will not that be sufficient? What need is
there then of your additional fines and whipping? I own I
do not think as you do, for, if I thought what you call a
sin was really such, I could not presumptuously commit
it. But, how can it be believed that heaven is angry at my
having children, when to the little done by me toward it,
God has been pleased to add his divine skill and admirable
workmanship in the formation of their bodies, and crowned
the whole by furnishing them with rational and immortal
souls?

"Forgive me, gentlemen, if I talk a little extravagantly
on these matters; I am no divine, but if you, gentlemen,
must be making laws, do not turn natural and useful actions
into crimes by your prohibitions. But take into your wise
consideration the great and growing number of bachelors
in the country, many of whom, from the mean fear of the
expenses of a family, have never sincerely and honorably

courted a woman in their lives; and by their manner of living leave unproduced (which is little better than murder) hundreds of their posterity to the thousandth generation. Is this not a greater offense against the public good than mine? . . . What must poor young women do, whom customs and nature forbid to solicit the men, and who cannot force themselves upon husbands, when the laws take no care to provide them any, and yet severely punish them if they do their duty without them; the duty of the first and great command of nature and nature's God, Increase and multiply: a duty, from the steady performance of which nothing has been able to deter me, but for its sake I have hazarded the loss of public esteem, and have frequently endured public disgrace and punishment; and therefore ought, in my humble opinion, instead of a whipping, to have a statue erected to my memory."

Franklin probably wrote *Polly Baker* in 1746, but its authorship was a mystery for many years. In 1818 Thomas Jefferson told a story that he claimed he had heard from Franklin in France in 1785. Abbé Raynal had written a book, *Histoire des Deux Indes;* Silas Deane and he were arguing about it in Franklin's presence, Deane claiming that there were numerous inaccuracies in it, specifically the story about Polly Baker, which could not be true because there was no law against bastardy in New England. The Abbé claimed that he had this story on very good authority. At this point they noticed that Franklin was shaking with laughter, and asked him why. "I will tell you, Abbé, the origin of that story," said Franklin. "When I was a printer and editor of a newspaper, we were sometimes slack of news and, to amuse our customers, I used to fill up our vacant columns with anecdotes and fables and fancies of my own; and this Polly Baker is a story of my making, on one of such occasions." Not the least disconcerted, the Abbé replied with a laugh, "Oh, very well, Doctor, I had rather relate your stories than other men's truths."

John Adams had something to say about *Polly Baker,* too. He said it was one of Franklin's many "outrages to morality and decorum."

The most famous of Franklin's light writings are whimsical rather than humorous—the bagatelles. These are the several gay and light little pieces which came from his press in Passy, most of which were inspired by, or dedicated to one or the other of his charming female neighbors. He originally set up the press, probably in 1777, to print documents relating to the work of the American commissioners. The earliest known Passy imprint is an invitation to dinner to celebrate July 4, 1779. During the last years in France the press was busy. He employed two or three men to help him cast type, compose, and print; but it is possible that he set and printed at least some of the bagatelles, in French and English, himself. The first one was for Madame Brillon and was inspired by a trip to an island which he had made in her company where they had seen many ephemeraes—May flies. It is called *The Ephemera.*

YOU MAY REMEMBER, my dear friend, that when we lately spent that happy day in the delightful garden and sweet society of the Moulin Joly, I stopped a little in one of our walks, and stayed some time behind the company. We had been shown numberless skeletons of a kind of little fly, called an ephemera, whose successive generations, we were told, were bred and expired within the day. I happened to see a living company of them on a leaf, who appeared to be engaged in conversation. You know I understand all the inferior animal tongues: my too great application to the study of them is the best excuse I can give for the little progress I have made in your charming language. I listened through curiosity to the discourse of these little creatures; but as they, in their national vivacity, spoke three or four together, I could make but little of their conversations. I found, however, by some broken expressions that I heard now and then, they were disputing warmly on the merit of two foreign musicians, one a cousin, the other a *moscheto;* in which dispute they spent their time, seemingly as regardless of the shortness of life as if they had been sure of living a month. Happy people, thought I, you live certainly under a wise, just and mild government, since you have no public grievances to complain of, nor any subject of contention but the perfections and imperfections of foreign music! I turned my head from them to an old grayheaded one, who was single on another leaf, and talking to himself. Being amused with his soliloquy, I put it down in writing, in hopes it will likewise amuse her to whom I am so much indebted for the most pleasing of all amusements, her delicious company and heavenly harmony.

"It was," said he, "the opinion of learned philosophers of our race, who lived and flourished long before my time, that this vast world, the Moulin Joly, could not itself subsist more than eighteen hours; and I think there was some foundation for that opinion, since, by the apparent motion of the great luminary that gives life to all nature, and which in my time has evidently declined considerably toward the ocean at the end of our earth, it must then finish its course, be extinguished in the waters that surround us, and leave the world in cold and darkness, necessarily producing universal death and destruction. I have lived seven of those hours, a great age, being no less than four hundred and twenty minutes of time. How very few of us continue so long! I have seen generations born, flourish, and expire. My present friends are the children and grandchildren of the friends of my youth, who are now, alas, no more! And I must soon follow them; for, by the course of nature, though still in health, I cannot expect to live above seven or eight minutes longer. What now avails all my toil and labor, in amassing honey-dew on this leaf, which I cannot live to enjoy! What the political struggles I have been engaged in, for the good of my compatriot inhabitants of this bush, or my philosophical studies for the benefit of our race in general; for, in politics, what can laws do without morals? Our present race of ephemerae will in a course of minutes become corrupt, like those of other and older bushes, and consequently as wretched. And in philosophy, how small our progress! Alas! art is long and life is short! My friends would comfort me with the idea of a name, they say, I shall leave behind me; and they tell me I have lived long enough to nature and to glory. But what will fame be to an ephemera who no longer exists? And what will become of all history in the eighteenth hour, when the world itself, even the whole Moulin Joly, shall come to its end, and be buried in universal ruin?

"To me, after all my eager pursuits, no solid pleasures now remain, but the reflection of a long life spent in meaning well, the sensible conversation of a few good lady ephemerae, and now and then a kind smile and a tune from the ever amiable Brillante."

For Madame Helvétius he wrote the bagatelle relating his conversation with M. Helvétius in Elysium. Then it was Madame Brillon's turn again, and he wrote *The Whistle:*

I AM CHARMED with your description of Paradise, and with your plan of living there; and I approve much of your conclusion that, in the meantime, we should draw all the good we can from this world. In my opinion, we might all draw more good from it than we do, and suffer less evil, if we would take care not to give too much for whistles. For to me it seems that most of the unhappy people we meet with are become so by neglect of that caution.

You ask what I mean? You love stories, and will excuse my telling one of myself.

When I was a child of seven years old, my friends on a holiday filled my pockets with coppers. I went directly to a shop where they sold toys for children; and, being charmed with the sound of a whistle that I met by the way in the hands of another boy, I voluntarily offered and gave all my money for one. I then came home, and went whistling all over the house, much pleased with my whistle, but disturbing all the family. My brothers, and sisters, and cousins, understanding the bargain I had made, told me I had given four times as much for it as it was worth; put me in mind of what good things I might have bought with the rest of the money; and laughed at me so much for my folly, that I cried with vexation; and the reflection gave me more chagrin than the whistle gave me pleasure.

This however was afterward of use to me, the impression continuing on my mind; so that often, when I was tempted to buy some unnecessary thing, I said to myself, "Don't give too much for the whistle"; and I saved my money.

As I grew up, came into the world, and observed the action of men, I thought I met with many, very many, who *gave too much for the whistle.*

When I saw one too ambitious of court favor, sacrificing his time in attendance on levees, his repose, his liberty, his virtue, and perhaps his friends, to attain it, I have said to myself, "This man gives too much for his whistle."

When I saw another fond of popularity, constantly employing himself in political bustles, neglecting his own affairs, and ruining them by that neglect, "He pays, indeed," said I, "too much for his whistle."

If I knew a miser, who gave up every kind of comfortable living, all the pleasure of doing good to others, all the esteem of his fellow citizens, and the joys of benevolent friendship, for the sake of accumulating wealth, "Poor man," said I, "you pay too much for your whistle."

When I met with a man of pleasure, sacrificing every laudable improvement of the mind, or of his fortune, to mere corporeal sensations, and ruining his health in their pursuit, "Mistaken man," said I, "you are providing pain for yourself, instead of pleasure; you give too much for your whistle."

If I see one fond of appearance, or fine clothes, fine houses, fine furniture, fine equipages, all above his fortune, for which he contracts debts, and ends his career in a prison, "Alas!" say I, "he has paid dear, very dear for his whistle."

In short, I conceive that great part of the miseries of mankind are brought upon them by the false estimates they have made of the value of things, and by their giving too much for their whistles.

Yet I ought to have charity for these unhappy people, when I consider that, with all this wisdom of which I am boasting, there are certain things in the world so tempting, for example, the apples of King John, which happily are not to be bought; for if they were put to sale by auction, I might very easily be led to ruin myself in the purchase, and find that I had once more given too much for the whistle.

At no time in his life, regardless of age or illness or cares, or the pressure of portentous events, did Franklin lose his sense of humor—his feeling that life and his relation to it was something about which there was a gaiety and a lighter side which made everything more bearable and made many things more understandable. He once wrote of his desire to end his life with a worth-while accomplishment, but what he said applies equally to his philosophy of humor. "Life, like a dramatic piece, should not only be conducted with regularity but, methinks, it should end handsomely. Being now in the last act, I begin to cast around for something fit to end with. Or, if mine be more properly compared to an epigram, as some of its lines are but barely tolerable, I am very desirous of concluding with a bright point."

CHAPTER XIV

FOURSCORE YEARS

ॐ

Benjamin Franklin was an old man when he went to France in 1776. When he returned to America in 1785, he was a very old man—four months short of his eightieth birthday. It was almost forty years since he had retired as a prosperous tradesman to devote his later life to philosophy. The demands of public service had deferred that dream. Instead, politics and diplomacy had kept him far from his home and family for half a lifetime. Now, surely, he could relax in the late evening of his life with the very few old friends that were left and his grandchildren, most of whom he had never seen. It was not to be.

The day after he returned the speaker and members of the General Assembly called and made a speech. Next day it was the provost and professors from the University with an address to the man who had first projected the Academy. The following day a committee from the Constitutional Society, who favored the status quo in relation to the state constitution, asked him to stand for election to the Supreme Executive Council. They were too late—he had already agreed to run on the ticket of the Anti-Constitutionalists, the moderates who wanted to revise the constitution. The Constitutionalists nominated him too, as did the

Mechanics Party. He was elected first to the Council, then to the presidency—the governorship of Pennsylvania.

"I had on my return some right . . . to expect repose," wrote Franklin, "and it was my intention to avoid all public business. But I had not firmness enough to resist the unanimous desire of my country folks, and I find myself harnessed again in their service for another year. They engrossed the prime of my life. They have eaten my flesh and seem resolved now to pick my bones." In another letter he said, "Though I apprehend they expect too much of me, and that without doing the good proposed I shall find myself engaged again in business more troublesome than I have lately quitted."

The old sage did not work too hard at being governor. His prestige was the important thing; the day-by-day routine of government could be left to younger men. The octogenarian was on the side of progress. To Bishop Shipley he wrote, "You seem desirous of knowing what progress we make here in improving our government. We are, I think in the right road of improvement, for we are making experiments. I do not oppose all that seem wrong, for the multitude are more effectually set right by experience, than kept from going wrong by reasoning with them; so that I have no doubt of our obtaining in a few years as much public felicity as good government is capable of affording, as I think we are daily more and more enlightened."

The old man observed events with the optimism of youth. To Thomas Jefferson he reported:

As to public affairs. . . . The disposition to furnish Congress with ample powers augments daily, as people become more enlightened, and I do not remember ever to have seen during my long life more signs of public felicity than appear at present throughout these states; the cultivators of the earth who make the bulk of our nation having had good crops, which are paid for at high prices with ready money, the artisans too receive high wages, and the value of all real estate is augmented greatly. Merchants and shop-keepers, indeed, complain that there is not business enough, but this is evidently not owing to the fewness of buyers, but the too great numbers of sellers, for the consumption of goods was never greater, as appears by the dress, furniture, and manner of living of all ranks of the people.

To Polly Hewson, nee Stevenson, he described a little of his personal life, and the social side of Philadelphia.

I HAVE FOUND my family here in health, good circumstances, and well respected by their fellow citizens. The companions of my youth are indeed almost all departed, but I find an agreeable society among their children and grandchildren. I have public business enough to preserve me from ennui, and private amusement besides in conversation, books, my garden and cribbage. . . . Cards we sometimes play here, in long winter evenings; but it is as they play at chess, not for money, but for honor, or the pleasure of beating one another. This will not be quite a novelty to you, as you may remember we played together in that manner during the winter at Passy. I have indeed now and then a little compunction in reflecting that I spend time so idly; but another reflection comes to relieve me, whispering: "You know that the soul is immortal; why then should you be such a niggard of a little time, when you have a whole eternity before you?" So, being easily convinced, and, like other reasonable creatures, satisfied with a small reason, when it is in favor of doing what I have in mind to do, I shuffle the cards again, and begin another game.

Franklin's personal wealth had tripled since the Revolution as a result of the rise in real estate values. Partly for profit and partly for fun he started to build houses. He told his sister: "I have ordered an addition to the house I live in, it being too small for our growing family. There are a good many hands employed, and I hope to see it covered in before the winter. . . . I hardly know how to justify building a library at an age that will so soon oblige me to quit it; but we are apt to forget that we are grown old, and building is an amusement."

When he finished the addition to his house he had another "first" to add to the many of his long life. His library was the largest and finest private book collection in America. To make it more convenient and comfortable, he devised his last three inventions: a fan which worked with the touch of his foot; a chair that converted into a small stepladder like present-day kitchen stools; and a mechanical hand for picking books off high shelves. This latter device was in constant use in grocery stores until supermarkets introduced self-service.

Franklin had long dreamed of returning to the scientific career of his middle age when his public life was over. Shortly before he left France he had written to fellow scientist Ingen- housz, "Rejoice with me, dear friend, that I am once more a free man after fifty years service in public affairs. And let me know soon if you will make me happy the little remainder of my life by spending the time with me in America. I have instruments, if the enemy did not destroy them all, and we will make plenty of experiments together." (The British officers who lived in Franklin's house during the occupation of Philadelphia did little damage. Most significant loss was a Franklin portrait stolen by Major André, of Arnold infamy, which remained in England until 1906 and now hangs in the White House.) The old man had little time for scientific experiments in his final years.

Franklin hoped that he might visit Boston before he died, but business and health conspired against it. His kidney stone soon made movement difficult. Walking and riding in a carriage was painful. To a friend in France he said, "I have sometimes wished I had brought with me from France a balloon suffi- ciently large to raise me from the ground. In my malady it would have been the easiest carriage for me, being led by a string held by a man walking on the ground." But his pen was busy writing to his Passy neighbors, to the Shipleys, to Polly Hewson coaxing her to come to America. His interest in the affairs of man did not dim.

In 1786, a feeling was growing that the Articles of Confederation under which the colonies had first been joined were not sufficient for a United States. A constitution which better defined the central government was needed. Although Franklin was not among those who were deeply disturbed by the weakness of the Articles, he favored the Constitutional Convention in a letter to Jefferson. "The delegates generally appointed . . . are men of character . . . so that I hope good from their meeting. Indeed if it does not do good it must do harm, as it will show that we have not wisdom enough among us to govern ourselves and will strengthen the opinion of some political writers that popular governments cannot long support themselves." Not among the Pennsylvania delegates appointed in December, Franklin was added in March, 1787, and took his seat when the Constitutional Convention assembled on May 25.

The Constitution was not Franklin's document, any more than it was Washington's. But the former from the floor and the latter from the chair exerted a powerful influence in guiding the younger Constitution framers toward agreement through compromise. Three of Franklin's important ideas—a single legislature, a plural executive, and no salaries for top government officers—were turned down by the Convention.

Franklin spoke at length on the matter of salaries—or, rather, he wrote a speech which was read for him. In it he said:

I THINK I SEE inconveniences in the appointment of salaries; I see none in refusing them, but, on the contrary, great advantages.

There are two passions which have a powerful influence in the affairs of men. These are ambition and avarice; the love of power and the love of money. Separately, each of these has great force in prompting men to action; but when united in view of the same object, they have in many minds the most violent effects. Place before the eyes of such men a post of honor, that shall at the same time be a place of profit, and they will move heaven and earth to obtain it. . . .

And of what kind are the men that will strive for this profitable pre-eminence through all the bustle of cabal, the heat of contention, the infinite mutual abuse of parties, tearing to pieces the best of characters? It will not be the wise and moderate, the lovers of peace and good order, the men fittest for the trust. It will be the bold and the violent, the men of strong passion and indefatigable activity in their selfish pursuits. These will thrust themselves into your government and be your rulers.

The motion on salaries was seconded by Alexander Hamilton to bring it before the body and, after Franklin's speech, it was postponed and forgotten. James Madison said that "It was treated with great respect, but rather for the author of it than from any conviction of its expediency or practicability."

Greatest stumbling block at the Convention was the question of representation in the legislature. Massachusetts, Pennsylvania and Virginia, with almost 40 per cent of the prospective voters, wanted it in terms of population. The ten smaller states wanted equal representation for each state. When debate on this became so acrimonious that it seemed the Convention might break up without agreement, Franklin made the first of his conciliatory speeches:

IT HAS GIVEN ME great pleasure to observe that till this point, the proportion of representation, came before us, our debates were carried on with great coolness and temper. If anything of a contrary kind has, on this occasion, appeared, I hope it will not be repeated; for we are sent hither to consult, not to contend, with each other, and declarations of a fixed opinion, and of determined resolution never to change it, neither enlighten nor convince us. Positiveness and warmth on one side naturally beget their like on the other, and tend to create and augment discord and division in a great concern, wherein harmony and union are extremely necessary to give weight to our counsels, and render them effectual in promoting and securing the common good. . . .

He next poured oil on the turbulent assembly—still wrangling about representation—in a speech moving that sessions be opened with prayer.

THE SMALL PROGRESS we have made, after four or five weeks' close attendance, and continual reasonings with each other, our different sentiments on almost every question, several of the last producing as many noes as ayes, is, methinks, a melancholy proof of the imperfection of human understanding. We indeed seem to feel our own want of political wisdom, since we have been running all about in search of it. We have gone back to ancient history for models of government, and examined the different forms of those republics which, having been originally formed with the seeds of their own dissolution, now no longer exist, and we have viewed modern States all round Europe, but find none of their constitutions suitable to our circumstances.

In this situation of this assembly, groping, as it were, in the dark, to find political truth, and scarce able to distinguish it when presented to us, how is it happened, sir, that we have not hitherto once thought of humbly applying to the Father of Lights to illuminate our understandings? In the beginning of the contest with Britain, when we were sensible of danger, we had daily prayers in this room for the Divine protection. Our prayers, sir, were heard—and they were graciously answered. All of us who were engaged in the struggle must have observed frequent instances of a superintending Providence in our favor. To that kind Providence we owe this happy opportunity of consulting in peace on the means of establishing our future national felicity. And have we now forgotten that powerful Friend? or do we imagine we no longer need its assistance? I have lived, sir, a long time, and the longer I live the more convincing proofs I see of this truth, that God governs in the affairs of men. And if a sparrow cannot fall to the ground without his notice, is it probable that an empire can rise without his aid? We have been assured, sir, in the sacred writings that "except the Lord build the house, they labor in vain that build it." I firmly believe this, and I also believe that without his concurring aid we shall succeed in this political building no better than the builders of Babel; we shall be divided by our little, partial, local interests, our projects will be confounded, and we ourselves shall become a reproach and a byword down to future ages. And, what is worse, mankind may hereafter, from this unfortunate instance, despair of establishing government by human wisdom, and leave it to chance, war, and conquest.

I therefore beg leave to move—

That henceforth prayers, imploring the assistance of Heaven and its blessing on our deliberations, be held in this assembly every morning before we proceed to business; and that one or more of the clergy of this city be requested to officiate in that service.

It is strange that this suggestion came from Franklin the freethinker—and was ignored by the majority of church members at the convention. Franklin wrote on the edge of the manuscript of his motion, "The Convention, except for three or four persons, thought prayers unnecessary." But the motion diverted the hotheads and calmed things down. Two days later, the doctor made a compromise motion. "The diversity of opinions," he said, "turns on two points. If a proportional representation takes place, the small states contend that their liberties will be in danger. If an equality of votes is to be put in its place, the large states say that their money will be in danger. When a broad table is to be made, and the edges of the planks do not fit, the artist takes a little from both and makes a good joint. In like manner here both sides must part with some of their demands, in order that they may join in some accommodating proposition."

This led to the appointment of a committee, with one delegate from each state, which formulated the basis of the two-house legislature. Franklin made the motion which recommended: (1) In the first branch of the legislature (the House of Representatives) there should be one representative from each state for every 40,000 of its inhabitants (changed to 30,000 before the Constitution was signed); (2) All bills for raising or appropriating money should originate in the first branch and not be subject to alteration or amendment in the second; (3) In the second branch (the Senate) the states should have equal votes.

This was Franklin's great contribution to the Constitution. Without it, and his influence, the delegates might have dispersed without agreement. For the time, there might not have been a Constitution. For the remainder of the Convention, the old man had little to say until the last day. Then, when the engrossed document was read by the secretary, James Wilson rose to read a speech Franklin had written.

I CONFESS that I do not entirely approve of this Constitution at present; but, sir, I am not sure I shall never approve it; for having lived long, I have experienced many instances of being obliged, by better information or fuller consideration, to change opinions even on important subjects, which I once thought right, but found to be otherwise. It is therefore that, the older I grow, the more apt I am to doubt my own judgment of others. Most men, indeed, as well as most sects in religion, think themselves in possession of all truth, and that wherever others differ from them, it is so far error. Steele, a Protestant, in a dedication, tells the Pope that the only difference between our two churches in their opinions of the certainty of their doctrine is, the Romish Church is infallible, and the Church of England is never in the wrong. But though many private persons think almost as highly of their own infallibility as that of their sect, few express it so naturally as a certain French lady who, in a little dispute with her sister, said: "But I meet with nobody but myself that is *always* in the right."

In these sentiments, sir, I agree to this Constitution, with all its faults—if they are such—because I think a general government necessary for us, and there is no form of government but what may be a blessing to the people, if well administered; and I believe further, that this is likely to be well administered for a course of years, and can only end in despotism, as other forms have done before it, when the people shall become so corrupted as to need despotic government, being incapable of any other. I doubt, too, whether any other convention we can obtain, may be able to make a better Constitution; for, when you assemble a number of men, to have the advantage of their joint wisdom, you inevitably assemble with those men, all their prejudices, their passions, their errors of opinion, their local interests, and their selfish views. From such an assembly can a perfect production be expected? It therefore astonishes me, sir, to find this system approaching so near perfection as it does; and I think it will astonish our enemies, who are waiting with confidence to hear that our counsels are confounded like those of the builders of Babel, and that our States are on the point of separation, only to meet hereafter for the purpose of cutting one another's throats. Thus I consent, sir, to this Constitution, because I expect no better, and because I am not sure that it is not the best. The opinions I have had of its errors I sacrifice to the public good. I have never whispered a syllable of them abroad. Within these walls were they born, and here they shall die. If every one of us, returning to our constituents, were to report the objections he has had to it, and endeavor to gain partisans in support of them, we might prevent its being generally received, and thereby lose all the salutary effects and great advantages resulting naturally in our favor among foreign nations, as well as among ourselves from our real or apparent unanimity. Much of the strength and efficiency of any government in procuring and securing happiness to the people, depends on opinion, on the general opinion of the goodness of that government, as well as of the wisdom and integrity of its governors. I hope, therefore, for our own sakes, as a part of the people, and for the sake of our posterity, that we shall act heartily and unanimously in recommending this Constitution, wherever our influence may extend, and turn our future thoughts and endeavors to the means of having it well administered.

On the whole, sir, I cannot help expressing a wish that every member of the convention who may still have objections to it would with me on this occasion doubt a little of his own infallibility and, to make manifest our unanimity, put his name to this instrument.

This was not quite the last word that Franklin spoke at the Convention. James Madison reports a final statement.

WHILE THE LAST MEMBERS were signing it, Dr. Franklin looked toward the president's chair at the back of which a rising sun happened to be painted, observed to a few members near him that painters had found it difficult to distinguish in their art a rising from a setting sun. "I have," said he, "often and often in the course of the session, and the

vicissitudes of my hopes and fears as to its issue, looked at
that behind the president without being able to tell whether it
was rising or setting. But now at length I have the happiness
to know that it is a rising and not a setting sun."

And he made a further famous remark about the historic
document: "Our new Constitution is now established and has
an appearance that promises permanency; but in this world
nothing can be said to be certain but death and taxes."

The Constitutional Convention was Franklin's last appearance on the national scene. His relationship with the Congress
of the country he had served so well ended on a sour note. He
felt that Congress might at least have thanked him for his years
of service and, perhaps, made some token expression of gratitude. To old friend Charles Thomson, secretary of Congress,
he wrote:

I MUST OWN, I did hope that, as it is customary in Europe,
to make some liberal provision for ministers when they return home from foreign service, the Congress would at least
have been kind enough to have shown their approbation of
my conduct by a grant of a small tract of land in their western country, which might have been of use and some honor
to my posterity. . . .

This is all to you yourself only as a private friend; for I
have not, nor ever shall, make any public complaint; and
even if I could have foreseen such unkind treatment from
Congress, their refusing me thanks would not in the least
have abated my zeal for the cause and ardor in support of it.
I know something of the nature of such changeable assemblies, and how little successors know of the services that have
been rendered to the corps before their admission, or feel
themselves obliged by such services; and what effect in
obliterating a sense of them during the absence of the serv-

ant in a distant country, the artful and reiterated malevolent insinuations of one or two envious and malicious persons may have on the minds of members, even of the most equitable, candid, and honorable dispositions; and therfore I will pass these reflections into oblivion.

"The envious and malicious persons" to whom Franklin referred were the Lees, Arthur and Richard Henry, much active in Congressional affairs, and John Adams. Arthur Lee was probably responsible for the rumor that a million livres that had passed through Franklin's hands were not accounted for. Franklin explained, and history proved, that this was a million that Beaumarchais had received before the American commissioners arrived in France. Also, when he had returned from France, he had submitted his accounts to the auditor of Congress—

WHICH HE EXAMINED . . . the difference between my statement and his being only seven sols, which by mistake I had overcharged; about threepence half-penny sterling.

At my request, however, the accounts were left open for the consideration of Congress, and not finally settled, there being some articles on which I desired their judgment. . . .

It is now more than three years that those accounts have been before that honorable body, and, to this day, no notice of any such objection has been communicated to me. But reports have, for some time past, been circulated here, and propagated in the newspapers, that I am greatly indebted to the United States for large sums that had been put into my hands, and that I avoid a settlement. This, together with the little time one of my age may expect to live, makes it necessary for me to request earnestly, which I hereby do, that the Congress would be pleased, without further delay, to examine those accounts.

Congress never replied to this letter.

Franklin made his will in July, 1788. By this time he had achieved world fame as a scientist and a seer, a politician and a philosopher. But he styled himself, "I, Benjamin Franklin, of Philadelphia, printer." The bulk of his estate went to relatives, particularly his daughter Sarah Bache and her husband Richard, with the request that, "in consideration thereof he would immediately after my decease manumit and set free his Negro man Bob." Son William received only some land in Nova Scotia. "The part he acted against me in the late war, which is of public notoriety, will account for me leaving him no more of an estate he endeavored to deprive me of." His sister received a house in Boston and fifty pounds a year; Temple some land in Georgia and a quit claim on a four-thousand-pound debt; Benny Bache, whom he had already set up in business, got his grandfather's share in the Library Company and all the type and printing materials in Philadelphia.

To his daughter Sarah also went a miniature of Louis XVI, surrounded by 408 diamonds, a gift from France, providing that "she would not form any of those diamonds into ornaments either for herself or daughters, and thereby introduce or countenance the expensive, vain and useless fashion of wearing jewels in this country." Austerity was the rule for poor Sally, even from the grave.

In a codicil to the will, made the next year, was another specific bequest. "My fine crab-tree walking-stick, with a gold head curiously wrought in the form of a cap of liberty, I give to my friend, and the friend of mankind, General Washington. If it were a scepter, he has merited it and would become it."

The main feature of the codicil was a scheme of philanthropy which was to run for two centuries. In line with his views on salaries for government officers, Franklin had not accepted his salary as President of Pennsylvania. This now amounted to two thousand pounds which he left to the citizens of Boston and Philadelphia.

I HAVE CONSIDERED THAT, among artisans, good apprentices are most likely to make good citizens, and, having myself been bred to a manual art, printing, in my native town, and afterward assisted to set up my business in Philadelphia by kind loans of money from two friends there, which was the foundation of my fortune, and of all the utility in life that may be ascribed to me, I wish to be useful even after my death, if possible, in forming and advancing other young men, that may be serviceable to their country in both these towns. To this end, I devote two thousand pounds sterling, of which I give one thousand thereof to the inhabitants of Boston, in Massachusetts, and the other thousand to the inhabitants of the city of Philadelphia, in trust, to and for the uses, intents, and purposes hereinafter mentioned and declared.

The said sum . . . shall be managed under the direction of the selectmen, united with the ministers of the oldest Episcopalian, Congregation and Presbyterian churches in that town, who are to let out the sum upon interest at the rate of 5 per cent per annum, to such young married artificers, under the age of twenty-five years, as have served an apprenticeship in the said town, and faithfully fulfilled the duties required in their indentures, so as to obtain a good moral character from at least two respectable citizens, who are willing to become their sureties, in a bond with the applicants, for the repayment of the moneys so lent, with interest. . . .

The funds did not work out as Franklin planned. He stipulated that no single loan, for the purpose of setting up a business, should exceed sixty pounds and this amount was soon insignificant for such purposes. Early in this century, Philadelphia transferred over $130,000 from Franklin's bequest to the Franklin Institute and currently has a balance of $134,835. Boston used some, with added help from Andrew Carnegie to build a technical school, Franklin Union, and now has $1,539,-791.

Franklin had not much time left. He said:

I AM GROWN SO OLD as to have buried most of the friends of my youth, and I now often hear persons whom I knew when children, called old Mr. Such-a-One, to distinguish them from their sons now men grown and in business; so that by living twelve years beyond David's period, I seem to have intruded myself into the company of posterity, when I ought to have been abed and asleep. Yet, had I gone at seventy, it would have cut off twelve of the most active years of my life, employed too in matters of the greatest importance; and whether I have been doing good or mischief is for time to discover. I only know that I intended well, and I hope all will end well.

He tried to continue his autobiography, but as his stone became worse he said, "Of late I am so interrupted by extreme pain, which obliges me to have recourse to opium, that between the effects of both I have but little time in which I can write anything."

He wrote to his friend Washington:

MY MALADY RENDERS my sitting up to write rather painful to me; but I cannot let my son-in-law Mr. Bache part for New York without congratulating you by him on the recovery of your health, so precious to us all, and on the growing strength of our new government under your administration. For my own personal ease I should have died two years ago; but, though those years have been spent in excruciating pain, I am pleased that I have lived them, since they have brought me to see our present situation. I am now finishing my eighty-fourth year, and probably with it my career in this life; but, whatever state of existence I am placed hereafter, if I retain any memory of what has passed here, I shall with it retain the esteem, respect, and affection with which I have long been, my dear friend, yours most sincerely,

B. FRANKLIN

In 1787 Franklin had become president of the first abolition society, an organization originally founded by Quakers with the resounding title: "The Pennsylvania Society for Promoting the Abolition of Slavery, and the Relief of Free Negroes Unlawfully Held in Bondage." Less than a month before his death he wrote his last public paper. Characteristically, it was a hoax, or parody, to make a point in connection with the betterment of his fellow man. The Abolition Society had presented a memorial to Congress, signed by Franklin, asking that body to exert itself to discourage the slave trade. James Jackson, of Georgia, had made a speech to the effect that Congress had no right to meddle—slavery was a matter for the states. Franklin wrote a parody in which he put Jackson's arguments in the mouth of the Dey of Algiers in a statement he was supposed to have made in 1687. He sent it to the *Federal Gazette,* signed "Historicus."

Allah Bismillah, etc. God is great, and Mahomet is his Prophet.

Have these *Erika* [Quakers] considered the consequences of granting their petition? If we cease our cruises against the Christians, how shall we be furnished with the commodities their countries produce, and which are so necessary to us? If we forbear to make slaves of their people, who in this hot climate are to cultivate our lands? Who are to perform the common labors of our city, and in our families? Must we not then be our own slaves? And is there not more compassion and more favor due to us as Mussulmen than to these Christian dogs? We have now above fifty thousand slaves in and near Algiers. This number, if not

kept up by fresh supplies, will soon diminish and be gradually annihilated. If we than cease taking and plundering
the infidel ships, and making slaves of the seamen and
passengers, our lands will become of no value for want
of cultivation; the rents of houses in the city will sink one
half; and the revenue of government arising from its share
of prizes be totally destroyed! And for what? To gratify
the whims of a whimsical sect, who would have us not only
forbear making more slaves, but even manumit those we
have.

But who is to indemnify their masters for the loss? Will the
state do it? Is our treasury sufficient? Will the *Erika* do it?
Can they do it? Or would they, to do what they think justice
to the slaves, do a greater injustice to the owners? And if
we set our slaves free, what is to be done with them? Few of
them will return to their countries; they know too well the
greater hardships they must there be subject to; they will
not embrace our holy religion; they will not adopt our manners; our people will not pollute themselves by marrying
with them. Must we maintain them as beggars in our streets,
or suffer our properties to be the prey of their pillage? For
men accustomed to slavery will not work for a livelihood
when not compelled. And what is there so pitiable in their
present condition? Were they not slaves in their own countries? . . .

I repeat the question, What is to be done with them? I
have heard it suggested that they may be planted in the
wilderness, where there is plenty of land for them to subsist
on, and where they may flourish as a free state; but they are,
I doubt, too little disposed to labor without compulsion, as
well as too ignorant to establish a good government, and
the wild Arabs would soon molest and destroy or again en-
slave them. While serving us, we take care to provide them
with everything, and they are treated with humanity. The
laborers in their own country are, as I am well informed,

worse fed, lodged and clothed. The condition of most of them is therefore already mended, and requires no further improvement. . . .

Let us then hear no more of this detestable proposition, the manumission of Christian slaves, the adoption of which would, by depreciating our lands and houses, and thereby depriving so many good citizens of their properties, create universal discontent, and provoke insurrections, to the endangering of government and producing general confusion. . . .

One of his last letters was to Ezra Stiles, President of Yale. Stiles had written asking for a portrait of Franklin for the university and then had continued, "As much as I know of Dr. Franklin, I have not an idea of his religious sentiments. I wish to know the opinion of my venerable friend concerning Jesus of Nazareth." To this the old man replied:

YOU DESIRE TO KNOW something of my religion. It is the first time I have been questioned upon it. But I cannot take your curiosity amiss, and shall endeavor in a few words to gratify it. Here is my creed. I believe in one God, the Creator of the universe. That He governs it by His providence. That He ought to be worshiped. That the most acceptable service we render to Him is doing good to His other children. That the soul of man is immortal, and will be treated with justice in another life respecting its conduct in this. These I take to be the fundamental points in all sound religion, and I regard them as you do in whatever sect I meet with them.

As to Jesus of Nazareth, my opinion of whom you particularly desire, I think his system of morals and his religion, as he left them to us, the best the world ever saw or is like to see; but I apprehend it has received various corrupting changes, and I have, with most of the present dissenters in England, some doubts as to his divinity; though it is a question I do not dogmatize upon, having never studied it, and think it needless to busy myself with it now, when I expect soon an opportunity of knowing the truth with less trouble. I see no harm, however, in its being believed, if that belief has the good consequence, as probably it has, of making his doctrines more respected and more observed; especially as I do not perceive that the Supreme takes it amiss, by distinguishing the unbelievers in His government of the world with any peculiar marks of His displeasure.

I shall only add, respecting myself that, having experienced the goodness of that Being in conducting me prosperously through a long life, I have no doubt of its continuance in the next, though without the smallest conceit of meriting such goodness.

Franklin was in bed for much of the last year of his life, frequently in great pain for which he was given sedatives. He died on April 17, 1790, aged eighty-four years and three months. His physician described the end: "A few days before he died he rose from his bed and begged that it might be made up for him so that he might die in a decent manner. His daughter told him that she hoped he would recover and live many years longer. He calmly replied, 'I hope not.' Upon being advised to change his position in bed, so that he might breathe easy, he said, 'A dying man can do nothing easy.'" These were his last words.

There have been many eulogies for Franklin, from the day after his death down to the present. One of the best was written only a few years ago by Carl Van Doren at the end of his great biography of Franklin:

FRANKLIN WAS NOT ONE of those men who owe their greatness merely to the opportunities of their times. In any age, in any place, Franklin would have been great. Mind and will, talent and art, strength and ease, wit and grace met in him as if nature had been lavish and happy when he was shaped. Nothing seems to have been left out except a passionate desire, as in most men of genius, to be all ruler, all soldier, all saint, all poet, all scholar, all some one gift or merit or success. Franklin's powers were from first to last in a flexible equilibrium. Even his genius could not specialize him. He moved through his world in a humorous mastery of it. Kind as he was, there was perhaps a little contempt in his lack of exigency. He could not put so high a value as single-minded men put on the things they give their lives for. Possessions were not worth that much, nor achievements. Comfortable as Franklin's possessions and numerous as his achievements were, they were less than he was. Whoever learns about his deeds remembers longest the man who did them. And sometimes, with his marvellous range, in spite of his personal tang, he seems to have been more than any single man: a harmonious human multitude.

But perhaps the one that Franklin would have preferred was one that he read shortly before his death in the last letter he received from his good friend and fellow Founding Father:

DEAR SIR: The affectionate congratulations on the recovery of my health, and the warm expressions of personal friendship, which were contained in your letter of the sixteenth instant, claim my gratitude. And the consideration that it is written when you were afflicted with a painful malady greatly increases my obligation for it.

Would to God, my dear sir, that I could congratulate you upon the removal of that excruciating pain under which you labor, and that your existence might close with as much ease to yourself as its continuance has been beneficial to our country and useful to mankind; or, if the united wishes of a free people, joined with the earnest prayers of every friend to science and humanity, could relieve the body from pain or infirmities, that you could claim an exemption on this score. But this cannot be, and you have within yourself the only resource to which we can confidently apply for relief, a philosophic mind.

If to be venerated for benevolence, if to be admired for talents, if to be esteemed for patriotism, if to be beloved for philanthropy, can gratify the human mind, you must have the pleasing consolation to know that you have not lived in vain. And I flatter myself that it will not be ranked among the least grateful occurrences of your life to be assured that, so long as I retain my memory, you will be recollected with respect, veneration, and affection by your sincere friend,

GEORGE WASHINGTON

Twenty thousand people escorted Dr. Franklin to his grave in Christ Church burying ground beside Deborah. Muffled bells tolled throughout Philadelphia, flags dropped to half mast throughout America, a company of artillery fired a salute over his grave. The House of Representatives went into mourning for a month, the National Assembly of France for three days. It occurred to no one to use the epitaph which Franklin had written for himself in 1728, when he was twenty-three years old. Its use might have appealed to the great man more than all the proper pomp and solemn splendor.

The Body

of

Benjamin Franklin

Printer

(Like the cover of an old book

Its contents torn out

And stript of its lettering and gilding)

Lies here, food for worms.

But the work shall not be lost

For it will (as he believed) appear once more

In a new and more elegant edition

Revised and Corrected

By

The Author.

INDEX

❧

Abolition, 293-95
Academy, *see* Pennsylvania, University of
Account of the Negotiations in London for Effecting a Reconciliation Between Great Britain and the American Colonies, 164
Adams, Abigail, 196, 254
Adams, John, 110, 177-78, 179, 181, 194-95, 196, 206, 207, 213-215, 217, 219, 222, 224-25, 232, 249, 254, 271, 289
Adams, John Quincy, 196, 249
Adams, Samuel, 147, 161
Advice on the Choice of a Mistress, 239
Aeronautics, Franklin's interest in, 227
"Age of Reason," 128
Air, fresh, 248
Albany plan, 93-98
Allen, William, 46
Almanacs, 48-67
Alphabet, proposed changes in the, 153
America, advice to, 1
American Philosophical Society, 3, 24, 38-40, 104
American Revolution, 95-97, 132, 172, 176-77, 178, 181-95, 203-8, 209, 216
American Weekly Mercury, 26, 36
André, Major, 280

Ants, 84
Apology for Printers, 118
Armonica, *see* Harmonica
Arnold, Benedict, 225, 280
Art of Procuring Pleasant Dreams, The, 247
Articles of Belief and Acts of Religion, 16
Articles of Confederation, 281
Aurora Borealis, 198-99
Autobiography, 4, 27, 30, 38, 49, 72, 97, 153, 236, 238, 292

Babies, raising of, 240
Bagatelles, 247, 256, 265, 271-73
Baker, Polly, speech of, 267-71
Balloons, 226-27
Bancroft, Edward, 182
Banks, Joseph, 226
Barbary powers, treaty with, 233
Barclay, David, 165-66, 169
Battery, 75
Beaumarchais, Caron de, 181, 193, 289
Bifocal spectacles, 232
Blackbeard, 5
Bond, Dr. Thomas, 91
Bonhomme Richard (ship), 203
Boston, Massachusetts, 291
Boston Massacre, 150
Boston Post, 5
Boston Tea Party, 160
Braddock, General Edward, 97, 100-1